New edition

Integrated Science

for Caribbean Schools

Book 2

Heinemann

Florine Dalgety   Carol Draper   David Sang

Heinemann Educational Publishers
Halley Court, Jordan Hill, Oxford OX2 8EJ
Part of Harcourt Education

Heinemann is the registered trademark of Harcourt Education Limited

© Florine Dalgety, Carol Draper, David Sang 2002

All rights reserved.

First published by Heinemann Educational Publishers in 2002

Design and cover by Jackie Hill 320 Design
Illustration by Joe Little and Keith Lemmon
Typeset by Magnet Harlequin, Oxford

ISBN 0 435 57589 9

Printed and bound in Spain by Edelvives

04 05 06 07 10 9 8 7 6 5 4 3 2

Acknowledgements

The publishers are grateful to the following people for reviewing this title during its development.

Sherril Gardner, Science Educator, Jamaica; Joy Gittens, Combermere School, Barbados; Mr Bertrand Harnanan, Standards Consultant, Trinidad; Pamela Hunte, Education Officer (Science), Ministry of Education, Youth Affairs and Sports, Barbados; Laurie O King, Senior Education Officer (Curriculum), Ministry of Education, Youth Affairs and Sports, Barbados; Natasha Lewis dos Santos, Queen's Royal College, Trinidad; Cheryl Remy, Science Education Lecturer, St Lucia; John Stringer, Educational Consultant, UK; R Worley, Advisor in the CLEAPSS School Science Service, UK

Photo acknowledgements

Cover photographs by David B Fleetham/OSF (green sea turtle) and PhotoDisc (wind turbine) Pages 9, 10 SPL; p. 13 Roger Scruton; p. 21 E Parker/Trip; p. 23, 25 Robert Harding Picture Library; p. 29 Michael Howes/Garden Picture Library; p. 36, Corbis; p. 40 Robert Harding Picture Library; p. 41 SPL; p. 42 Corbis; p. 45 Tropix; p. 50 B Turner/Trip; p. 54 Tom Ulrich/OSF; p. 64 PhotoDisc; p. 65 SPL; p. 68 National Medical Slide Bank (pellagra, rickets), SPL (scurvy); p. 70 Artie Photography; p. 73 SPL; p. 75 Jerry Alexander/Lonely Planet Images; p. 85 FLPA; p. 89 National Medical Slide Bank; p. 96 John Radcliffe Hospital/SPL; p. 99, Larry Mulvehill/SPL p. 100 SPL; p. 118 Trip; p. 120 Mediscan; p. 121 SPL; p. 122 Artie Photography; p. 128 Empics; p. 129 Colorsport; p. 130 Mediscan (arm in plaster), National Medical Slide Bank (X-ray images); p. 133 PhotoDisc (dog, horse), Bruce Coleman (snake); p. 134 OSF; p. 135 E&D Hosking/FLPA (albatross), Gerard Lacz/FLPA (ostrich); p. 136 SPL; p. 137 OSF; p. 138 FLPA (woodlouse), OSF (shrimp, millipede), Bruce Coleman (worm); p. 141 Artie Photography (students), SPL (batteries); p. 144 Corbis; p. 147, 148 Roger Scruton; p. 159 Alamy; p. 163, 166 SPL; p. 168 J Greenberg/Trip; p. 174 SPL; corner images by PhotoDisc

OSF, Oxford Scientific Films; SPL, Science Photo Library; FLPA, Frank Lane Picture Agency

Contents

Safety in the laboratory — iv
Colour ranges of pH indicators — vi

Unit 9: Looking at non-living things
9.1 States of matter — 1
9.2 Changing things — 5
9.3 Making crystals — 9
9.4 More about dissolving — 12
9.5 Elements, compounds and mixtures — 16
9.6 Separating things — 20
9.7 Acids and alkalis — 26
9.8 Acids and metals — 32
9.9 More about salts — 35

Unit 10: Resources for life
10.1 Air as a resource — 38
10.2 Soil as a resource — 44
10.3 Food chains and food webs — 52
10.4 Carbon and nitrogen cycles — 58

Unit 11: Systems in animals
11.1 Food and nutrition — 63
11.2 The digestive system — 77
11.3 Teeth — 85
11.4 Blood and the circulatory system — 92
11.5 Breathing and respiration in humans — 103
11.6 Excretion: getting rid of waste materials — 110
11.7 The effects of drug abuse — 115

Unit 12: Support and movement
12.1 Support and movement in humans — 124
12.2 Support and movement in animals — 133

Unit 13: Electricity and magnetism
13.1 Using electricity — 141
13.2 Using electricity safely — 147
13.3 Electrical circuits — 151
13.4 Electrical resistance — 157
13.5 Series and parallel circuits — 161
13.6 Static electricity — 163
13.7 Magnets and electromagnets — 168
13.8 Uses of electromagnets — 174

Questions — 177

Science words — 182

Index — 185

Safety in the laboratory

The laboratory (often called simply the 'lab') is a place of discovery and excitement. The following guidelines are given so that you can enjoy your lab sessions safely, without getting hurt.

Read this page very carefully. Ask your teacher to explain anything that you do not understand. These rules apply to all lab work, now and in the future.

Basic safety rules

- Do not enter the lab unless there is a qualified supervisor present.
- Always walk in the lab. Do not run or play around.
- Keep coats, bags and other belongings tidied away.
- Tie back long hair. Keep your hair well away from flames and hot objects.
- Nails should be neatly trimmed, and jewellery kept to the minimum – earrings should be small and not dangling.
- The teacher, laboratory attendant and laboratory technicians are responsible for the equipment in the lab. Do not touch any piece of equipment, unless instructed to do so by one of these adults. Sometimes a senior student may be given the responsibility of guiding you and your classmates through an experiment. Obey all instructions given.
- Do not interfere with fittings such as gas taps and electrical sockets. Seek adult help if something goes wrong with any of these things.
- Do not touch electrical sockets or switches with wet hands. Never allow any electrical appliance to come into contact with water, unless it is designed to do so. You might get a shock.
- Do not open gas taps before you are ready to light the gas. A build-up of gas in the immediate area can lead to an explosion, and you can be seriously hurt.

What you should know

- Locate the nearest staircase or fire escape that should be used in an emergency. Your teacher will explain the safety procedure and how to leave the lab if there is an emergency.

Safety in the laboratory

When conducting experiments

- ✓ Check all bottle labels carefully. Chemicals can be dangerous if not handled correctly. Never remove anything from the lab without permission.
- ✓ Wear eye protection (goggles), gloves, or other protective gear when told to do so, and do not take these items off until told to do so. The symbol on the left shows you when eye protection is needed.
- ✓ Use the amounts of materials stated in the instructions.
- ✓ When pouring liquids from a labelled bottle, ensure that the label is held towards the palm of the hand so that you can see the contents, and the chemical does not pour over the label.
- ✓ When heating material in a test tube, always point the mouth of the test tube away from yourself and others.
- ✓ If a piece of apparatus gets chipped or broken, tell a supervisor immediately.
- ✓ Surfaces should be kept clean. Immediately wipe away any spills. There should be special cleaning cloths for this purpose.
- ✓ Wash your hands thoroughly after handling chemicals, or after handling plant or animal material.
- ✓ Allow Bunsen burners, tripods, beakers, etc. to cool down before handling them, or wear protective gloves. Do not rest hot apparatus directly on the desk top. Use a heat-proof mat.
- ✗ Do not hold hot apparatus with your bare hands.
- ✗ Do not eat or drink in the lab.
- ✗ Do NOT mix chemicals unless told to do so. Ask for advice if instructions are not clear to you.
- ✗ Do NOT taste or drink ANY chemical in the lab unless told to do so by a RESPONSIBLE adult. If you accidentally get something in your mouth, spit it out and wash your mouth out with lots of water. Tell your teacher or supervisor. You will be taught the correct way to smell a chemical.

Safety icons

The following symbols, or icons, are used to warn of any possible hazards associated with activities. Make sure you know what they mean, and take notice of them.

| Corrosive | Toxic | Harmful or irritant | Highly flammable | Oxidizing | Danger! Care needed! |

Colour ranges of pH indicators

1 Litmus	acid neutral base	red mauve blue	
2 Universal indicator	pH 1 2 3 4 5 6 7 8 9 10 11 12 13 14		
3 Methyl orange	acid base		

Looking at non-living things

9.1 States of matter

> **Objectives**
>
> After studying this topic you should be able to:
> - classify things into solids, liquids and gases
> - describe the properties of solids, liquids and gases.

In Topics 1 and 2 of Book 1 you learned about the differences between living and non-living things, and how to put living things into groups, such as plants, animals, bacteria and fungi. In this unit we will look at non-living things.

We will first find out the main differences between solids, liquids and gases. All materials can be placed into one of these three groups, which are called the three states of matter. Some common examples are shown in Figure. 9.1.

Fig. 9.1 Everyday examples of solids, liquids and gases. (a) Solids, such as the coconut, are hard and have definite shape. (b) The water flows down the chute, just like all liquids. (c) The balloon fills evenly with gas, whatever its shape.

Brownian motion

In 1827 a Scottish scientist called Robert Brown noticed that pollen grains in water moved around randomly. He couldn't explain this restlessness. It took Albert Einstein in 1905 to explain that the movement is due to the water molecules bouncing off the pollen grains. The water molecules look like little children running around a playground, bumping into each other! The pollen grain is like a teacher, trying to stand still! But why does this happen?

A litre of air contains about 30 000 million million million molecules. Each of them is travelling at 450 metres a second. So each molecule will have around 5000 million collisions every second. These collisions will move particles such as pollen grains around. They are the cause of Brownian motion.

Diffusion

If you add a drop of ink to water, it will eventually colour all the water, even without stirring. This is called **diffusion**. The particles of ink spread from a place where they are concentrated to a place where they are not.

Diffusion is vital to the movement of substances in plants and animals. Nutrients and gases diffuse in and out of living cells.

Activity Liquids

You will need
- transparent containers (e.g. bottles, jugs, vases, beakers) of different shapes
- a measuring cylinder

Method
Pour 20 cm^3 of water into each container.

Discuss
1 Which container seems to have the most water?
2 Is 20 cm^3 of water always the same shape?

Activity Gases

You will need
- an air freshener or perfume spray

Method
1 Ask a friend to stand at the other end of the classroom, with the windows or shutters closed.
2 Spray a little air freshener or perfume.
3 Ask your friend to say when he or she can smell it.
4 Repeat this experiment with the windows or shutters open.

Discuss
1 How long does it take for your friend to smell the spray?
2 Does it take longer when the room is ventilated?

Activity More about gases

You will need
- balloons of different shapes but similar size

Method
1. Blow each balloon up to its largest size.
2. Tie the necks of the balloons.
3. Squeeze the balloons at different places.
4. Untie the necks and release the balloons.

Discuss
1. Why was it possible to make strange shapes with the balloons?
2. Why did the air not stay in the balloons after the necks were open?

We can hold solids. They have definite shape and volume. Liquids and gases are fluids. Fluids flow to take up the shape of the container that they are in. Liquids have definite volume but gases spread out in all directions (Fig. 9.2).

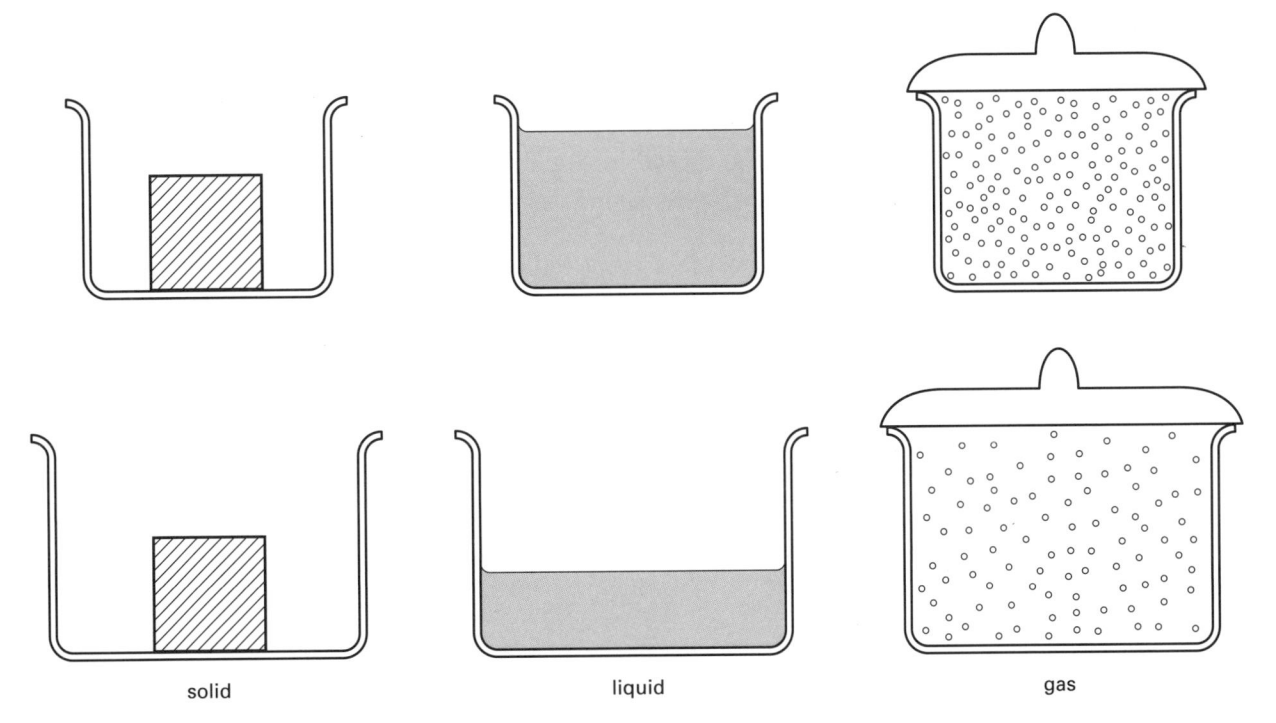

Fig. 9.2 Solids, liquids and gases.

9.1 Looking at non-living things

○ What you should know

- Matter can be divided into solids, liquids and gases.
- Solids have definite shape.
- Liquids take up the shape of the container.
- Gases have no shape or definite volume.
- You can pour some solids too – salt or flour, for example – but they don't form a flat top like a liquid.

② Questions

1 There are three states of matter. What are they called?

2 Look at the items in the following list, and say whether each is a solid, a liquid or a gas:

   stone, air, paper, wood, fruit juice, salt, milk, straw, bubbles in cola

3 Say whether each of the following statements is describing a solid, liquid, or gas (some may apply to more than one):
   a It can be sent through a pipe.
   b Things can float in it.
   c I can sit on it.
   d I can fill a bottle with it.
   e I can cut it with a knife or saw.

4 Fill in each blank space in the following sentences using either the word 'shape' or the word 'volume'.
   a Solids have a definite _____ and _____.
   b Liquids have a definite _____ but flow to take the _____ of their containers.
   c Gases have no set _____ and they spread out to fill the available space.

Looking at non-living things

9.2 Changing things

▶ Objectives

After studying this topic you should be able to:

- describe what happens when things are heated or cooled.

In the laboratory we use a Bunsen burner or spirit lamp to heat things. At home we use paraffin (kerosene), gas, electricity or charcoal.

→ Activity What happens when things are heated?

You will need
- tin lids
- a Bunsen burner or a spirit lamp
- a tripod
- candle wax
- sugar
- lipstick
- soil
- cooking oil
- ice
- salt

Eye protection must be worn

Danger!
Some substances may spit when heated

Method

1. Arrange the apparatus as shown in Figure 9.3.
2. Place a little of one of the materials (a small piece if it is solid, a quarter teaspoonful if it is powdered, and a few drops if it is liquid) on the tin lid.
3. Warm the substance on the lid gently, and gradually increase the heat. Observe what happens.
4. Repeat with each of the other substances.
5. Your teacher may be able to heat a few other substances that are dangerous for you to heat; for example, magnesium ribbon or ammonium dichromate.

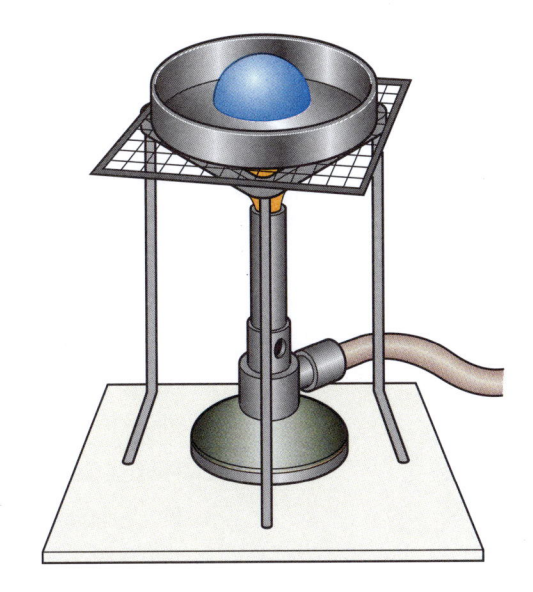

Fig. 9.3 Observe what happens when you warm different things.

Record
Record your observations in a table like Table 9.1 overleaf.

Discuss
Did the substances change when they were heated? Which ones changed from a solid to a liquid, or from a liquid to a gas? Did the sugar and the ice change in the same way?

9.2 Looking at non-living things

Table 9.1 Heating substances.

Name of substance	What I observed	
	Gentle heat	Stronger heat

What do you think would happen if you cooled substances? Let us find out. Why not do this activity at home. Let members of the family know what you are doing so that they do not interfere.

➔ Activity Cooling substances

You will need
- access to the refrigerator or an ice bucket
- two drink bottle covers
- a tin can lid
- water
- cooking oil
- other common household substances

Method
1. Place the two bottle covers on a tin can lid.
2. Fill one cover with water and the other with cooking oil.
3. Place the lid with the covers in the freezing chamber of the refrigerator. Note the time.
4. Check after half an hour and record your observations.
5. Allow another half an hour to pass, then remove the covers from the refrigerator. Record your observations. Try cooling other substances.

Discuss
Were the results what you expected? How were they a surprise?

Boiling and freezing points

The boiling point of a liquid is the temperature at which it boils and becomes a gas. For a pure liquid at normal pressure, this is always the same. The boiling point for pure water is 100°C. However, adding another material to the water can change this boiling point. In Book 1, Topic 6.1 you investigated the effect that adding salt had on the boiling point of

Changing things 9.2

water. You will have found that salty water boiled at a higher temperature than pure water.

The freezing point of a liquid is the temperature at which it becomes solid. The freezing point of pure water is 0°C. Adding another material to the water can change the freezing point, as you will see in the next activity.

➔ Activity Getting colder

You will need
- a beaker of crushed ice
- a thermometer
- salt

Method
1 Take the temperature of a beaker of ice – using crushed ice brings the thermometer closer to the ice and so gives a better reading.
2 Take out the thermometer, stir in some salt, put the thermometer back and take readings over the next few minutes.

Discuss
What happened when you added salt to the ice?

In some cold countries, salt is sprinkled on wet roads. The salt lowers the freezing point of the water, and so the weather has to get even colder before the roads get icy and slippery. This makes it much safer to drive in the winter.

Changes of state

Cooling and heating do opposite things to a substance. Let us look at water. If we cool it in the freezer, it freezes to form ice, which is a solid. If we then heat the ice by taking it out of the freezer and placing it in a warm room, it melts to become water again. When the water changes from a liquid to a solid, or from a solid to a liquid, we say that it changes state.

Water also changes state when we heat it in a kettle (Fig. 9.4). The water gives off water in the form of water vapour; in other words it evaporates. As the temperature rises the water evaporates faster and faster, until eventually the water boils. The water vapour comes out of the

steam (gas)

Fig. 9.4 How many changes of state are occurring when the kettle is boiling?

9.2 Looking at non-living things

spout as a gas called steam, which then cools to form water droplets. You can see water vapour – you cannot see steam. This change from a gas to a liquid is called condensing. It is the opposite to evaporation or boiling. 'Steam', confusingly, is the everyday word for clouds of water droplets. Evaporation is when a liquid changes to a gas – vapour – at a temperature below its boiling point.

As you have seen, some substances undergo other changes when they are heated. The sugar, for example, melted at first, then it changed to a dark liquid and gave off water vapour. We use the term 'change of state' only when the same substance changes between solid, liquid and gas.

Sublimation

This is the change of a material from solid to vapour without passing through a liquid stage. You can see it at pop concerts and plays when dry ice (solid carbon dioxide) changes to swirls of carbon dioxide vapour to give 'smoke' or 'fog' on stage (see page 41).

Water ice sublimes slowly at ordinary pressure – but more quickly at low pressures. The food industry uses this to freeze-dry food (such as coffee) by making water ice sublime at low pressure.

What you should know

- Substances change when they are heated or cooled.
- Changes of the same substance from solid to liquid, or from liquid to gas, or from solid to gas, and vice versa, are called changes of state.
- Freezing, melting, condensing and evaporating all cause changes of state.

Questions

1. Fill in the gaps in the following sentences using words from the list: condense, evaporate, freeze, melt

   a Heating causes a solid to _____ to a liquid, and a liquid to _____ to a gas or vapour.

   b Cooling causes a gas to _____ to a liquid, and a liquid to _____ to a solid.

2. Name some fuels that can be burned to produce heat.

3. What changes take place when a candle burns? Where are the solid, liquid and gas?

Looking at non-living things

9.3 Making crystals

▶ Objectives

After studying this topic you should be able to:
- explain how to make a solution of something
- describe the appearance of a freshly grown crystal
- make models of crystals
- explain why crystals cleave or split when tapped.

Have you ever looked closely at the salt that you use in cooking or sprinkle on your food? It can look like a coarse powder, hard crumbs, pebbles or even a rock, depending on what sort you buy. Whatever form it takes, you are looking at **crystals** of salt (or sodium chloride, to use its proper chemical name).

If you add some salt to a glass of water, and stir for long enough, the salt crystals disappear. They have dissolved, to form a mixture with the water. This mixture is called a **solution** of salt in water. The substance that is dissolved is called the **solute**, and the liquid in which it dissolves is called the **solvent**. In this case, salt is the solute and water is the solvent.

Most solids that dissolve in water are in the form of crystals. They are described as being crystalline. If you look at crystals under a microscope you see that they have flat sides and sharp edges (Fig. 9.5). Crystals have a definite shape, although with household salt, for example, the true shape is often impossible to see because the crystals have been broken up in the manufacturing process. To see crystals clearly, we need to grow them ourselves.

Fig. 9.5 Crystals of calcite (which is also known as dog-tooth spar).

▶ Activity Growing crystals

You will need
- a glass jar
- a glass rod or wooden stick
- alum crystals
- nylon or cotton thread
- water

9.3 Looking at non-living things

Method

1. Make a saturated solution of alum by dissolving alum in water at room temperature until no more dissolves.
2. Tie a single crystal of alum with the thread.
3. Tie the other end of the thread to the glass rod or stick.
4. Carefully lower the alum crystal into the saturated solution (Fig. 9.6).
5. Leave for a few days and observe what happens.

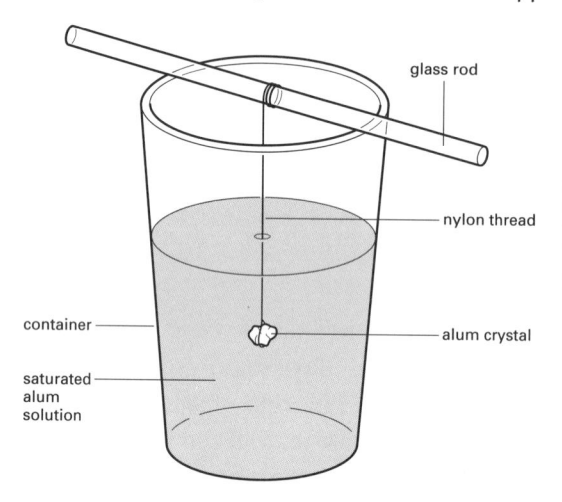

Fig. 9.6 An alum crystal suspended in alum solution (left). Well-developed alum crystals form delicate fronds (above).

When a crystal is split into pieces, for example by tapping it gently with a hammer, the pieces have flat, smooth sides like the crystal you started with. Why is this? You learnt in primary school that scientists believe that everything is made up of very tiny particles. The particles that make up crystals are arranged in layers, rather like layers of egg trays. Splitting, or cleaving, a crystal in this way is like separating the layers in the stack of egg trays.

Would you like to make models of crystals? You can do this at home.

❓ Finding out

Sulphur crystals

Crystals of sulphur (Fig. 9.7) may be found near volcanoes. The sulphur was once deep in the Earth. When the volcano erupted the liquid sulphur was thrown out. As it cooled the sulphur crystallized. Find out the names of some other naturally occurring crystals.

Fig. 9.7 Sulphur crystals.

9.3 Making crystals

→ Activity Crystal models

You will need
- genip (ackee or chenette) seeds, or marbles
- wood glue

Method A
1. Arrange and glue together 16 seeds or marbles in the shape of a square.
2. Repeat this three more times.
3. Carefully stack the squares so that you get a cube.

Method B
1. Arrange and glue together 16 seeds to make a square.
2. In a similar way make a square of nine seeds.
3. Make a square with four seeds.
4. Carefully stack the squares so that you get a pyramid (you need to put a single seed at the top).

Discuss
1. What do the seeds/marbles represent?
2. Look how layers can be stacked to make different shapes.
3. What shape would you get if you glued the base of one pyramid against the base of another pyramid?
4. Think of some other shapes you can make in this way.

○ What you should know

- When a substance dissolves it forms a solution. The substance is called the solute, and the liquid in which it dissolves is the solvent.
- When no more solute will dissolve, the solution is said to be saturated.
- Crystals can be grown in saturated solutions.
- Crystals have definite shapes with flat sides and sharp edges.

ⓠ Questions

1. You have been given a solid material. How would you find out whether it is a crystal?

2. In the sentences below, fill in the blank spaces using the correct words taken from the following list:

    crystals, dissolve, solute, solution, solvent

    a Stirring salt _____ in water makes them _____ to form a _____.

    b The salt is the _____ and the water is the _____.

Looking at non-living things

9.4 More about dissolving

▸ Objectives

After studying this topic you should be able to:

- describe how heating and cooling affect the way in which a substance dissolves in a solvent
- say why bubbles form in fizzy drinks
- name some common solvents.

As we learned in the previous topic, a solute is a substance that dissolves in a solvent. We say that the solute is soluble in the solvent. So, for example, salt is soluble in water.

Is there a limit to how much solute can dissolve in a solvent? Have you ever added so much sugar to your drink that even with much stirring some sugar crystals remain at the bottom of the container?

▸ Activity How much solid will dissolve in water?

You will need

- three test tubes
- a measuring cylinder
- a Bunsen burner or a spirit lamp
- spatulas (or other measures)
- a thermometer
- solids, such as sodium carbonate (washing soda [irritant]), potassium nitrate (oxidizing agent), magnesium sulphate

Eye protection must be worn

Danger! Point the tube away from people

Danger! Care needed when handling chemicals!

Method

1. Pour 5 cm^3 of water into a test tube.
2. What can you use to measure the solid? You must add it to the water a little at a time, using exactly the same amount each time. You choose.

   Add one of the solids to the water, a little at a time using your measure, until no more dissolves after shaking the test tube. Record how many measures you added.
3. Heat the solution to about 70°C and then add more solute until no more dissolves. Measure the temperature using the thermometer. Record how many measures you added.
4. Leave to cool.
5. Repeat the procedure for each of the other solids.

9.4 More about dissolving

Record
Make a record of your observations in a table like Table 9.2.

Table 9.2 Dissolving solids.

Substance	Number of measures added	
	to cold water	when heated

Discuss
1 Is there a limit to the amount of solid that will dissolve in a given quantity of water at a given temperature?
2 Is the amount that will dissolve the same for each solid?
3 What happens when the solution cools?
4 Why did we use the same amount of water for each solid?
5 Why should we measure each solid in the same way?

For all solids there is a limit to the amount that will dissolve in a given quantity of water at a given temperature. When no more solid will dissolve in the water the solution is said to be **saturated** at that temperature.

Do gases dissolve in water? What happens if you shake a bottle of soft drink before you open it? It fizzes. The fizz is caused by trapped gas. The more gas that is trapped, the more bubbles are produced. The gas must have been dissolved in the liquid (Fig. 9.8).

The bubbles in your soft drink are carbon dioxide gas. When the drink was made, carbon dioxide was dissolved in it. By squeezing the gas in under pressure, the makers were able to get more carbon dioxide to dissolve. When you release the pressure by opening the cap the extra gas that was squeezed in bubbles out. Some remains dissolved, however, and gives the drink its pleasant, slightly acid, taste.

Fig. 9.8 A fizzy drink contains dissolved gas. This escapes as bubbles when you open the bottle, especially if you have shaken the bottle before opening it.

9.4 Looking at non-living things

➡ Activity Dissolving carbon dioxide in water

You will need
- a test tube of carbon dioxide gas (your teacher will provide this)
- a beaker of water

Method
1. Hold the test tube upside down in the water (Fig. 9.9).
2. Let it stay there for some time (several hours).
3. Observe what happens.

Discuss
Why does the level of the water in the tube rise?

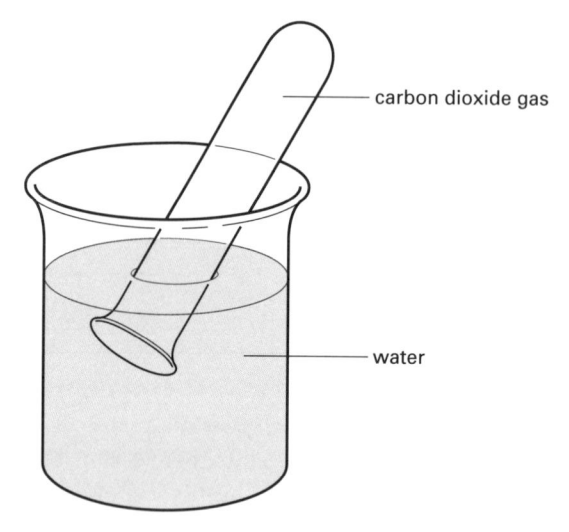

Fig. 9.9 Dissolving carbon dioxide gas in water.

Air, which is a mixture of gases, can dissolve in water. If you look carefully at a beaker of water that has been warmed up as it stands in the Sun, you will see tiny bubbles of gas (air) forming on the sides. Fish breathe the oxygen dissolved in water in order to live.

Other solvents: Water is a very useful solvent. However, not all substances we need to use as solutions can be dissolved in water. Some will dissolve in other liquids such as paraffin (kerosene), turpentine or propanone (also called acetone). These other liquids are solvents too.

⚠ **Danger!**

Note:
Solvents such as turpentine, white spirit, propanone and paraffin (kerosene) are highly flammable. Make sure there are no naked flames nearby when handling such substances.

❓ Finding out

Identifying solvents

Read the labels of varnishes, paints and cough medicines. Name the solvents that are common:

a. to cough medicines
b. to varnishes

Can you identify the solvents? Are there any solvents that are used for all cough medicines and all varnishes?

9.4 More about dissolving

Concentration and dilution

The **concentration** is the amount of the dissolved substance – the solute – present in a solution. It is the strength of the sugar in a cup of tea, for example. You can increase the concentration of a solution by removing solvent. If you leave a saucer of salt water on the windowsill, the water (the solvent) will evaporate and the solution will become more concentrated.

Dilution is reducing the concentration of a solution by adding more solvent. For example, it is adding water to fruit syrup to make squash. Five-fold dilution of a solution means adding enough solvent to give you five times the volume you started with.

What you should know

- You can dissolve more of a given substance by heating the solvent.
- When a hot saturated solution is cooled, crystals of the solute may form.
- Some solvents are better than others at dissolving a given substance.
- Gases may also dissolve in liquids.

Questions

1. What is a saturated solution?

2. How would you make crystals from a saturated solution?

3. Fill in the blank spaces in the following sentence by using one word from each of the following pairs: solution or solute; decreases or increases.

    For solids, the amount of _____ that will dissolve in a solvent _____ with temperature.

4. Name a gas that is soluble in water.

5. Find out more about how soft drinks – especially 'carbonated' fizzy drinks – are made.

6. Why is it important to aquatic life that oxygen dissolves in water?

7. Full cola cans sink in water. Full diet-cola cans float. Devise an investigation to find out why.

Looking at non-living things

9.5 Elements, compounds and mixtures

▶ Objectives

After studying this topic you should be able to:
- describe the properties of elements, compounds and mixtures
- say what a chemical symbol is
- say what a chemical formula is
- write down an equation to represent a simple chemical reaction.

As we have said before, scientists believe that all matter is made up of very tiny particles. These particles are called **atoms**. They are too small to see, even with the most powerful microscopes. Substances that contain only one type of atom are called **elements**. Common elements are oxygen, nitrogen, carbon and hydrogen. Gold, silver and platinum are examples of much rarer elements. In their natural state, most elements do not occur on their own but are combined with other elements. Substances formed when elements combine are called **compounds**.

Many elements were first isolated during the eighteenth and nineteenth centuries, and today we know of 92 elements that occur naturally. More than ten other elements have been created artificially in laboratories, but these do not occur in nature. Elements are usually extracted from their compounds. There are several million known compounds.

▶ Activity Making a compound

You will need
- lime juice
- sodium hydrogencarbonate (sodium bicarbonate)
- a test tube

Method
Place a teaspoonful of sodium hydrogencarbonate in a test tube and add some lime juice.

Discuss
What do you see?

When you added lime juice to sodium hydrogencarbonate you made a compound. The compound was carbon dioxide, which you saw as a fizzing, or gas bubbles, being given off inside the test tube. The carbon dioxide was made by the lime juice reacting with the sodium hydrogencarbonate. We can write that sentence another way:

lime juice + sodium hydrogencarbonate → carbon dioxide + other substances

9.5 Elements, compounds and mixtures

Carbon dioxide is made up of the elements carbon and oxygen. Carbon occurs in coal, pencil lead and diamonds. In this form, although it is in contact with oxygen in the air, it does not react. Sometimes simply mixing elements together is not enough to make them combine. We may have to do other things, such as heating them.

Mixtures

Look at some freshly dug soil. From a distance it looks an even colour, but as you get closer you can see stones and pebbles, and perhaps bits of dead leaves. If you take a sample of soil and shake it with some water in a test tube, you will see even more different things, including particles of different colours. Soil is an example of a **mixture**. It is made up of various substances that can be separated quite easily, and its make-up changes depending on where it comes from.

Air is another mixture that is all around us. It contains several different gases, including oxygen, which we need to breathe. Other gases present in air include nitrogen, carbon dioxide and water vapour. Air can also contain dust particles, smoke and traffic fumes, depending on where you are.

→ Activity Comparing mixtures and compounds

You will need
- iron filings
- sulphur
- a magnet
- a hand lens
- a beaker
- a clean tin lid or a test tube
- a Bunsen burner

Eye protection must be worn

Danger!
Point the test tube away from people!

Method
1 Mix a spatulaful each of clean iron filings and sulphur thoroughly in a beaker.
2 Touch the mixture with the magnet.
3 Examine the mixture with a hand lens.
4 Add another spatulaful of iron filings.
5 Mix thoroughly again.
6 Now test if the magnet still attracts the iron filings.
7 Put some of the mixture of iron and sulphur on a clean lid, or in a test tube.
8 Heat the mixture for about 2 minutes and allow it to cool.
9 Look at the result with a hand lens.
10 Test the new substance with a magnet.

Discuss
What are the differences between the mixture of iron and sulphur and the solid formed when the mixture is heated?

9.5 Looking at non-living things

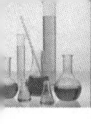

Heat is necessary for the elements iron and sulphur to combine to form the compound called iron(II) sulphide. We can show this reaction as:

iron + sulphur → iron(II) sulphide

In compounds the atoms are joined together to form **molecules**. So each molecule of iron(II) sulphide is made from one iron atom and one sulphur atom (Fig. 9.10). Molecules of other compounds may be made from two, three or more atoms.

iron   sulphur   iron(II) sulphide

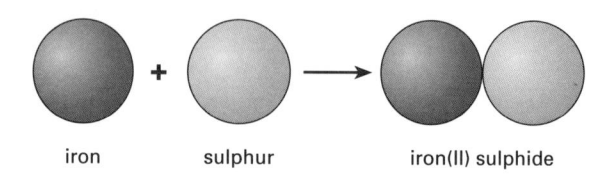

Fig. 9.10 Model showing the formation of a molecule of iron(II) sulphide.

Breaking down compounds: We learned earlier that most elements have to be extracted from their compounds. When certain compounds are heated they break down (or decompose). This is what happens to sugar when we heat it. In some cases one (or more) of the elements of the compound is released in the process. Decomposition of compounds also takes place when an electric current passes through a liquid or solution. This process is called **electrolysis**.

Elements and their compounds

Compounds behave differently from the elements that make them up. In this way compounds are different from mixtures, which behave according to the properties of their ingredients.

Elements in compounds are always combined in a fixed ratio. This means that any molecule of a given compound always has the same number of atoms of each of its elements. For water, whatever its source, two atoms of hydrogen are combined with one atom of oxygen. A carbon dioxide molecule is always made up of one atom of carbon and two atoms of oxygen.

Symbols and formulas

Every element has a name. It can also be written in a shorthand way using a symbol. For example, the symbol for hydrogen is H, the symbol for oxygen is O, the symbol for sulphur is S (all fairly easy to remember!) and the symbol for iron is Fe (not so obvious; it comes from the Latin word for iron, *ferrum*).

? Finding out

Properties of compounds

Find out the properties of hydrogen and oxygen (which form water) and also the properties of sodium and chlorine (which form common salt). Are any properties of the elements also found in the compounds they make?

Elements, compounds and mixtures — 9.5

The symbol stands for one atom of the element. A single molecule of a compound can be represented by the symbols of its combining elements. Hence water is written as H_2O (the '2' below the line after the 'H' symbol shows that there are two hydrogen atoms in each water molecule). This is the **chemical formula** for water. In the same way, we can write the chemical formula for iron(II) sulphide as FeS.

Above we saw how iron and sulphur react when heated to form the compound iron(II) sulphide. We wrote this down in words as:

iron + sulphur → iron(II) sulphide

This is called the **reaction equation**. Now, if we use the chemical symbols instead of words we get:

Fe + S → FeS

You will learn to use symbols and formulas as you use the substances in science.

What you should know

- All matter is made up of atoms.
- An element consists of only one type of atom.
- Elements combine in exact amounts to form compounds.
- It is usually difficult to separate the elements in a compound.
- A mixture may contain varying amounts of substances.
- It is usually easy to separate the ingredients of a mixture.
- Elements and compounds can be written down using chemical symbols.
- The starting materials and the products of a chemical reaction can be written down as a chemical equation.

Questions

1. What do we call a substance that contains two or more elements that are chemically combined? What is the main difference between such a material and a simple mixture of two elements?

2. When carbon burns in air it reacts with the oxygen in air to form carbon dioxide. The chemical symbols are: C for carbon, O_2 for oxygen, and CO_2 for carbon dioxide. Write the chemical equation for this reaction using the symbols.

3. Combining two or more substances can produce useful new substances. Think of some everyday examples of this – in cooking, building, gardening, etc.

Looking at non-living things

9.6 Separating things

> ### Objectives
>
> After studying this topic you should be able to:
> - describe the different types of mixtures
> - describe how filters, chromatography and distillation are used to separate the parts of a mixture
> - give examples of how these separation methods are used
> - outline the separation of sugar from sugar cane
> - outline the separation of petrol and other oils from crude oil.

Many everyday materials are mixtures, for example, soil, air, sea water, milk and ink. We may want to separate one or more substances from the rest of a mixture. For example, if salt can be removed from sea water we can obtain water that is fit to drink.

There are various methods for separating the parts of mixtures. Which method we choose depends on the properties of the substance we want to separate. For example, we might want to separate solid particles from a liquid, or we might want to separate a solute from a solvent. Some of the following methods are useful:

- add water to dissolve a soluble substance;
- allow solids to settle and pour off (decant) the liquid at the top;
- use a filter to separate the solids from the liquid;
- filter the liquid, then heat it to evaporate the solvent, leaving a solute to crystallize out.

There are two sorts of mixtures – **heterogeneous** and **homogeneous**. In heterogeneous mixtures you can see the separate parts quite easily (e.g. soil; salt/sand mixture). In homogeneous mixtures the parts are so well mixed together that the mixture seems to be one substance (e.g. salt solution, crude oil).

Filtration

> ### Activity Separating mud from water
>
> **You will need**
> - some muddy water
> - a filter apparatus like the one shown in Figure 9.11
> - filter paper
> - distilled water

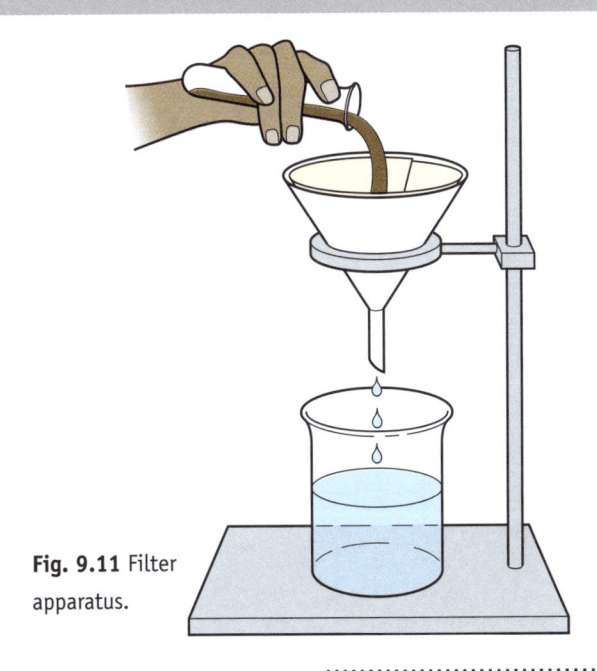

9.6 Separating things

Fig. 9.11 Filter apparatus.

Method
1. Fold the filter paper into quarters.
2. Open out the filter paper into a cone.
3. Wet the inside of the filter funnel with distilled water.
4. Place the cone of filter paper in the filter funnel. Moisten it with a little distilled water to keep the cone in place.
5. Pour the muddy water through the filter paper.

Discuss
1. What is left behind in the filter funnel?
2. What collects in the beaker? Is the water completely clear? Do you think it is pure water or a solution?

The activity above shows the process called **filtration**; the liquid that comes through the filter paper is called the **filtrate**, and the solid that remains on the filter paper is called the **residue**.

Filtration is not only used to separate undissolved solid from a solution. Air filters are used in motor vehicles to remove harmful particles from the air entering the engine. Gas masks are worn when poisonous gases are present, for example, when tear gas is used in riots. What are filter-tip cigarettes meant to filter?

Evaporation

Evaporation is an important process. Salt is obtained by letting the water evaporate from a salt solution. Look at the photograph of the salt flats in Figure 9.12. Why do we only get salt lakes/flats in parts of the world with lots of sunshine? Did you know there's a salt lake in Anguilla?

Fig. 9.12 Salt flats are produced when the water evaporates from a salt lake.

Activity Separating salt from sand

You will need
- a mixture of salt and sand
- a Bunsen burner
- a test tube containing 10 cm^3 of water
- a filter apparatus (Fig. 9.13)
- an evaporating dish or tin lid

9.6 Looking at non-living things

Method

1. Add two spatulas of the salt/sand mixture to the test tube water.
2. Shake the test tube for a minute.
3. Pour the mixture through the filter funnel and collect the filtrate (clear liquid) in a beaker.
4. Look at the residue in the filter paper. What is it?
5. Pour half of the filtrate into an evaporating dish.
6. Gently heat the evaporating dish until the water has evaporated. Does the residue look like salt?

Eye protection must be worn

Danger! Mixture may spit!

Discuss

1. Why is it possible to separate this mixture by first adding water, then filtering?
2. What other mixtures can you separate by first adding a solvent?

Fig. 9.13 Separating salt from sand.

Chromatography

What happens when the juices of some fruits get on your blouse or shirt? The juices of some plants were used long ago as natural dyes. Do you think they are good dyes, or do they wash out? If curry falls on the tablecloth, does it spread evenly? What colour is the outer ring?

We can show that there are different dyes in black ink by doing a similar experiment.

→ Activity Paper chromatography

You will need
- two strips of filter paper
- two test tubes
- black ink
- two matchsticks
- two paperclips
- dye

Method

1. Put an ink spot 2 cm from the end of one piece of paper and a dye spot 2 cm from the end of the other paper.
2. Place each strip in a test tube with a little water, by suspending the paper as shown in Figure 9.14.

Discuss

Draw what happens to the spot in each case. How many different colours can you see coming from each spot?

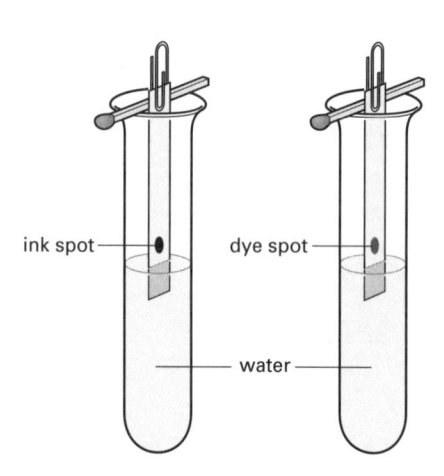

Fig. 9.14 Paper chromatography.

Separating things 9.6

This activity shows a type of separation called **chromatography**. Chromatography separates the different chemicals in substances such as dyes or inks. The more lines there are the more substances were in the original dye.

As you can see, we choose different separation techniques according to the type of mixture we have. In our daily activities we use many separation techniques.

➔ Activity Separating mixtures in the home

Think of a process used in the home that involves separation of a mixture. Write out the process in stages. Identify the stage(s) involving separation. What techniques are used? How is each technique suited to the mixture it separates? How is the equipment used similar to/different from the equipment you would use in the science laboratory at school?

In some industrial processes too, separation techniques are evident, as the two examples that follow will show.

Separating sugar

The Caribbean is known as a producer of sugar and rum. Rum originated in the Caribbean during the seventeenth century.

The cane farmers know at what stage the sugar cane is ready to be cut (Fig. 9.15). The cane is cleaned and chopped, and then crushed between huge rollers to extract the juice (Fig. 9.16). The juice is collected in pipes and pumped into large tanks where it is purified by adding lime (this is not the fruit, but the chemical calcium hydroxide). It is then gently heated to boiling. When this happens sediment settles out and the clear juice is extracted from the top. This sediment still has some juice in it, and is passed into drums that keep turning. This separates the sediment from the juice.

The juice is now passed to the boilers. Here the water is evaporated until the liquid becomes like syrup with some crystals in it. The evaporation can be taken further in special pans, which are made so that the sugar does not burn. Finally

Fig. 9.15 Cutting sugar cane.

Fig. 9.16 Sugar cane is crushed between huge rollers.

9.6 Looking at non-living things

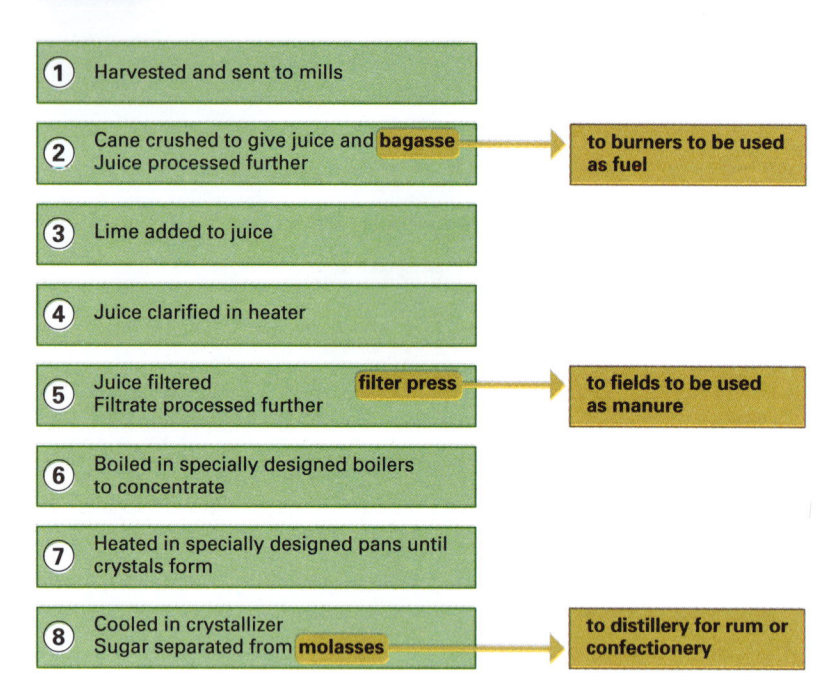

1. Harvested and sent to mills
2. Cane crushed to give juice and **bagasse** → to burners to be used as fuel
   Juice processed further
3. Lime added to juice
4. Juice clarified in heater
5. Juice filtered **filter press** → to fields to be used as manure
   Filtrate processed further
6. Boiled in specially designed boilers to concentrate
7. Heated in specially designed pans until crystals form
8. Cooled in crystallizer → to distillery for rum or confectionery
   Sugar separated from **molasses**

sugar crystals are obtained in a syrupy liquid called molasses. To separate the sugar from the molasses the mixture is put into revolving baskets which are spun very fast. The sugar crystals remain in the baskets while the molasses is forced out of the holes and is collected. The molasses is used to make rum. The stages in producing sugar are shown in Figure 9.17.

Fig. 9.17 Stages in producing sugar.

fraction	use
gases	
petrol (gasoline)	
paraffin (kerosene)	
diesel oil	
lubricating oil	
fuel oil	
bitumen	

Fig. 9.18 The different substances obtained from crude oil.

Separating crude oil

Another separation process that is carried out in the Caribbean is the purification of oil. Oil is obtained from rocks beneath the ground or the sea bed. It is brought out by drilling oil wells through the rocks. The oil comes out as a mixture called **crude oil**, which contains several different kinds of oil.

As you know, we use oil for different purposes (Fig. 9.18). Some is used in car and aeroplane engines, some is burned at home, and some is used to lubricate things so that they run smoothly. These different kinds of oil all come from crude oil, using a process called **distillation**. This takes place in an oil refinery (Fig. 9.19). The different oils boil at different temperatures. As each oil reaches its boiling point, it changes to a vapour, which can be piped off and then condensed back to a liquid. The main types of oil in crude oil are petrol (gasoline), which boils at the lowest temperature, paraffin (kerosene) and diesel oil.

When we split up a natural product, like crude oil, into parts like this, we call the parts fractions, and the process is called **fractional distillation**.

Separating things   9.6

Fig. 9.19 The Willemstad oil refinery at Fort Nassau, Curaçao, N. Antilles.

What you should know

- Mixtures can be homogeneous or heterogeneous.
- Mixtures can be separated by filtration, distillation or chromatography.
- Sugar cane produces a mixture of sugar and molasses.
- Crude oil is a mixture of petrol (gasoline), paraffin (kerosene), diesel oil and other types of oil. These are separated by a process called fractional distillation.

Questions

1 How would you separate the following mixtures?
   a A soluble salt in a solvent.
   b An insoluble material suspended in a liquid.
   c Two powders, one of which is a magnetic metal.

2 Name a naturally occurring mixture that is separated on an industrial scale by fractional distillation. What properties of the substances in the mixture make this a suitable method?

3 Find out more about fractional distillation and petroleum products from the internet. Sites you might like to try are the Institute of Petroleum (www.petroleum.co.uk) and the American Petroleum Institute (www.api.org).

4 The release of chemicals can damage the environment. Research an example – an oil spill, the release of waste into a river – and the pollution that resulted. How was this pollution tackled?

Looking at non-living things

9.7 Acids and alkalis

▶ Objectives

After studying this topic you should be able to:

- give examples of some common acids and alkalis
- outline a simple test to show whether a substance is acidic or alkaline
- describe how the pH scale measures the strength of acids and alkalis.

You have probably tasted lime juice and vinegar. We describe the taste as 'sour' or 'acid'. In fact, both lime juice and vinegar contain chemical compounds called **acids**. You may know of other acids. Some, such as the acid in a car battery, are much stronger than lime juice, and can attack metals and other materials. Our skin and eyes can also be damaged if they get splashed by strong acids.

Acids react with another group of chemical compounds called **bases** (or **alkalis**). An alkali is a soluble base. The product formed when an acid reacts with a base is called a **salt**. (Do not confuse this term 'salt' with the common salt we use in cooking, which is properly called sodium chloride.)

How acidic?

1 Litmus	acid	red
	neutral	mauve
	base	blue
2 Universal indicator	pH 1	
	2	
	3	
	4	
	5	
	6	
	7	
	8	
	9	
	10	
	11	
	12	
	13	
	14	
3 Methyl orange	acid	
	base	

Fig. 9.20 The colour ranges of three common indicators. This is shown in colour on page vi.

It can be a bit unpleasant to taste lime juice and vinegar, but we come to no harm. However, we cannot go around tasting unknown things to see if they are acidic or not. This would be very dangerous! Instead we use substances called indicators. These are similar to the dyes that are used to colour our clothes. An indicator tells us if a substance is an acid or an alkali. It shows different colours in acid and in alkali. A substance that is neither acid nor alkali is described as neutral.

There are various types of indicator. The colour changes produced by three common indicators are shown in Figure 9.20. So, for example, litmus gives just three colours. Using indicators like **litmus** only allows you to tell whether a substance is acidic, alkaline or neutral. However, it does not allow you to compare two substances and tell which is the more acidic.

We measure how acidic or alkaline something is by the pH scale (Fig. 9.21). This is a number scale from 0 to 14. Acidic substances have a low pH, less than 7 (the lower the pH, the stronger the acid); neutral substances have a pH of 7; and alkaline substances have a high pH, greater than 7 (the higher the pH, the stronger the alkali).

9.7 Acids and alkalis

> **Did you know?**
>
> Litmus is a dye used as an indicator. It turns red with acids and blue with alkalis. Neutral substances have no effect.

Universal indicator is the name of a special indicator that has different colours at different pH values and so allows you to compare the acidity of different substances.

pH 0 1 2 3 4 5 6 7 8 9 10 11 12 13 14

neutral

acidic ← → alkaline

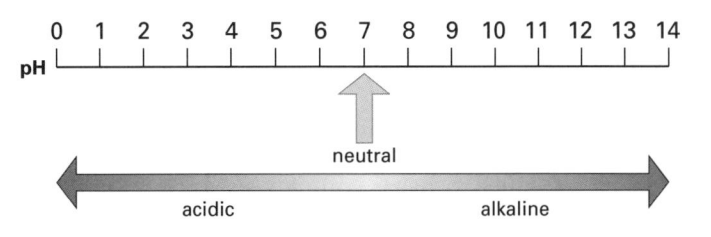

Fig. 9.21 The pH scale.

→ Activity Finding out pH values

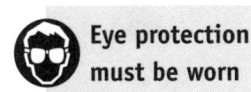

You will need

- test tubes
- lemon or lime juice
- an antacid (e.g. sodium hydrogencarbonate)
- dilute sodium hydroxide solution (corrosive)
- salt water
- detergent (washing powder)
- universal indicator paper
- vinegar
- ammonia solution
- dilute sulphuric acid (car battery acid [corrosive])
- sodium carbonate (washing soda) solution (irritant)
- sour milk
- drinking water
- methylated spirits (flammable)

> **Eye protection must be worn**
>
> **Danger!**
>
> Care needed when handling chemicals!

Method

1 Put about 1 cm depth of the liquid to be tested in a test tube. You will need to add water to dry materials.
2 Add a piece of universal indicator paper.
3 Match the colours with the colours on the chart to find the pH.
4 Test some other materials. Your teacher will guide you.

Record

Record your observations in a table like Table 9.3.

Substance	Colour of universal indicator paper	pH	Acid or alkali?
Vinegar	Red		Acid

Table 9.3 Acid or alkali?

Discuss
1. Which substances are acidic? Which are alkaline?
2. What is the strongest alkali?

Neutralization

From the last activity, you can begin to understand why we study acids and bases together. Some people think of them as chemical opposites. Let us see what happens to the pH of an alkali when we add some acid.

➡ Activity Neutralizing an alkali

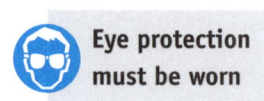

You will need
- an alkali solution (sodium hydroxide [corrosive])
- an acid (dilute nitric acid [corrosive] or hydrochloric acid [irritant])
- a measuring cylinder
- a beaker or test tube
- a plastic syringe
- universal indicator solution or paper

Eye protection must be worn

Danger! Care needed when handling chemicals!

Method
1. Put 10 cm³ of the alkali solution into the beaker (Fig. 9.22).
2. Add two drops of indicator solution or a piece of indiator paper.
3. Add 1 cm³ of acid solution at a time from the syringe.

Record
Observe the colour of the indicator after each addition of acid and record it in a table like Table 9.4.

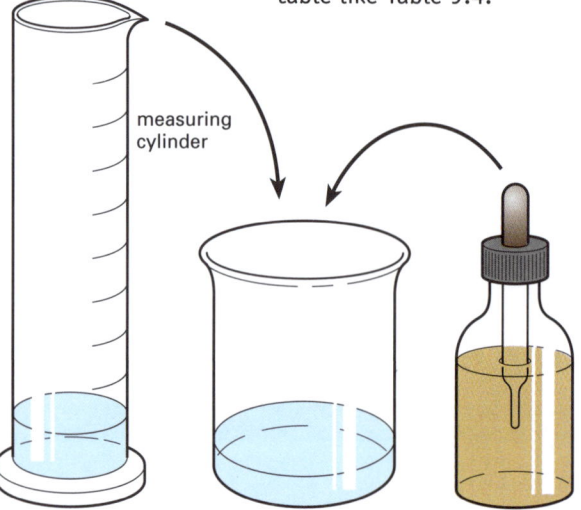

Measure 10 cm³ alkali and add 2 or 3 drops of indicator solution

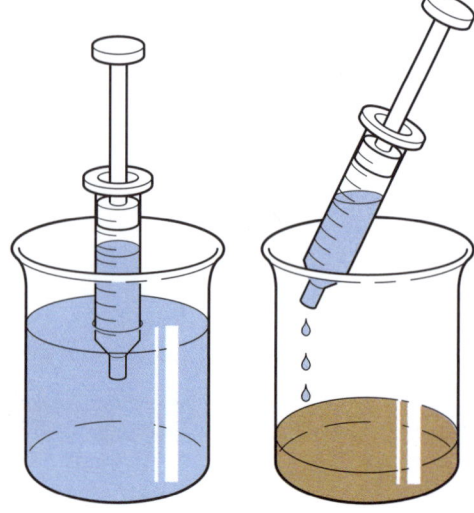

Fill syringe with acid solution

Add acid to alkali from syringe

Fig. 9.22 Method for neutralizing an alkali.

9.7 Acids and alkalis

Table 9.4 Adding acid to alkali.

Volume of acid (cm³)	Colour	pH

Discuss
What volume of the acid was needed to bring the pH of the solution to 7?

....

When acid is added to alkali so that the solution becomes pH 7, or neutral, we say that the acid has neutralized the alkali. In the same way we can add alkali to an acid, and so neutralize the acid. When an acid neutralizes an alkali or vice versa, a salt is formed.

Finding out

Soil acidity

Plants and animals that live in the soil prefer the pH to stay within a certain range, usually 4 to 8 (Fig. 9.23). If the soil is too acidic or too alkaline, it becomes difficult for a farmer to grow crops. He/she must then adjust the soil pH. How do you think this is done?

Much of the Caribbean has soil based on limestone, which is calcium carbonate. What pH range would you expect soil from limestone to have? Find out if you are right. What does your answer teach you about the pH of salts? Would you expect the soil everywhere in a country to have the same pH?

Fig. 9.23 A meter is used to test the pH of the soil.

Activity Soil pH values

Hygiene: wash your hands thoroughly after handling soil.

You will need
- several test tubes or glass jars
- universal indicator paper

Method
1. Collect and label soil samples from different places, for example the school grounds, the seashore, a river bed, a vegetable garden, an old compost heap, a freshly dug plot of land.
2. Add water to each soil sample. Shake well.
3. Allow to settle and test the liquid with universal indicator paper.

Discuss
1. Which soil sample had the highest pH?
2. Which soil sample had the lowest pH?
3. Why do you think that was?

Products of neutralization

As we have already mentioned, when an acid and alkali neutralize each other they form a new substance called a salt:

acid + alkali (or base) → salt + water

9.7 Looking at non-living things

Salts are named after the acids and bases from which they are made. So, all salts made from hydro*chloric* acid are called *chlorides*. In the same way, all salts made from *sulphuric* acid are called *sulphates*; and ones made from *nitric* acid are called *nitrates*. Every salt has at least two parts to its name. Let us now look at some examples.

- If the alkali you use is *sodium* hydroxide and the acid you use is hydro*chloric* acid, you will get the salt called *sodium chloride*.
- If you use *potassium* hydroxide and *sulphuric* acid, the salt you get is called *potassium sulphate*.
- If you use *ammonia* solution and *nitric* acid the salt you get is called *ammonium nitrate*.

Activity Making a salt

You will need
- alkali solution (e.g. sodium hydroxide solution [corrosive])
- acid (e.g. nitric acid [corrosive])
- a beaker
- a measuring cylinder
- an evaporating dish
- a measuring cylinder
- a Bunsen burner
- a tripod and gauze

Danger! Care needed when handling chemicals!

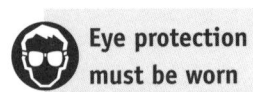

Eye protection must be worn

Danger! Danger of spitting!

Method
1. Measure out 10 cm^3 of the alkali.
2. Add just sufficent acid to neutralize all the alkali (the amount you discovered in the activity on page 28!).
3. Place this solution in the evaporating dish and heat over a beaker of boiling water (see Fig. 9.24).
4. Continue heating until almost all the water in the evaporating dish has evaporated.

Discuss
1. What is left in the evaporating dish? What does it look like?
2. What is the chemical name of this substance?

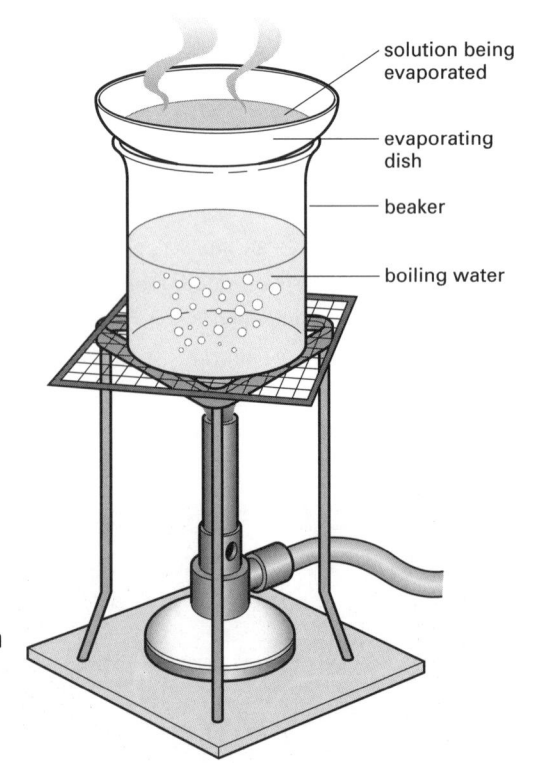

Fig. 9.24 Evaporating the solution of a salt.

Acids and alkalis 9.7

What you should know

- Acids react with alkalis (or bases) to form salts.
- We can test whether a substance is acidic or alkaline using an indicator.
- The strength of an acid or alkali is measured on the pH scale.
- Acids have pH values less than 7; alkalis are greater than pH 7.
- Salts are named after the alkali and acid from which they are formed.

Questions

1. Say whether the following values or indicator colours mean that a substance is acidic, neutral or alkaline:

   a. a pH value of 8

   b. litmus paper that has turned blue

   c. a pH value of 3

   d. a pH value of 7

   e. litmus paper that has turned red

2. Name the salts that you will get if you react the following alkalis and acids:

   a. Sodium hydroxide and sulphuric acid

   b. Potassium hydroxide and sulphuric acid

   c. Ammonia solution and hydrochloric acid

3. Look around your home for common acids (often in foods) and alkalis (often in cleaning materials). Make a list of them.

9.8 Acids and metals

▶ Objectives

After studying this topic you should be able to:
- describe what happens when certain metals react with acids
- outline the properties of hydrogen.

We have found out what happens to acids when they are neutralized by alkalis. What happens when we add an acid to a metal?

➔ Activity Acids and metals

You will need
- dilute hydrochloric acid (irritant) and dilute sulphuric acid (corrosive)
- small pieces of different metals, such as aluminium foil, iron, lead, copper, zinc granules and magnesium ribbon
- several test tubes

⚠ Danger!
Care needed when handling chemicals!

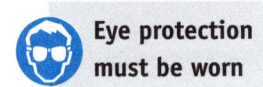

Eye protection must be worn

Method
1. Put some dilute hydrochloric acid into a test tube.
2. Add small pieces of one of the metals.
3. Repeat with different metals.
4. Repeat the whole experiment with dilute sulphuric acid.

Record
Copy Table 9.5 into your workbook and use it to record your observations.

Table 9.5 Reacting metals with acids.

Metal	Dilute hydrochloric acid	Dilute sulphuric acid

Discuss
1. Was any gas given off when the metal was dropped into the acid? (Was there any fizzing?)
2. Did the metal disappear?
3. Did the tube get warm?

Acids and metals 9.8

4 If the metal reacted with the acid. How reactive was it?
5 Which metal was the most active?
6 Place the metals in an order of reactivity. Think about how quickly the metal reacts, how much fizzing there is, and how warm the test tube gets.

Here then is another way of making salts. We can say:

> metal + acid → salt + gas

We shall find out what the gas is in our next experiment.

It should be pointed out that this is not a general method of making salts. Sometimes it does not work. Certain metals do not react with dilute acids. The method can only be used for the more active metals.

Now let's investigate the gas given off when zinc reacts with dilute sulphuric acid.

→ Activity What's the gas?

Danger!
Care needed when handling chemicals!

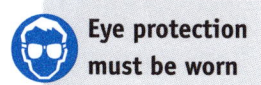

Eye protection must be worn

You will need
- an apparatus set up like the one shown in Figure 9.25
- dilute sulphuric acid (corrosive)
- pieces of zinc

Method
1 Pour some dilute acid down the funnel into the flask containing pieces of zinc.
2 Collect the gas that comes off in a test tube.
3 Test the gas with a lighted taper as shown in Figure 9.26.
4 Evaporate the solution left in the flask, using the apparatus shown in Figure 9.24.

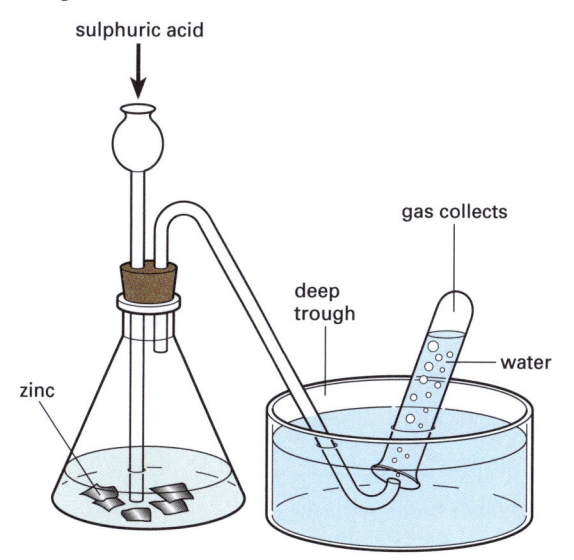

Fig. 9.25 Collecting the gas given off when zinc reacts with dilute sulphuric acid.

Fig. 9.26 Testing the gas with a lighted taper.

9.8 Looking at non-living things

Discuss
1 What colour was the flame when you tested the gas with a lighted match?
2 What remains in the evaporating dish when all the water has been evaporated?

The gas given off is called hydrogen. Hydrogen is colourless and insoluble in water. It burns with a blue flame, but does not allow things to burn in it. It forms an explosive mixture with oxygen. Even so, it could be used as a fuel for cars and other vehicles in the future.

Where do you think the hydrogen comes from? Remember that metals like zinc and magnesium are elements.

The hydrogen comes from the acid.

For some metals – those which are active when placed in acids – we can say that the metal reacts with acid to form hydrogen and a salt:

acid + metal → salt + hydrogen

Did you know?

Hydrogen is the lightest gas known; it is much less dense than air. For this reason it was used in the past to fill the bags of airships. However, it sometimes caused explosions and fires, the most famous being the destruction of the German airship *Hindenburg* in 1937. After that, airships used the non-flammable gas helium instead of hydrogen.

What you should know

- Certain metals react with dilute sulphuric acid or hydrochloric acid to form a salt and hydrogen.
- The hydrogen released comes from the acid.

Question

1 The sentences below describe some of the properties of hydrogen. Fill in each blank space using a word from the following list:

blue, colourless, helium, insoluble, less, more, oxygen, red, soluble

a Hydrogen forms an explosive mixture with _____.
b Air is much _____ dense than hydrogen.
c Hydrogen burns with a _____ flame.
d Hydrogen is _____ in water.

Looking at non-living things

9.9 More about salts

▷ Objectives

After studying this topic you should be able to:

- describe what happens when a carbonate reacts with an acid
- describe how metal oxides react with acids
- say what we mean by a chemical 'base'.

Carbonates

As we have seen already, salts are formed by neutralizing acids or alkalis, and by reacting certain metals with acids. They can also be made by reacting carbonates with acids, or by reacting metal oxides with acids.

→ Activity How carbonates react with acids

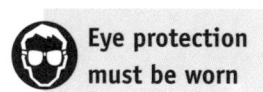

You will need

- test tubes
- a measuring cylinder
- dilute sulphuric acid (corrosive), hydrochloric acid (irritant) or nitric acid (corrosive)
- lime water (calcium hydroxide solution [irritant])
- samples of solids: washing soda (sodium carbonate [irritant]), baking soda (sodium hydrogencarbonate, sometimes called sodium bicarbonate), eggshells, seashells, coral

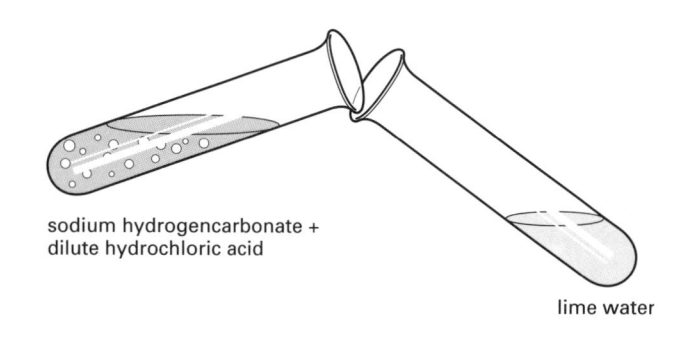

⚠ **Danger!**

Care needed when handling chemicals!

👓 Eye protection must be worn

sodium hydrogencarbonate + dilute hydrochloric acid

lime water

Fig. 9.27 Testing for carbon dioxide gas with lime water (calcium hydroxide solution).

Method

1. Pour about 10 cm^3 of the dilute acid into a test tube.
2. Add one of the solids – a little at a time – until no more will react.
3. Test some of the gas coming off with lime water as shown in Figure 9.27.
4. Evaporate the solution (see page 30) to collect the salt formed.

Discuss

1. What happens when you add the solid carbonates?
2. What happens to the lime water when you test the gas?

From this activity you will see that some shells and coral, as well as household chemicals such as washing soda (sodium carbonate), react with dilute acids to give off carbon dioxide. You can test for this with lime water (the lime water becomes milky if carbon dioxide is present).

The other products of this reaction are a salt and water. So the reaction is:

acid + carbonate → salt + carbon dioxide + water

Metal oxides

A metal oxide is a compound containing just two elements in combination: one is a metal, the other is oxygen. Examples are aluminium oxide, magnesium oxide and zinc oxide. A layer of metal oxide forms on the surface of some metals, such as aluminium or zinc, because the metal reacts with oxygen in the air. You can scrape off this layer of metal oxide to reveal the shiny metal underneath.

Some metal oxides can dissolve in water and form alkalis. But many metal oxides will not dissolve in water. They will, however, react with acids to form salts. They act as bases. The reaction is:

metal oxide + acid → salt + water

Activity A metal oxide and an acid

You will need
- copper(II) oxide
- dilute sulphuric acid (corrosive)
- test tubes
- a Bunsen burner

Eye protection must be worn

Danger! Care needed when handling chemicals!

Method
1 Put a little copper(II) oxide in a test tube.
2 Add dilute sulphuric acid and warm gently.
3 Add more copper(II) oxide, bit by bit, until no more dissolves.
4 Filter the solution to remove excess copper(II) oxide (see Fig. 9.11).
5 Evaporate the clear blue solution, as before (see page 30), to prepare the salt, but do not boil all the water away. When some solid starts to form around the edge, set it aside to cool slowly.

Discuss
You have prepared a salt called copper sulphate (Fig. 9.28). If you repeated the experiment using nitric acid, what salt would you get?

9.9 More about salts

Fig. 9.28 Copper sulphate has many uses. It is used in Bordeaux mixture, which is sprayed on crops to kill harmful fungi.

Bases

We have seen in Topic 9.7 how acids are neutralized by alkalis such as sodium hydroxide. The alkali and acid react together to form a salt and water. We have just seen how metal oxides react with acids. Again, the reaction produces a salt and water.

The oxides and hydroxides of metals are described as bases. They react with acids to form a salt and water only. The reaction is:

$$\text{acid} + \text{base} \rightarrow \text{salt} + \text{water}$$

Ammonia is another example of a base. Some bases dissolve in water to form alkalis.

Although carbonates form salts with acids, they are not bases because the reaction produces carbon dioxide as well as salt and water.

What you should know

- Acids can be neutralized by adding carbonates or hydrogencarbonates to them. A salt and water are formed and carbon dioxide gas is given off.
- Acids also react with bases to form a salt and water.
- Bases include hydroxides and oxides of metals, and ammonia.

Questions

1. Which of the following will give off carbon dioxide gas when dilute acid is added?

    a zinc carbonate

    b zinc oxide

    c sodium hydrogencarbonate

    d sodium hydroxide

    e magnesium oxide

2. In each of the reaction equations below, replace 'X' with the correct word chosen from the following list:

    alkali, carbonate, chloride, hydrogen, oxygen, water

    a acid + X $\rightarrow$ salt + water + carbon dioxide

    b metal oxide + acid $\rightarrow$ salt + X

    c acid + metal $\rightarrow$ salt + X

3. We use ammonia in many different ways in the home, in agriculture and industry. Research some of its uses.

Resources for life

10.1 Air as a resource

▶ Objectives

After studying this topic you should be able to:
- list the different gases found in air
- describe some simple tests for oxygen and carbon dioxide
- outline the biological and industrial importance of the gases in air.

Air is all around us. Most of the time we don't give it much thought. If it's windy we can feel it, and sometimes we can smell chemicals carried on it. Animals and plants need to breathe air to stay alive. Even animals and plants that live underwater depend on the air dissolved in water. Without air things will not burn.

Air is also used for many industrial and manufacturing purposes. By cooling it in a special apparatus it can be made into a liquid and its constituents separated.

What is air?

So what is air made of, and why is it so important for living things? We can begin to find out by doing a few simple experiments.

➔ Activity What part of air is used up in burning?

You will need
- a candle
- a basin
- a glass jar
- a tin lid

⚠ **Danger!**

Care needed!

Method
1. Fix the candle on the tin lid and light it.
2. Half fill the basin with water and float the candle in the water.
3. Turn the jar upside down and carefully lower it over the lighted candle so that the mouth of the jar just touches the water surface (Fig. 10.1).
4. Observe what happens.

Fig. 10.1 Testing air with a burning candle.

Discuss
1. When did the water put the flame out?
2. How much of the air in the jar was used up by the burning candle?

10.1 Air as a resource

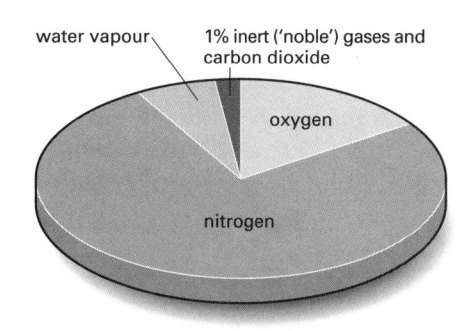

Fig. 10.2 The composition of air.

You should have observed that roughly one-fifth of the air inside the jar was used up by the burning candle. This part is made up of oxygen, the gas that allows things to burn. The remainder of the air does not allow things to burn. We know this because the candle in the experiment went out.

The part of the air that was left in the jar is a mixture of gases. These include nitrogen, carbon dioxide, water vapour and small amounts of various noble gases (or inert gases) (Fig. 10.2).

Detecting gases in air

Gases in the air, such as oxygen and carbon dioxide, have no smell or taste. They are detected by chemical reactions.

→ Activity Reactions of oxygen and carbon dioxide

Danger!
Care needed!

Eye protection must be worn

You will need
- four stoppered labelled test tubes of oxygen
- four stoppered labelled test tubes of carbon dioxide
- bicarbonate indicator
- splints
- calcium hydroxide solution (lime water [irritant])

Method
1. Hold a burning splint in a tube of each gas.
2. Hold a glowing splint in a tube of each gas.
3. Add about 2 cm³ of calcium hydroxide solution to a test tube of each gas. Shake the tube.
4. Add about 2 cm³ of bicarbonate indicator to a test tube of each gas and shake the tube.

Record
Copy Table 10.1 and use it to record your observations.

Table 10.1 Reactions of oxygen and carbon dioxide.

Experiment	Oxygen	Carbon dioxide
1 Burning splint		
2 Glowing splint		
3 Calcium hydroxide solution		
4 Bicarbonate indicator		

Oxygen will cause a glowing splint to relight, and a burning splint to burn more brightly. Carbon dioxide puts out a flame, causes lime water to go milky, and changes bicarbonate indicator from purple to yellow (the colour change shows that carbon dioxide is acidic).

Oxygen

As we have just seen, oxygen is used when things burn. It is also the gas that living organisms take from the air when they breathe. Oxygen is needed by most living organisms, including all plants and animals. They use it to release energy from food in a process called **respiration**. You will look at this more closely in Topic 11.5.

Oxygen is produced by plants, algae and other organisms that perform the process of **photosynthesis**. This process uses light energy (from the Sun) to convert carbon dioxide and water into food and oxygen (see Book 1, Topic 5.1).

Pure oxygen gas is distributed in pressurized cylinders and used for various industrial purposes, including welding. It is also used in the breathing apparatus worn by divers (Fig. 10.3), and in equipment for helping sick people to breathe in hospital.

Oxygen occurs not only as a gas in air but also as an element in a wide range of chemical compounds, including all major foodstuffs.

Fig. 10.3 This breathing apparatus contains a mixture of compressed air and oxygen. It allows the diver to stay underwater for up to two hours.

Carbon dioxide

Although present in only small amounts in air, carbon dioxide is another gas that is very important for living organisms. It is produced by animals and plants as a product of respiration. However, it is a vital raw material for photosynthesis in plants. Without carbon dioxide, plants could not make their own food. Since all animals depend on plants, directly or indirectly, as a source of food, they too would suffer.

Carbon dioxide is one of the key links in the transfer of carbon between living things and the environment. We shall look more closely at this carbon cycle in Topic 10.4.

Did you know?

Solid carbon dioxide is called dry ice. It is very cold: −78°C! When water is added, dry ice gives off carbon dioxide gas (Fig. 10.4). This is because at normal temperatures and atmospheric pressure dry ice changes directly from a solid to a gas (it sublimes). You have probably seen dry ice being used in films and on stage at rock concerts to create artificial mist and fog. Because it is much colder than water ice, dry ice is used in industry to keep things at very low temperatures.

Fig. 10.4 Dry ice sublimes (changes from solid directly to gas) when mixed with water, giving off carbon dioxide gas.

Nitrogen

Nitrogen gas makes up the biggest proportion of air, over three-quarters of the total in terms of volume. Although it is not as chemically reactive as oxygen and carbon dioxide, nitrogen plays an important role in nature. Some of the nitrogen gas is converted to nitrates by soil bacteria. Plants absorb these nitrates, and use them to make proteins and other nitrogen-containing compounds. Proteins are used by all living organisms as chemical 'building blocks', essential for growth and repair of tissues.

Humans have invented a chemical process for taking nitrogen gas from the atmosphere and combining it with hydrogen to make ammonia. Ammonia is used in the chemical industry to make various chemical products, including fertilizers, dyes and explosives.

The reactions involving nitrogen from the air are examined in more detail when we look at the nitrogen cycle in Topic 10.4.

Water vapour

We have already discussed the importance of water vapour in the air when we studied the water cycle in Book 1, Topic 3.2. The amount of water vapour in air varies greatly from place to place. As you might expect it is often very high in places near the sea – and in the Caribbean that means most places! It is also very high after a rainstorm. You may have heard people say 'It is very humid today' when they mean that there is a lot of water vapour in the air.

10.1 Resources for life

Some substances, for example table salt, react with the water vapour in the air. They can be protected by placing small bags (or sachets) of **desiccants**, such as silica gel, in the containers. Desiccants are materials that easily absorb water (the word 'desiccate' means to dry). In the laboratory cobalt chloride paper changes from blue to pink in the presence of water vapour.

→ Activity Testing for water vapour

You will need
- cobalt chloride paper which has been warmed so that it is blue
- silica gel desiccant
- a jar with a lid
- forceps

Method
1. Leave pieces or strips of cobalt chloride paper in various parts of the room and outside in the school grounds. Use forceps to handle the cobalt chloride paper because the moisture on your hands would make it change colour.
2. Place a piece of cobalt chloride paper in a jar with the desiccant.

Discuss
1. What happens to the pieces of cobalt chloride paper? Do they all change colour?
2. What do your results tell you about humidity in and around the school?
3. What weather changes might give you different results?

⚠ Danger!

Cobalt chloride paper is toxic and may sensitize your skin. Handle with forceps.

Noble gases

Air contains very small amounts of certain other gases – the noble gases or inert gases. They are helium, neon, argon, krypton, xenon and radon. Because they are chemically unreactive, they have a wide range of uses. For example, helium is much lighter than air and does not burn or explode, so it can be used as the lifting gas for weather balloons and airships. It is also mixed with oxygen in the breathing apparatus used by deep-sea divers. Both helium and argon are used in welding. Fluorescent lamps are filled with argon or a mixture of inert gases, and advertising signs are often lit with neon-filled lamps (Fig. 10.5).

Fig. 10.5 Neon advertising signs are a familiar sight in many cities. The neon gas inside the lamps glows orange-red, but other colours are produced by adding various chemicals to the neon.

Air as a resource 10.1

◘ What you should know

- Air is a mixture of gases, including nitrogen, oxygen, carbon dioxide, water vapour and the noble gases.
- Oxygen encourages burning, whereas carbon dioxide will put out a flame.
- Organisms breathe air to obtain oxygen. This is used to extract energy from food by the process called respiration.
- Carbon dioxide in the air is used by plants and other green organisms to make food by the process called photosynthesis. Carbon dioxide is also a by-product of respiration.
- Over three-quarters of air is nitrogen gas. This is extracted by certain soil bacteria and made into nitrates, which are absorbed by plants and used to make proteins.
- The gases of air can be separated and used for a wide range of industrial purposes.

@ Questions

1. Carbon dioxide is used in some types of fire extinguisher. This is an example of how science can be applied to useful products.

    a Why is carbon dioxide used?

    b Carbon dioxide is heavier than air. Why is this is an advantage when putting out a fire?

    c In some extinguishers, an acid is mixed with another chemical to produce carbon dioxide when it is needed. What type of chemical do you think this is? (Hint: Revise 'Acids'.)

2. As you climb up a high mountain the air pressure slowly falls and the air gets 'thinner'. Why do you think breathing becomes more difficult?

3. Which of the following gases is the odd one out, and why? Nitrogen, argon, hydrogen, oxygen, helium, carbon dioxide.

4. Find out more about the noble gases. How do they produce the vivid colours in advertising lights?

Resources for life

10.2 Soil as a resource

> **Objectives**
>
> After studying this topic, you should be able to:
> - describe the structure of soil
> - explain how soil is formed
> - describe the importance of soil to the ecosystem
> - explain the importance of soil conservation.

Soil is a thin layer covering a large part of the land on the Earth's surface. The only bits of land that are not covered with some kind of soil are bare rocks. Soil is an important natural resource. It is the home or habitat of many plants and animals. People cultivate the soil on farms and in gardens to grow food. Good-quality soil also means there is good grass for grazing animals.

The parts of soil

Look carefully at the section through the soil shown in Figure 10.6. This is called a soil profile. It shows that there are two layers of soil above the rock. The top darker layer is the **topsoil**. It is very fertile and is where most animals live and where most plant roots are found. It is fertile because it contains a lot of **humus**. Humus consists of the dead and decaying remains of animals and plants. Beneath the topsoil is the lighter

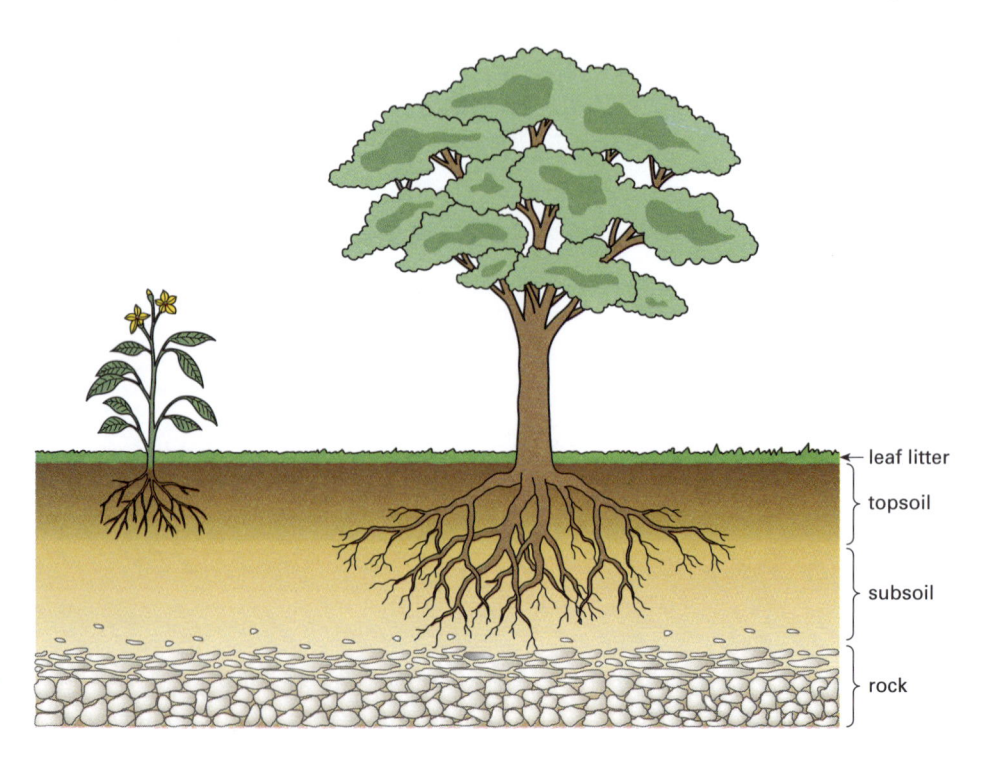

Fig. 10.6 A section through soil showing the layers.

— leaf litter
— topsoil
— subsoil
— rock

coloured **subsoil**, which has very few animals and plant roots and therefore less humus. The roots of large trees grow down into this layer. Below the subsoil is slightly weathered rock (with particles) on top of the solid rock. You can see these layers if you look at the side of a quarry or at recently dug soil when a road is being cut through high ground (Fig. 10.7).

Now you are going to look at soil more closely.

Fig. 10.7 The soil has been dug out down to the underlying rock. The topsoil is the very dark layer at the top.

→ Activity Investigating the parts of the soil

Hygiene: Wash your hands thoroughly after handling soil.

You will need
- a large jar or other transparent container
- a spoon or glass rod for stirring the soil
- water
- a sample of soil from the school area

Method
1. One-third fill the container with soil.
2. Add water up to a level about 5 cm below the rim.
3. Stir the soil and water mixture thoroughly.
4. Allow the mixture to settle for about 30 minutes.

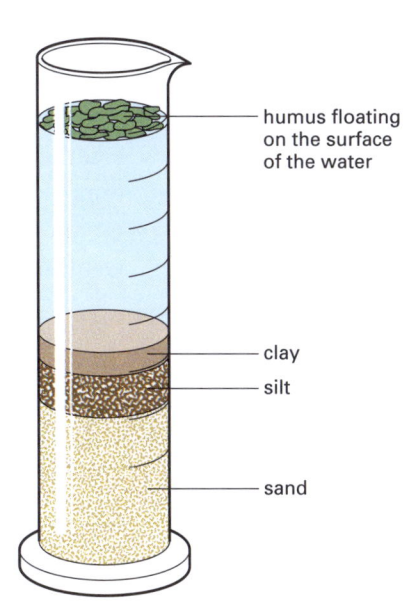

Fig. 10.8 Investigating the parts of soil.

Record
Examine the container carefully without shaking it and draw what you can see. Use the drawing in Figure 10.8 to help you.

Discuss
1. What can you see at the bottom of the container?
2. Why are there different layers at the bottom of the container?
3. Why do you think the water is cloudy?
4. What is floating on the top of the water?

❓ Finding out

Compost heaps

People with gardens often make a compost heap from the waste plant material in the garden. For example, dead plants, flowers and leaves, and unwanted trimmings of vegetables or roots are all piled up in a heap. They rot down over many months with the help of bacteria. The compost can then be spread and dug in around new plants to supply them with extra nutrients. This is an example of **recycling** plant material in the garden.

Find out what other materials can be used to make compost. Perhaps some gardening books will tell you. How long does it take for the compost to form? How can you tell when it is ready to spread on your garden? How hot can a compost heap become? Why does it have this high temperature?

In the experiment, you observed that the soil is made up of different parts. You saw that the largest, heaviest particles sank to the bottom. These were gravel particles. Above this were smaller particles of sand, then a layer of even smaller particles of silt. The water was cloudy because it contained the smallest clay particles. The lightest things floating at the top were mainly bits of leaves and stems and other plant material.

Soil particles: Gravel, sand, silt and clay particles are formed from the weathering of rocks. Wind, rain, flowing water, and hot and cold temperatures gradually wear the rocks away and the particles are carried off and then deposited somewhere else. You will learn more about the weathering of rocks in Book 3, Topic 14.4.

Soil water: Soil also contains water. Even if soil sometimes looks or feels dry at the surface, if you dig down far enough, it is damp. Soil water forms a thin film around the soil particles. It contains dissolved mineral salts. Water and mineral salts are needed by plants and are absorbed through the roots. (We learnt about this in Book 1, Topic 5.20.)

Air: Air is also found in the spaces between the soil particles. It contains oxygen needed by soil animals and plant roots for respiration.

Humus: When plants and animals die, they decay (rot) to form humus. Humus is rich in nutrients for living plants, for example nitrates. It sticks to the soil particles, and causes the formation of lumps of soil known as soil crumbs.

Now you know about the contents of soil, go back to the drawing you made in the previous activity and see if you can add more labels.

Activity Does soil contain air?

Method
1 Repeat the previous activity, but this time add a big lump of soil to the water.
2 Stir it thoroughly to break up the lump and watch the water closely.

Record
Draw what you can see. Can you see bubbles in the water?

Discuss
1 If you saw air bubbles, where was the air before you stirred the soil and water?
2 Why is air important in healthy soil?

⊙ Activity Feeling soil texture

Hygiene: Wash your hands thoroughly after handling soil.

You will need
- samples of clay soil, sandy soil and loam (a dark, rich soil)
- some water

Method
1 Examine each sample of soil in turn. How does each type of soil feel when rubbed between the palms of your hands? Try rolling the soil into a ball.
2 Slowly add enough water to just wet a handful of soil of each type. Do not add too much water.
3 Take a sample of each type of damp soil in turn, and rub it between your palms. How does the damp soil feel? Can you roll the wet soil into sausages?

Record
Copy Table 10.2 and write in your results for each type of soil.

Table 10.2 Results of feeling different types of wet and dry soils.

Type of soil	How dry soil feels	How wet soil feels	Can you make a soil sausage?
Sandy soil			
Clay soil			
Loam			

Discuss
1 Which type of dry soil rolled into a ball easily?
2 Which type of wet soil rolled into a ball easily?
3 Which type of soil did not roll into a ball when wet or dry?
4 Which type of soil made the best soil sausage?

10.2 Resources for life

Although there are many different types of soil all over the world, it is convenient to divide soils into three main types based on the type and size of the soil particles.

Sandy soil: This contains more sand particles than clay particles. The particles of sand in a sandy soil are larger than the particles in a clay soil, so there are bigger air spaces between the particles. If you pour water onto sandy soil, the water passes easily through these spaces. Sandy soils are warm but do not hold much water – they drain easily. Soil water contains dissolved salts, so when the water soaks through, the salts pass through too and are lost.

Clay soil: This contains more clay particles than sand particles. In a clay soil, the particles are smaller and closer together. There is less air and the soil quickly fills up with water – a clay soil drains poorly. A wet clay soil feels sticky because the particles stick together. Clay soils are usually cold and wet.

Loam: This contains similar amounts of sand and clay particles. It is a very fertile soil.

Which of these three types of soil is found in your school area?

Living things in the soil

Living things in soil range in size from microscopic animals, plants and bacteria, to larger invertebrates such as earthworms, insect larvae, beetles, ants, mites, millipedes, snails and spiders (Fig. 10.9). The insects

Fig. 10.9 Examples of animals found in soil. (Note that they are not drawn to scale!)

10.2 Soil as a resource

and other small soil-dwelling animals are food for vertebrate animals, such as lizards and certain birds. Other animals burrow into the ground to make their homes, for example, the agouti.

Plants generally put down their roots in the soil. Other plant parts found in soil include bulbs, corms and rhizomes (see Book 1, Topic 5.5). Fungi are also important inhabitants of soil, as can be seen by the many different types of moulds, toadstools and mushrooms that develop when conditions are damp.

Some activities of living things can benefit the soil, but others can harm it.

- Earthworms are very useful animals in soil. They take in soil and get nutrients from the humus. Very fine soil passes out of their bodies (often seen on the surface as worm casts). They break down (or till) the soil for us, and move it about, and their burrows help air to penetrate the soil.
- Plant roots growing closely together help to stop soil particles from blowing away in high winds. In this way, plants protect the soil.
- The activities of bacteria are also very important. They help to break down dead plants and animals.

Remember that some activities of living things can be harmful to the soil. For example, certain bacteria remove nitrogen from the soil. You will learn more about this in Topic 10.4.

➔ Activity Looking at small animals in the soil

Hygiene: Wash your hands thoroughly after handling soil and animals.

You will need
- some rich garden soil
- a flexible lamp with a 25 W bulb or a very powerful torch
- a large funnel (preferably plastic) containing some pebbles
- a beaker or jar with a tight-fitting lid
- a stand and clamp to support the funnel
- a hand lens

Method
1. Figure 10.10 shows you how to set up the experiment.
2. Place the pebbles in the funnel to stop the soil from falling through, but do not block

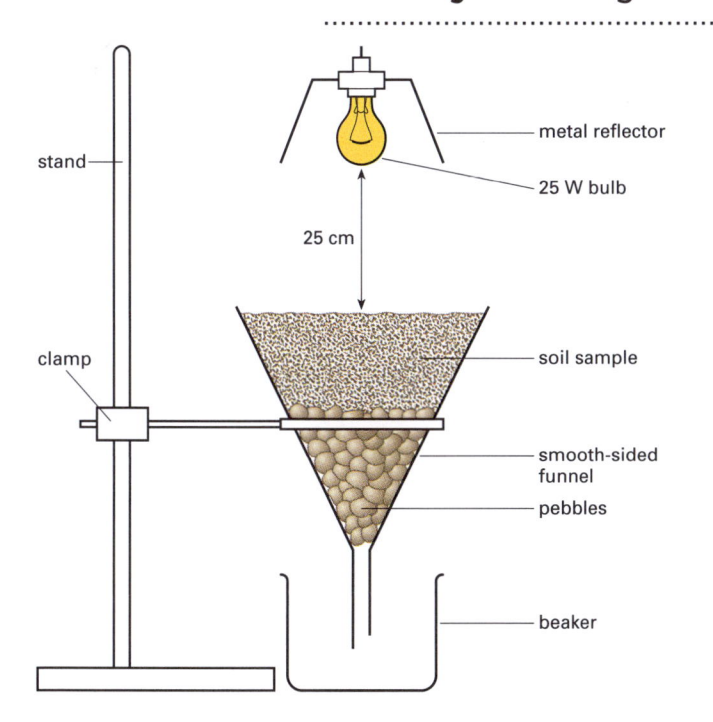

Fig. 10.10 Observing small animals in the soil.

the hole completely. Put the soil in the funnel before you place it over the beaker in case some soil seeps through.

3 Switch the lamp on.

4 The animals in the soil will crawl away from the light, down through the soil and should drop into the beaker. Do not bring the lamp so close to the soil that you harm the animals.

Record

Identify the animals you collected, using books and pictures. You will need to use a hand lens. Figure 10.9 shows some of the animals you might find.

How soil is formed

The forces of nature – climate, wind and water – change rock to soil. This process is called weathering. You will learn more about this in Book 3, Topic 14.4

The forces of nature gradually break down large rocks into smaller and smaller particles, eventually forming soil. Organic matter such as dead leaves and plants and animal remains decay to form **humus**, which is an important part of soil because it is rich in nutrients. In some areas, volcanic ash provides a particularly rich supply of mineral nutrients (Fig. 10.11).

Fig. 10.11 The lava and ash from this volcano in St Kitts produced a rich soil in which sugar cane grows well.

Lime and peat

The type of rock in an area can affect the soil. For example, if there are limestone rocks in the area, the soil will contain a lot of lime. Limestone is made of calcium carbonate and so the plants growing in this type of soil will obtain a good supply of calcium. Calcium carbonate also makes the soil more alkaline (see Topic 9.7). Adding lime to poor soil or to soil that is too acid adds calcium, makes it less acid and also helps soil particles to form clumps, and so make soil crumbs.

In marshy or swampy areas, the soil is often waterlogged. The dead plant material does not completely rot down because there is not enough air. This partly decayed plant material forms peat. When you add peat to soil, it makes it more acid. When there is more air, peat rots down further and forms humus. Both humus and peat make a soil more acid.

Soil as a resource 10.2

Plants have adapted to living in these types of soil. Some plants can only grow well in acid soils, some plants grow best in alkaline soils and others grow best in neutral soils (neither acid nor alkaline).

Soil in coastal areas contains a lot of salt. Some plants grow well in this type of soil, for example, coconut trees.

? Finding out

The plants in your neighbourhood

Work in groups and make a list of the plants you can see growing at school and nearby. In the first activity in this topic, you examined a sample of soil from your school area. What sort of soil was it? Does it affect the types of plants growing in your area?

What you should know

- Soil is a thin layer covering most of the land on the Earth's surface.
- It is a home (or habitat) for many animals and plants.
- The two main layers of soil are topsoil (more fertile) and subsoil (less fertile).
- Soil consists of mineral particles, water, air, humus and living organisms.
- The three main types of soil are clay soils, sandy soils and loam.
- The first soil formed when life began on Earth.
- Lime makes soil become alkaline. Peat makes soil become acid.

Questions

1. What are the names of the two main layers of soil you can see if you walk through a cutting made for a new road?

2. What are the main non-living parts of the soil?

3. How is humus formed in soil?

4. Why is soil rich in humus considered to be good soil?

5. What happens if you add lime to some soil?

6. What is peat, how is it formed and in what sort of places would you find it?

7. Find out how soil is formed today. What do the Sun's heat, ice, water and glaciers have to do with soil formation?

Resources for life

10.3 Food chains and food webs

▶ Objectives

After studying this topic you should be able to:

- explain how green plants and similar organisms capture the Sun's energy by photosynthesis
- describe how organisms release the energy in food through respiration
- outline the different levels of a food chain
- describe what is meant by a food web.

Fig. 10.12 A simple food chain. The plant provides food for the mouse, which in turn becomes food for the snake.

In Book 1, Topic 4.1 we saw that the Sun's rays are the main source of energy for life on Earth. Plants, algae and other plant-like organisms capture some of the Sun's energy and convert it into food. This food energy is used not only by the plants themselves, but by animals that eat the plants. Suppose that a plant uses some of its food to make berries. A mouse comes along and eats some of the berries. Then the mouse is eaten by a snake. Energy originally captured by the plant becomes food for the mouse; then the mouse becomes food for the snake. So energy, in the form of food, moves from plant, to mouse to snake. This is a simple **food chain** (Fig. 10.12). All animals and plants are part of such food chains.

Now let us take a closer look at the first vital step in any food chain – the capture of the Sun's energy.

Photosynthesis

Plants, algae, some bacteria and certain other organisms are able to make their own food using light, carbon dioxide and water (Fig. 10.13). This is called photosynthesis (photo- means 'light'). It produces oxygen, which we need to breathe, and food for us to eat.

A plant captures the energy in the Sun's rays by means of a special green pigment in leaves and other parts. This pigment is called chlorophyll. All the various shades of green you can see in plants are the result of

Food chains and food webs 10.3

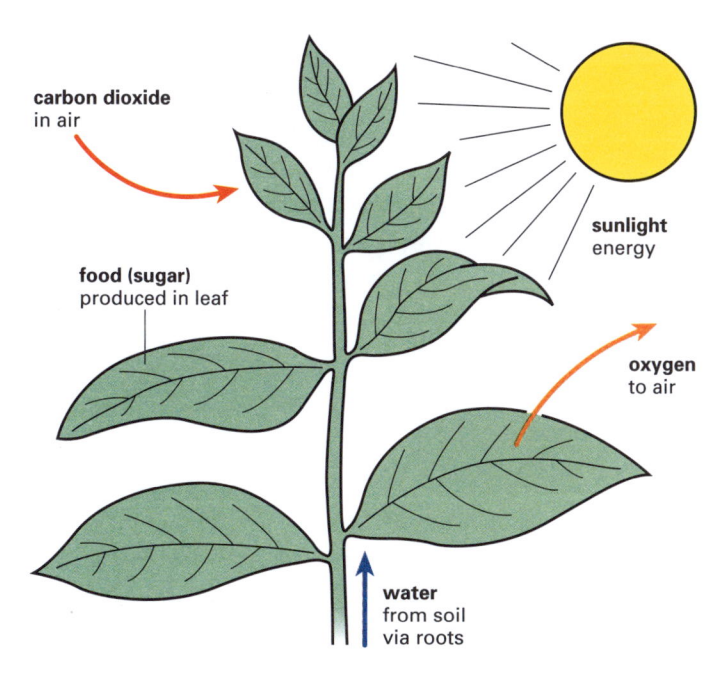

Fig. 10.13 The essential steps of photosynthesis.

chlorophyll. The other raw materials of photosynthesis are water, which the plant absorbs from the soil via its roots, and carbon dioxide, which enters the plant's leaves from the air.

Photosynthesis mainly takes place in the leaves. The water and carbon dioxide are converted into substances called **carbohydrates**. Sugar and starch are common carbohydrates made by plants. Sugar is soluble and can be moved around the plant in the form of sap. Starch is insoluble and serves as a food store for the plant, for example in roots or seeds.

Go back to Topic 5.1 in Book 1 to revise photosynthesis.

Respiration – unlocking energy

When animals eat plants or other animals, the energy locked in the food has to be released. Plants also need chemical energy from their food to do their work. In all organisms, a special process called respiration releases this energy from the food. During this process, carbon dioxide is produced, and this goes into the air. In most cases, respiration requires a supply of oxygen from the air.

We can see that respiration and photosynthesis have opposite effects on energy:

- Respiration uses oxygen, breaks down food and unlocks chemical energy. Carbon dioxide is released to the air.
- Photosynthesis converts carbon dioxide and sunlight energy to chemical energy in food. Oxygen is given off to the air.

Topic 11.5 examines respiration in greater detail.

Producers and consumers

Plants use carbohydrates as fuel, to provide them with energy when and where it is needed. They use the energy to make all the other substances that plants require, such as fats, proteins and vitamins. These are the 'building blocks' that the plants need to grow, make flowers, produce seeds, and perform all their other functions.

Animals also need energy, proteins, fats and other substances in order to function. But they depend on plants or other animals to supply them. In

10.3 Resources for life

our example in Figure 10.12, the mouse feeds on the berries; it probably also feeds on many other types of food produced by plants, such as seeds and roots. Plants and similar organisms are called **producers** – they make food that other organisms eat. The mouse is called a **primary consumer** – it consumes food made by a producer. When the mouse is caught by the snake it becomes food for the snake. The snake is called a **secondary consumer** – it eats a primary consumer. In some food chains there may be **tertiary consumers**, which eat the secondary consumers. All food chains have producers and consumers.

> **? Finding out**
>
> **What do you eat?**
>
> Animals that eat only plants are called **herbivores**. Animals that eat other animals are called **carnivores**. Animals that eat both animals and plants are called **omnivores**.
>
> Name some examples of each type of animal. What type of animal are humans?

Different ways of getting food

Predators and prey: The lion hunts for its food by chasing other animals, killing and eating them. Eagles and other hawks also hunt for their food (Fig. 10.14). Name some other hunters and the food that they catch. Animals that hunt for food are called **predators**. Animals that are hunted for food are the **prey**. An animal can be a predator but become prey to another animal. Name an example of a predator.

Decomposers: Bacteria, fungi and some simple animals have very different ways of getting food. They release **enzymes** onto their food. The enzymes break down the food into substances that can then be absorbed by the organism's body.

Fig. 10.14 This osprey is an expert predator, using its talons to catch prey.

These organisms perform the vital task of breaking down, or decomposing, dead plants, animals and other organisms – they are called **decomposers**. As we saw in Topic 10.2, decomposition is important in forming humus in soil. The actions of decomposers mean that substances in the dead organisms are returned to a form that living plants can use again. Also, this breakdown produces food particles that are eaten by earthworms, beetles, woodlice and many other invertebrates. Decomposers are nature's recyclers.

However, decomposers can have unwanted effects too. They are responsible for rotting of food – their actions cause the horrible smell that comes from rotting meat and fruit! Also, they attack the timbers of buildings and furniture, creating the need for treatments and repairs.

> **Did you know?**
>
> Scientists use knowledge of food chains and food webs to help farmers control pests. The pink mealy bug is an insect that recently showed up in the Caribbean. It caused extensive damage to crops in Grenada and has been found in many other countries in the region. Caribbean scientists learnt about organisms that feed on the mealy bug from other countries where the mealy bug is naturally found. They are now importing these predators, breeding them, and releasing them into the Caribbean environment, where they are successfully destroying the mealy bug. (This way of controlling pests is called biological control.)

Food chains

Let us now look at food chains more closely. In drawing a food chain we use arrows to show the direction in which food (or energy) passes from one organism to another. Our simple three-step food chain involving the plant, the mouse and the snake (Fig. 10.12) would be drawn as shown in Figure 10.15.

plant (producer) ⟹ **mouse** (primary consumer) ⟹ **snake** (secondary consumer)

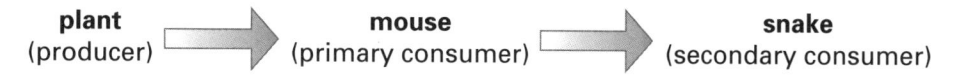

Fig. 10.15 A three-step food chain.

Activity Drawing food chains

Look at the following list of organisms:

snake, goat, lizard, blackbird, hawk, caterpillar, kiskadee, grass, guava

Draw as many food chains as you can. In each case start with the grass or guava.

Finding out

Food chains in water

Food chains also exist in rivers, ponds, lakes and the sea. In the sea, for example, microscopic plants and animals called plankton play an important part in many food chains. Small fish, such as herrings and sardines, feed on plankton. In turn, these small fish are eaten by larger fish.

Work out food chains for large fish like the kingfish or shark. How can you put humans in your food chains?

10.3 Resources for life

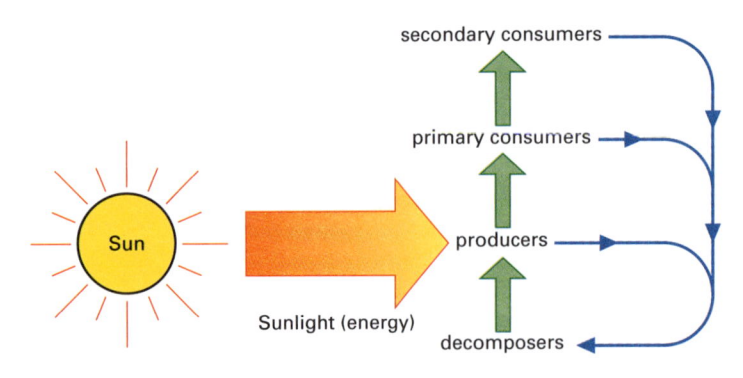

Fig. 10.16 The basic pattern of a food chain.

All the food chains you have studied have the same basic pattern. If we start with the producers at the first level, energy flows from producers to primary consumers to secondary consumers (and possibly to tertiary consumers). And when any of these die, their energy flows to the decomposers, who return it to the producers (Fig. 10.16).

Food webs

It is unusual for herbivores and carnivores to eat only one type of plant or animal. For example, a bird is unlikely to eat only caterpillars; it may eat moths, worms, grubs or even grasshoppers as well. This means that in the garden there would be several different food chains linking the bird to a variety of organisms. Such a network of food chains is called a **food web**.

➔ Activity Food webs

Look at Figures 10.17 and 10.18.

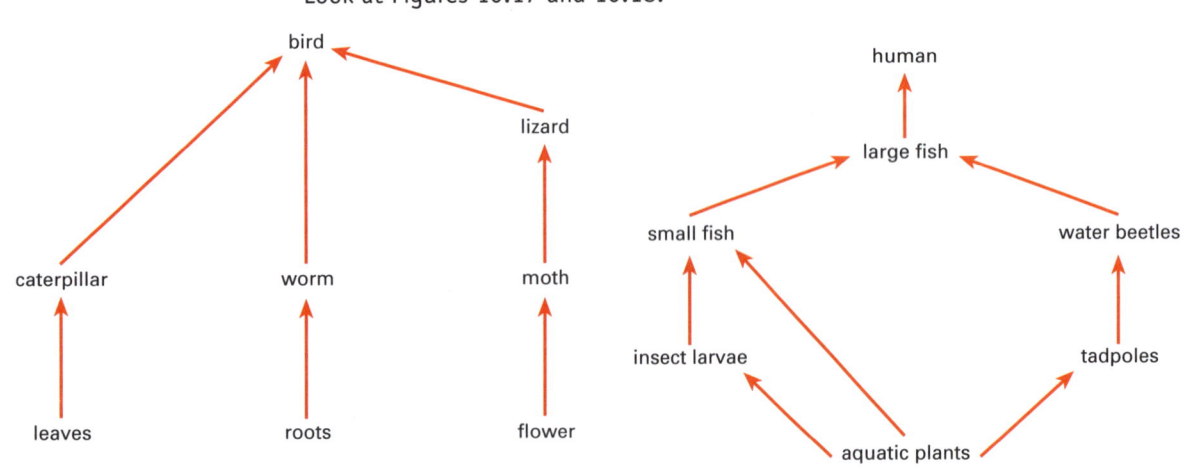

Fig. 10.17 Garden (terrestrial) food web.

Fig. 10.18 Freshwater food web.

Discuss

1. In each food web identify the different feeding levels – producer, and primary, secondary and tertiary consumers.
2. What is likely to happen to the other organisms in the freshwater food web if the insect larvae were all to die?
3. Draw a food web for the animals in your garden or school grounds.

Food chains and food webs 10.3

What you should know

- Most of life on Earth depends on energy from the Sun.
- Plants, algae and similar organisms convert the energy in sunlight to chemical energy stored in food. This process is called photosynthesis.
- Organisms release the chemical energy in food by the process of respiration.
- The way in which organisms feed on each other can be shown as a food chain.
- Any food chain has two basic levels: producers and consumers.
- Decomposers are important in many food chains.
- Food chains are usually interlinked to form a food web.

Questions

1. What raw materials do plants use to make food by photosynthesis? What are the end products?

2. What is the scientific name for an animal that eats meat?

3. What is a herbivore?

4. What are the end products of respiration?

5. Some deep-sea food chains, where sunlight cannot penetrate, are dependent on bacteria that can use energy from sulphur and other sources. Use CD-ROMs and the internet to research these deep-sea food chains.

Resources for life

10.4 Carbon and nitrogen cycles

▶ Objectives

After studying this topic you should be able to:
- describe the carbon cycle and say why it is important
- describe the nitrogen cycle and say why it is important
- outline some of the effects that human activities have on these cycles.

We have already learnt in Topic 10.1 that carbon and nitrogen are major elements found in air. Carbon occurs in combination with oxygen as carbon dioxide, while nitrogen is present as nitrogen gas. But these two elements are also among the most important elements found in living organisms and other materials on Earth.

Carbon is everywhere around us. It is present in a huge variety of natural compounds. All the major compounds of living organisms – such as carbohydrates, proteins and fats – contain carbon. Other major deposits include the fossil fuels – coal, oil and natural gas – as well as limestone rocks.

Nitrogen is a key component of proteins, which occur in all living organisms. It is also found in the soil in the form of nitrates, ammonia and other compounds that are essential for the growth of plants.

Both these elements are continually moving – for example from the air into living organisms and back again, or into the soil and then back to the air. These circulation movements form the nitrogen and carbon cycles. When considered throughout the world, these cycles involve vast amounts of the elements concerned. However, they are easier to think about if we simply look at the main processes involved. Remember that soil contains air, and that air dissolves in water.

Carbon cycle

Carbon dioxide occurs as a gas in air and is also dissolved in water, for example in ponds, lakes and seas. As we saw in Topic 10.3, the process of photosynthesis converts carbon dioxide to carbohydrates (Fig. 10.19). This is performed by plants, algae and certain other organisms. As these are eaten by animals, the carbon enters the food chain, and is converted into the huge variety of carbon-containing compounds found in living things.

Animals, plants and other organisms give out carbon dioxide through the process of respiration. This immediately returns some of the carbon to the air. After their death, these organisms are likely to be broken down by fungi, bacteria and other decomposers, which through their own respiration return yet more carbon to the air as carbon dioxide.

Carbon and nitrogen cycles 10.4

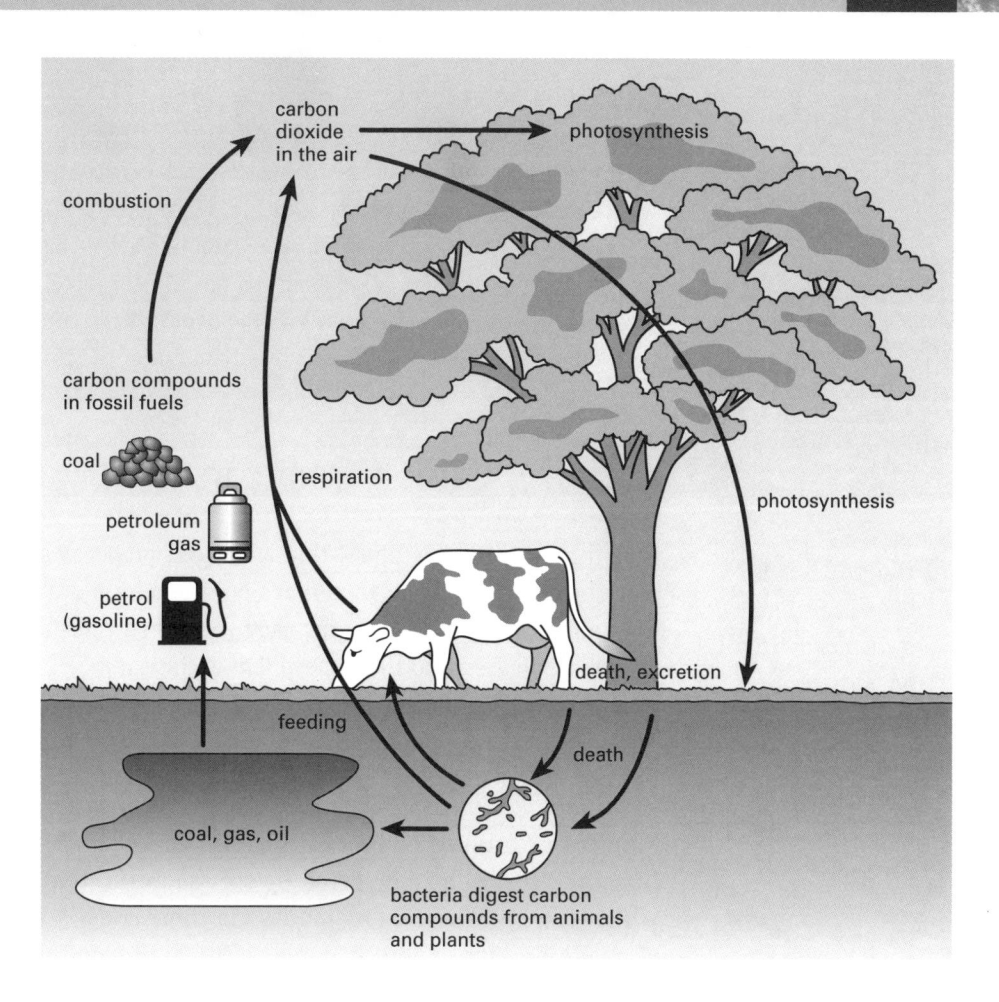

Fig. 10.19 The carbon cycle.

In swamps, or if the soil is very wet, the remains of organisms may not be completely broken down but instead are converted to peat. Over millions of years, the peat may be transformed into coal. Peat and coal, along with oil and natural gas, form huge underground deposits of carbon. When we burn these deposits as fuel – whether in power stations or in vehicle engines – we release the carbon back into the air as carbon dioxide. Limestone (or calcium carbonate) rock is another vast deposit of carbon. This is formed by the accumulation of the lime-rich shells of aquatic animals on the seabed.

Effects of humans: Wood, coal, peat, oil and natural gas are all carbon-rich fuels. Humans burn these fuels to provide heat and power. Over the last two to three hundred years the growth of industry has led to a great increase in the use of these fuels, and to a rise in the amounts of carbon dioxide released into the atmosphere when they are burned. Scientists now believe that the increased amount of this gas in the Earth's atmosphere is causing the surface to heat up. This climate change or global warming is seen by many people as one of the greatest threats to our planet. We return to this subject in Book 3, Topic 18.3.

10.4 Resources for life

> **Did you know?**
>
> It is estimated that most of the world's carbon, about 70%, is dissolved in the oceans as hydrogencarbonate and carbonate ions. Live and dead aquatic organisms make up just 4% of total carbon. Another 22% is held in deposits of limestone, peat, coal, oil and natural gas. All the world's land plants and animals put together account for only about 3% of the total carbon, while carbon dioxide in air represents less than 1% of the total.

→ Activity Carbon from cars

Each litre of petrol (gasoline) that a car uses produces about 2.2 kg of carbon dioxide. Select a typical car, perhaps one used by your family or a teacher, and work out how much fuel it burns each year. Then calculate the amount of carbon dioxide it releases into the atmosphere each year.

> **Did you know?**
>
> Have you noticed on your way to and from school that there are many traffic jams? In many Caribbean countries the number of vehicles on our roads is increasing rapidly. What effect will this have on the atmosphere?

Nitrogen cycle

Plants and animals cannot absorb nitrogen gas directly from the air. Instead it has to be converted by soil bacteria to ammonia and nitrates, which can be absorbed by plants via their roots. This conversion is called nitrogen fixation, and it is done by the actions of **nitrogen-fixing bacteria** (Fig. 10.20). Some of these bacteria live freely in the soil, whereas others live in partnership with the roots of certain plants (called **legumes**).

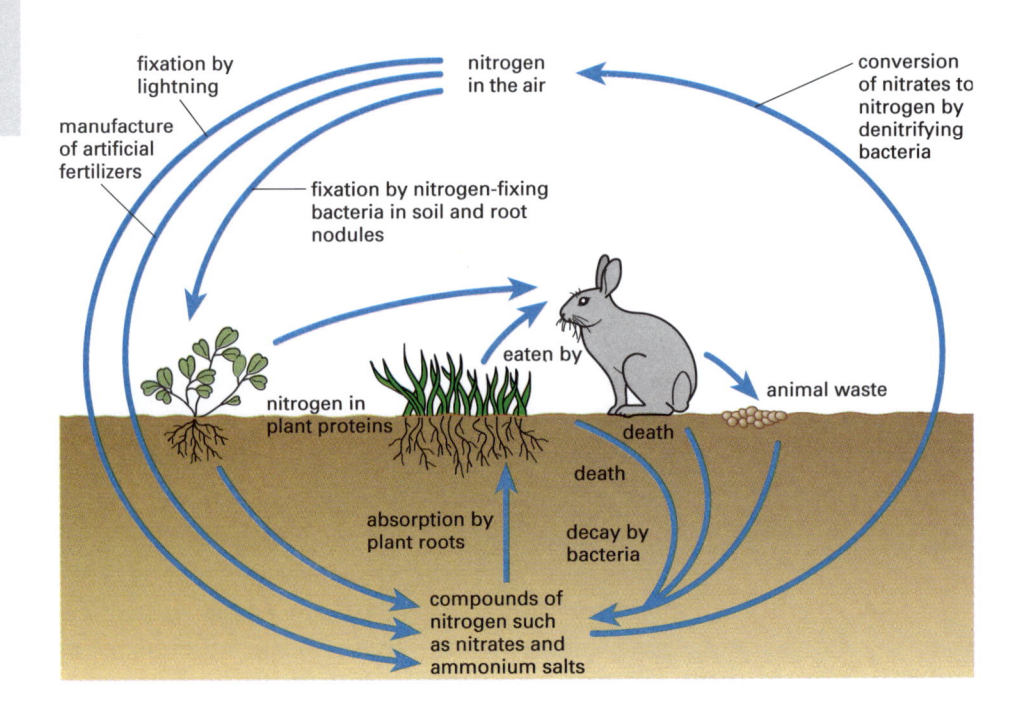

Fig. 10.20 The nitrogen cycle.

Carbon and nitrogen cycles — 10.4

Lightning and cosmic radiation from outer space also convert some nitrogen gas into nitrates in the Earth's atmosphere. These airborne nitrates then dissolve in rainwater droplets and enter the soil in rainfall. Another source of ammonia is the manufacture of artificial fertilizers using nitrogen gas from air.

Nitrogen absorbed by plants enters the various food chains, where it is incorporated into proteins and other compounds of living organisms. Some will pass though animals that eat the plants, and be returned to the soil in the form of faeces and urine. Some will simply return to the soil when the plant drops its leaves or fruits. Nitrogen is also returned to the soil when an organism dies and its remains decompose. Here bacteria change the various nitrogen-containing compounds of the dead organisms into nitrates that plants can use.

As well as containing nitrogen-fixing bacteria, soil also contains other types of bacteria – **denitrifying bacteria** – that break down the nitrates to form nitrogen gas. This then returns to the air, so completing the cycle.

Effects of humans: Growing crops year after year removes more nitrogen from the soil than is replaced by natural processes. Farmers add artificial fertilizers to soil to boost nitrogen levels, and so maintain crop production. However, much of this added nitrogen is lost, or leached, by water seeping through the soil. It enriches streams and rivers and causes abundant growth of algae – a process called eutrophication. The algae prevent other plants from obtaining sunlight and oxygen, so these plants die. There is then intense activity, and hence respiration, by decomposers, which removes virtually all the dissolved oxygen in the water. The result is a stagnant, lifeless body of water.

Nitrogen is also pumped into the atmosphere as nitrogen dioxide gas and other nitrogen oxides. These come from vehicle exhausts, factory chimneys and other sources, and are a major cause of air pollution (see Book 3, Topic 18.3).

❓ Finding out

Nitrogen-fixing plants

Peas and beans belong to a family of plants called **legumes**. The roots of these plants have small nodules. These nodules contain special nitrogen-fixing bacteria, which form a very useful partnership with the plant. The bacteria convert, or 'fix', nitrogen gas and produce ammonia, which the plant uses to make proteins. In return, the plant supplies the bacteria with food.

Find out about other plants that fix nitrogen in this way. What effect do such plants have on soil fertility? How do farmers make use of such plants?

10.4 Resources for life

➔ Activity On the nitrogen cycle

Make a large poster to show the nitrogen cycle. Share this poster with the rest of the school, and explain why the nitrogen cycle is important.

◯ What you should know

- The carbon cycle describes the movements of carbon between the atmosphere, organisms, and deposits such as coal and oil.
- The main natural processes in the carbon cycle are photosynthesis and respiration.
- Burning coal, oil and other fossil fuels releases carbon into the air as carbon dioxide.
- The nitrogen cycle describes the movements of nitrogen between air, living organisms and the soil.
- The main natural processes in the nitrogen cycle are nitrogen fixation and denitrification by soil bacteria.
- Some industrial processes also fix nitrogen from the air to make nitrogen fertilizers and other compounds.

Ⓠ Questions

1. In ponds and seas most of the photosynthesis is performed by microscopic algae. From where do these underwater organisms get their carbon?

2. How might planting trees affect the carbon cycle?

3. In what form do plant roots take up nitrogen from the soil?

4. Name and describe a nitrogen-containing gas that is given out in the exhaust fumes of a typical car.

5. Write a letter to a farmer advising him/her of some ways of improving his/her soil and growing more crops.

Systems in animals

11.1 Food and nutrition

▶ Objectives

After studying this topic you should be able to:

- explain that food is needed for energy, growth, repair of worn-out tissues and protection against diseases
- explain that our diet is the food we need every day
- list the types of food needed to have a healthy, balanced diet
- explain that the type of diet depends on your age, sex, lifestyle and health
- describe the dietary and energy needs of different types of people.

We need food to provide us with energy for all our activities, including heat energy to maintain our body temperature. We also need it to grow and to repair and replace worn-out tissues. Food keeps the body healthy and helps to protect it from diseases.

In Topic 10.3, you learned that plants, algae and certain bacteria can make their own food by photosynthesis. You also learned that animals are herbivores (feed on plants), carnivores (eat other animals) or omnivores (eat both plants and animals). Humans are omnivores and eat plants and animals (meat and animal products such as eggs, cheese and milk, for example).

Fig. 11.1 Eating a meal is very enjoyable.

The food we eat every day is our diet (Fig. 11.1). The substances we need every day are: **carbohydrates**, fats, **proteins**, **vitamins**, mineral salts and water. We call these food substances nutrients. We need to have a sensible diet and not eat too many or too few of these food substances. In other words, to keep healthy, we need to have a balanced diet (Fig. 11.2). Now we will look at these important nutrients in more detail.

🅖 Did you know?

Your teacher is made up of about 65% water and so are you! The body also contains about 18% protein, 10% fat, 5% carbohydrates and 2% other substances.

What we need in a balanced diet

Carbohydrates: Carbohydrates are energy-giving foods and include starch and sugar. There are different types of sugar. Glucose is one of the simplest sugars. Other sugars include sucrose or cane sugar, which comes from the stems of sugar cane; lactose or milk sugar, which comes from milk; fructose or fruit sugar, which comes from fruit. Sugar beet is also an

11.1 Systems in animals

Fig. 11.2 These foods are all important in a balanced diet.

important source of sugar (sucrose). The sugar is stored in the swollen roots.

Starch is a very big molecule and is made from hundreds of smaller glucose molecules. Starch is made by plants in photosynthesis and is the form in which carbohydrates are stored in plants. Bread, rice, cereals, yams and Irish potatoes are important sources of starch in our diet. Animals cannot store carbohydrates in the form of starch. Instead, the smaller glucose molecules are built up into **glycogen**. So in animals, glycogen is a big, energy-storing molecule.

You learned in Book 1, Topic 2.1 that plant cells have cell walls made of cellulose. Cellulose is also a very big carbohydrate molecule. It is very tough and rubbery and cannot be digested by humans. But we need it in our diet because it gives the food we eat some bulk and helps the food to move along the gut. You will learn more about this in Topic 11.2. The plant fibres in our food are known as **roughage**. Cereals and brown bread provide us with roughage.

Fats and oils: Fats and oils are also important energy-giving foods. In many mammals, a layer of fat is stored around the main body organs and beneath the skin. Fat helps to insulate the body from losing heat. Fats and oils are very big molecules and are made up from smaller molecules called fatty acids and glycerol.

Fats are solid at normal room temperature and you need to heat them to melt them. Oils are liquid at room temperature (for example, olive oil and corn oil). Oil can also be obtained from soya beans and peanuts. Margarine is made from a mixture of plant oils. Butter and lard are obtained from animals (cattle and pigs). Animal fats and egg yolks contain cholesterol, which is needed by the body for many things. The problem is that if there is too much cholesterol in the diet, this can lead to heart disease (Topic 11.4).

Proteins: These are body-building substances, used when the body is growing and for repair of worn-out cells and tissues. Milk, egg white, cheese, meat, fish, rice and beans are good sources of proteins. Proteins are very big molecules and are made from smaller molecules called **amino acids**. Amino acids are the 'building blocks' of proteins. Enzymes are also proteins. You will learn about enzymes in Topic 11.2.

Food and nutrition   11.1

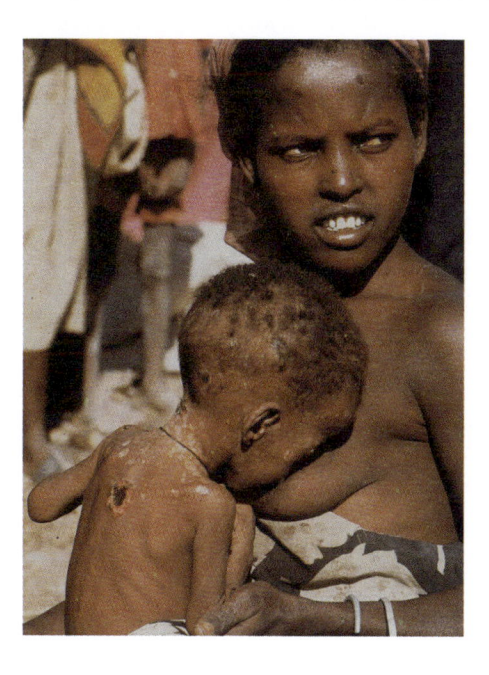

In many poor countries, people do not get enough proteins in the diet. Growing children are particularly affected. Often, the mother's milk may not have enough protein because she herself has a poor diet. Children become ill with a **deficiency disease** known as **kwashiorkor** (Fig. 11.3). They become very weak and tired. They may look fat, but this is because their bodies are swollen with fluid.

Fig. 11.3 This child has kwashiorkor. Notice its thin hair and sores on its skin. It is also very thin.

➔ Activity Testing foods for starch, sugar, proteins and fats

You will need
- different types of food to test, for example: granulated sugar (white sugar you add to your tea), banana, cassava, cooking oil, margarine, bread, milk, egg white, biscuits or any type of food you wish to test

- a pestle and mortar
- some test tubes
- a test-tube rack
- a Bunsen burner
- dilute iodine solution
- dilute copper sulphate solution
- dilute sodium hydroxide (irritant) or potassium hydroxide solution
- water
- a test-tube holder
- a beaker of cold water
- a tripod and gauze
- thin white paper or brown paper
- Benedict's solution

Method
1 If the food is liquid, you can carry out the tests immediately.
2 If the food is solid, grind it down using the pestle and mortar and then add some water.
3 Table 11.1 shows you some simple tests you can carry out to see if your food sample contains starch, sugar, proteins and fats. Some foods may contain more than one of these substances.

11.1 Systems in animals

Table 11.1 How to test samples of food for starch, sugar, fat and protein.

Substance you are testing for	Name of test and method	What you will see if the test is positive
Starch	**The iodine test:** Iodine solution is a brown liquid. Place a small amount of the food you are testing in a test tube. Add about 3 drops of iodine solution.	Iodine will change colour to blue-black in the presence of starch.
Sugar **⚠ Danger!** Do not heat the test tube directly in the flame of the Bunsen burner as the hot liquid may spurt out.	**Benedict's test:** 1 One-quarter fill the test tube with the food solution. 2 Add an equal quantity of Benedict's solution (blue in colour). 3 Mix by agitating the test tube gently. 4 Half-fill the beaker with water. This is your water bath (Fig. 11.4). Heat the water in the water bath until it boils. 5 Using your test-tube holder, carefully place your test tube in the boiling water and leave it for about 2 minutes. 6 Remove, observe and place the test tube in the rack to cool down.	If sugar is present in the food, a green, brown or red colour will develop. **Eye protection must be worn**
Fat	**The paper test for fats:** Rub a small amount of food onto some paper.	A greasy mark on the paper means that fat is present. If you hold the paper up to the light, you can see through it.
Protein **Eye protection must be worn**	**The biuret test:** 1 One-quarter fill the test tube with the food solution. 2 Place your test tube in the rack. Carefully add a few drops of dilute sodium hydroxide or potassium hydroxide solution (corrosive). 3 Add a few drops of dilute copper sulphate solution. 4 Observe.	The mixture should become clear after the potassium or sodium hydroxide is added. If protein is present, a purple colour should develop when the dilute copper sulphate is added.

Systems in animals

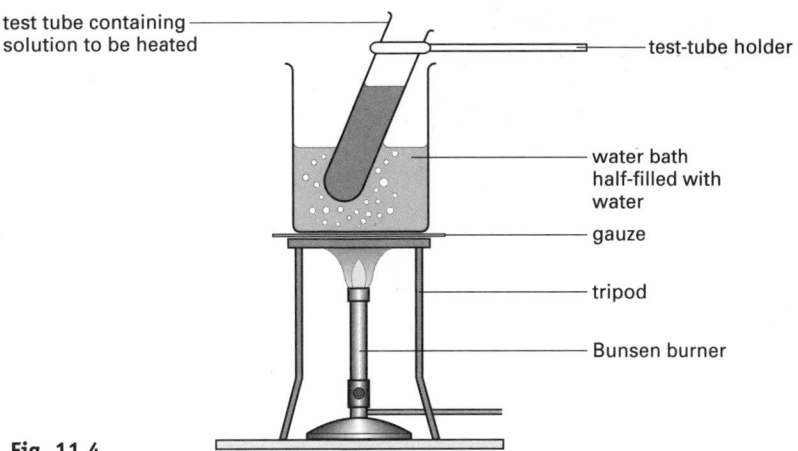

Fig. 11.4

Results

Copy Table 11.2, listing the foods you have tested, and write your results (yes or no) in the spaces.

Table 11.2 Results of the food tests.

Food sample being tested	Does it contain starch?	Does it contain sugar?	Does it contain fat?	Does it contain protein?
Granulated sugar				
Banana				
Cassava				
Cooking oil				
Margarine				
Bread				
Milk				
Egg white				
Biscuits				

Discuss

1 Which types of food are a good source of carbohydrates?
2 Which types of food are a good source of fats?
3 Which types of food are a good source of proteins?
4 The tests do not tell you how much of each nutrient is present. Why is that important? Which nutrients are needed in a balanced diet?

11.1 Systems in animals

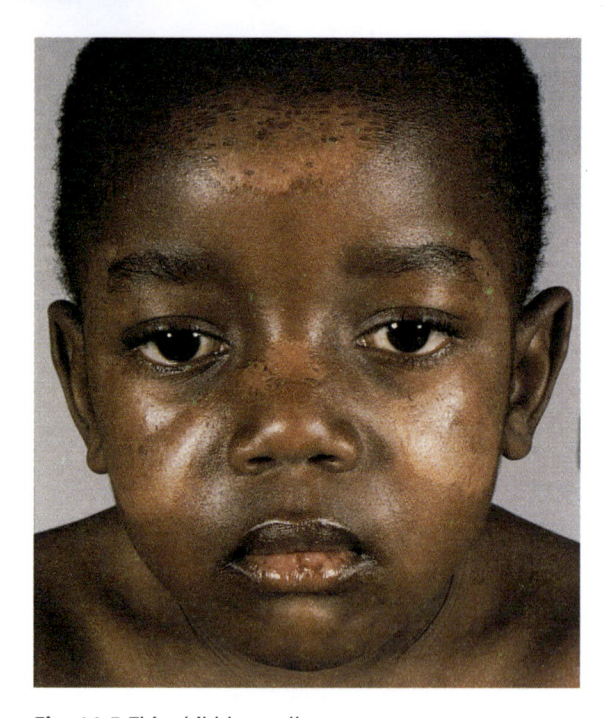

Fig. 11.5 This child has pellagra.

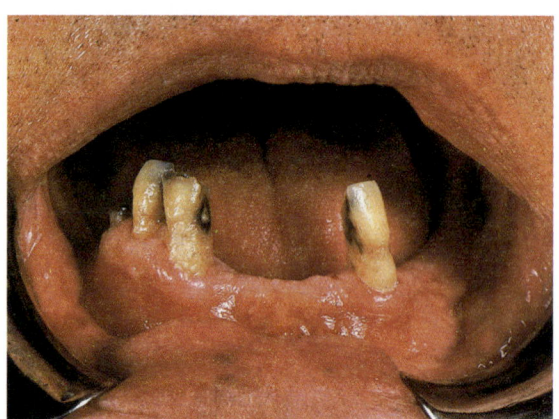

Fig. 11.6 Scurvy leads to bleeding gums and loss of teeth.

❓ Finding out

How were vitamins discovered?

You have learned that vitamins are needed in very small amounts, but even so are essential for our health. Find out about how some of the vitamins were discovered, using books, encyclopedias and the internet. These are some names you could look up to help you: Gowland Hopkins (an English scientist), Christian Eijkman (a Dutch scientist), Joseph Goldberger (an American doctor).

Water: Water is used for transporting things in cells and living systems. The chemical reactions inside cells take place in a watery solution. You need to drink at least a litre of water a day and can live for only a few days without water. Some animals never drink water. They get enough water from the solid food they eat. Cucumber has a high percentage of water. Name some other foods that contain large amounts of water.

Mineral salts and vitamins: These are important, usually in small amounts, to help the body to work properly. When they are missing from the diet, they result in deficiency diseases. Tables 11.3 and 11.4 list some of the main mineral salts and vitamins, the best food sources and the deficiency diseases that people can get if they do not have enough of them in their diet.

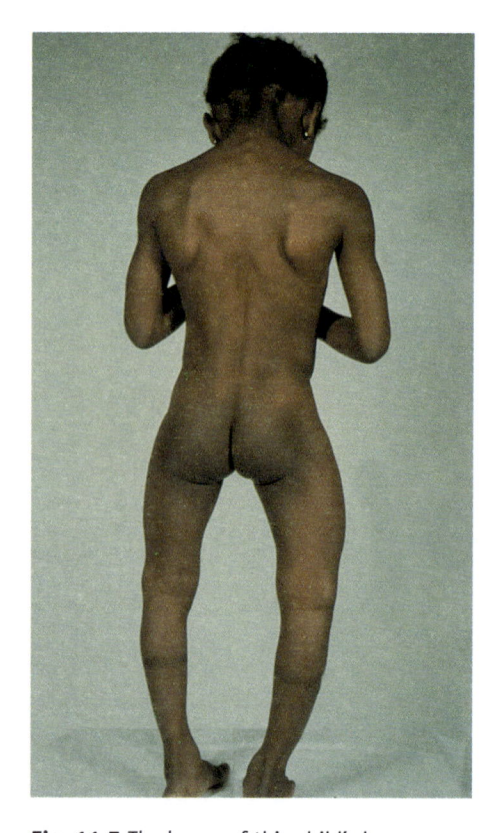

Fig. 11.7 The bones of this child's legs are misshapen and bent. The bones are too soft to take the child's weight. Rickets is caused by lack of vitamin D and calcium in the diet.

Table 11.3 Some information about vitamins.

Name of vitamin	Why it is needed	Food source	Deficiency disease
Vitamin A	helps us to see in dim light	carrots, fish liver oil	**night blindness:** the cornea (outer covering of the eye) becomes very thick and can even cause the person to become blind
Vitamin B	needed for respiration in the cells	fish, meat, liver, yeast, cereals	**pellagra:** (Fig. 11.5) sickness, rash (often shaped like a necklace), swollen tongue, upset stomach
			beri-beri: weak muscles, paralysis, the person could die
Vitamin C	keeps the inner surfaces of the body healthy, especially the mouth	citrus fruit, such as oranges and limes	**scurvy:** (Fig. 11.6) bleeding, especially of the gums, loosening teeth
Vitamin D	helps the bones to take up calcium in the diet	fish liver oil, made in the skin in sunlight	**rickets:** bones stay soft and become misshapen (Fig. 11.7)

Table 11.4 Some information about mineral salts.

Name of mineral	Why it is needed	Food source	Deficiency disease
Sodium	helps nerves and muscles to work properly	common salt (sodium chloride), which is present in most food	**cramp:** (muscles contract very painfully after sweating a lot); can easily be cured by taking salt tablets
Calcium	needed for healthy bones and teeth, healthy muscles and to help blood to clot	cheese, milk and fish	**rickets** (Fig. 11.7)
Iron	needed to make haemoglobin in the red blood cells (see Topic 11.4)	red meat, liver, kidneys, drinking water	**anaemia:** (see Topic 11.4); can be cured by taking iron tablets
Iodine	needed to make thyroxine in the thyroid gland (see Book 3, Topic 16.2)	sea foods, drinking water, often added to the salt we put on our food	**goitre:** swollen neck caused by the thyroid gland swelling up

11.1 Systems in animals

➲ Activity Making a wallchart

Work in groups. Collect pictures from magazines and/or do some drawings of the main foods that are good sources of all the necessary parts of a balanced diet. For example, an orange is a good source of vitamin C. Send for some literature published by the Caribbean Food and Nutrition Institute (CFNI), PO Box 140, Kingston 7, Jamaica. Your teacher will help you to do this. Display your chart in the classroom to remind you what you have learned about food.

Different types of diet

Some people need special diets. For example, babies drink only milk for the first few weeks of their lives. Some elderly people need to eat food that is easy to digest. People with diabetes need to regulate how much sugar and carbohydrate they eat.

Vegetarians are people who do not eat meat or fish. **Vegans** take this a stage further and do not eat any products from animals, such as milk and cheese. They choose to eat food from plant sources only.

Energy needs of the body

We measure the amount of energy in food in **kilojoules (kJ)**. We used to measure it in calories, and this term is still sometimes used. It was really confusing because what most people called calories were in fact Calories with the capital letter C. Each Calorie is in fact 1000 calories (with a small c)! You may still see energy in food recorded in Calories as well as kilojoules on food packets. You may also have heard people talking about 'counting their calories'. What they mean is that they study the energy content of the food they eat. They try to avoid putting on weight by working out the number of calories in certain foods and restricting how many calories they eat (Fig. 11.8).

Fig. 11.8 The labels on packets, jars and cans of food tell you about the ingredients (what the food contains) and the energy content.

A **food calorimeter** (Fig. 11.9) is a special apparatus used to find out the amount of energy in a weighed sample of food. The food sample is burned in pure oxygen and the amount of heat (energy) given out from the burning food is measured. The heat passes into the water and the thermometer measures the rise in the temperature. This is the amount of energy the food contains.

Food and nutrition 11.1

Fig. 11.9 A food calorimeter.

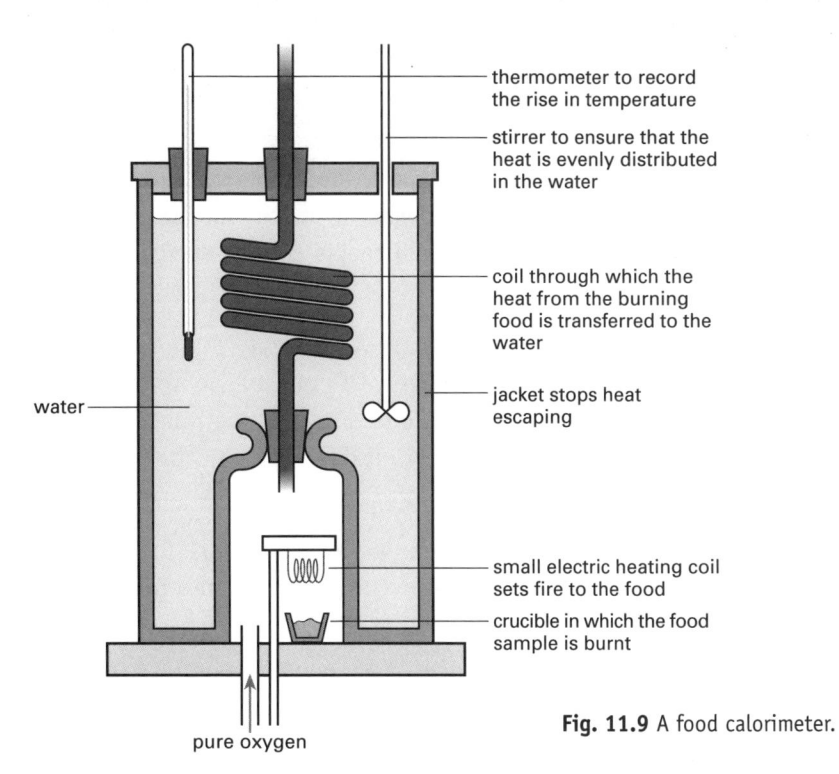

- 1 gram of carbohydrate contains 17 kJ energy.
- 1 gram of fat contains 39 kJ energy.
- 1 gram of protein contains 17 kJ energy.

Notice that 1 gram of fat contains over twice as much energy as 1 gram of carbohydrate or 1 gram of protein.

➔ Activity Energy in different types of food

Table 11.5 Energy in different types of food.

Food	Kilojoules (kJ) in each gram	Food	Kilojoules (kJ) in each gram
Butter	31.2	Lean beef	6.7
Chocolate	24.2	Egg	6.3
Sugar (white)	16.3	Yam	4.5
Lean pork	15.6	Ripe banana	4.0
Rice	14.0	Milk (cows')	2.9
Groundnut (peanut)	12.9	Potatoes	3.3
Bread (brown)	10.0	Mango	2.7
Salt fish	8.6	Beer	1.2
Chicken	7.7		

11.1 Systems in animals

Discuss

Study Table 11.5.

1. Which type of food contains most energy?
2. Which type of food contains least energy?
3. Which is your favourite food? Does it contain a lot of energy?
4. Why would people eat low-energy foods?

Table 11.6 shows roughly the amount of energy needed by people of different ages. Of course, the amount of energy you need also depends on what you do in a day. Sometimes you are very active and at other times, you relax or sit down more. The energy you need depends on:

- your age: old people need less food than active younger people
- your sex: males need more food because generally they have bigger, more muscular bodies than females of the same age;
- your lifestyle, for example, the type of work you do: people doing hard physical work or professional athletes need more food than people who work in offices.

Table 11.6 Amounts of energy needed every day by different people.

Description of person	Number of kilojoules (kJ) needed per day	
	female	male
1-year-old child	3800	4020
15–18-year-old	9600	12 600
Healthy active adult	10 500	12 400

Finding out

Many people in the world are starving

Some countries are very rich and people have enough food to eat. However, in the developing countries, many people are starving. These are the parts of the world (and the numbers involved) where people are starving: Africa (26%); the Caribbean (5%); the Far East (27%); Latin America (14%); the Middle East (10%). Find out about why people are suffering from starvation in these parts of the world. Also find out about international organizations that help these people. One example is Oxfam. Use books, encyclopedias, an atlas and the internet to help you.

Food and nutrition 11.1

Starvation

In many parts of the world, people do not have enough food to eat and so they starve. The bodies of starving people become wasted, thin and weak. General starvation is called **marasmus** (Fig. 11.10). If an adult person regularly gets less than 9000 kJ of energy per day, they are considered to be starving.

Fig. 11.10 This child is starving. His belly is swollen with fluid but you can see how thin his legs are.

Eating too much

Some people eat too much food and become overweight (Fig. 11.11). They eat more than their body needs for energy, growth and repair. The extra food is stored in their bodies, usually as fat around the organs and beneath the skin. Being too fat is known as **obesity**. Being obese causes many health problems, including diabetes, high blood pressure and a risk of a heart attack (see Topic 11.4). Some overweight people have an illness or an imbalance in body chemicals called hormones.

People lose weight by eating less food and also by exercising. How can exercising cause a person to lose weight?

Fig. 11.11 These people are overweight.

➔ Activity Healthy meals

Method
Look through everything you have learned about food in this topic and decide on the food you would choose to make your family a healthy meal. Remember that your selection should include everything you need to have a balanced diet and to provide enough energy.

Discuss
Have a class discussion about your menu. Think about these questions. Do they make you change your mind about your menu?

73

11.1 Systems in animals

1 How much does the food cost?
2 Where can you get the foodstuffs easily?
3 Does someone in your family need a special diet?
4 What do you know about how to cook the food?
5 What connection is there, if any, between the cost of food and how good it is for you?

Where does our food come from?

We can eat fresh food in our diet. For example, we may grow our own fruit and vegetables or buy locally grown produce from shops or markets. We may also get fresh meat that has been killed locally from the butcher. But much of our food comes from somewhere else. If a country does not grow all its own food for its people, then food may be imported from other countries. Food may also be imported because people like to eat a variety of food that cannot be grown in their own countries because the climate is unsuitable or because they want to eat some foods out of season. Food may also have to be transported from one part of a country to another.

If you cannot eat food while it is fresh, it will need to be preserved in a variety of ways to stop it going bad (see Book 1, Topic 7.3). We can preserve our own food, for example, by making jam or pickles, but we can also buy these products in the shops. Much of our food is processed and preserved on a large scale in factories.

The food industry in many countries is very large and continues to expand. This is because many people are working outside the home and want to have food that is easy to prepare. There are even 'ready-made' meals that only need to be heated up. But there are other things that we need to think about when we choose our food. These things include food additives and food contaminants.

➲ Activity Market research

Sometimes technology may be safe, practical and affordable but still not acceptable to people. Why is this? This activity should help you find an answer.

A group of young entrepreneurs in your community wants to start a business. They want to offer families easy-to-prepare, healthy meals. The meals are nutritious, local, safe, cheap and can be warmed up on conventional stoves and ovens and in the microwave. However, before they invest their money, they want to find out if the people in the community will buy the meals.

They want your group to do the market research. You must find out from 20 people if they would buy the meals, and the reasons for their answer. Decide on two or three questions you would ask.

Food and nutrition 11.1

Let each group member interview four or five people. Record their answers. Put your results together.

What reasons have people given for their decision? Do any of the reasons relate to their values? If so, describe these values.

Activity A flavour of the Caribbean

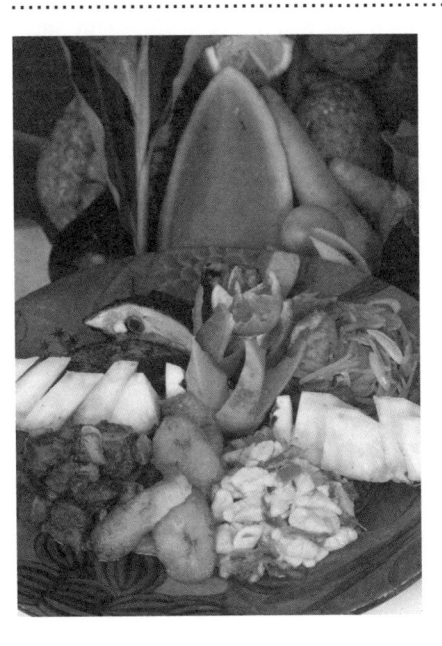

Each country in the Caribbean has its own food speciality. In Jamaica, ackee and saltfish or jerk chicken are cooked for special occasions (Fig. 11.12). The people of Barbados cook flying fish and coocoo. Trinidadians enjoy eating roti, callaloo and crab with dumplings. In Tobago, steamed fish is a favourite, and a special dish of the Guyanese is pepperpot. Peas and rice are eaten by people in all the Caribbean islands.

Fig. 11.12 Traditional food of Jamaica: jerk chicken, ackee with saltfish, goat meat and fried plantain.

A food guide known as the multimix principle is used in the Caribbean. It places the food that you eat into six groups:

- **Staples:** cassava, yams, bananas, plantains, potatoes.
- **Peas, beans and nuts:** red beans, black-eyed peas, lentils, pigeon peas.
- **Dark green leafy and/or yellow or orange vegetables:** e.g. patchoi, spinach, carrots, pumpkins, squashes.
- **Food from animals:** chicken, pork, beef, lamb, rabbit, fish.
- **Fruit:** water melon, cucumbers, mangoes, oranges, grapefruit.
- **Fats and oils:** peanuts, avocados, coconut, fish oils, fat from animals.

A multimix meal always contains a staple and at least one other food group. This mixture helps to provide people with a balanced diet.

Method
1. Plan a balanced meal using three groups from the multimix principle.
2. Keep a record of all of your meals for one week. Is your diet balanced? If not, how could you change it?

11.1 Systems in animals

What you should know

- Food is needed for energy, growth and repair of worn-out tissues and for protection against diseases.
- Nutrients such as carbohydrates, fats, proteins, vitamins, mineral salts, water and roughage are needed for a healthy balanced diet.
- Carbohydrates and fats are the main energy-giving foods; proteins are essential for growth and repair of tissues.
- Deficiency diseases occur when any of the main parts of the diet are missing.
- In some countries of the world, people do not have enough to eat and are starving.
- Some people need to have special diets, depending on their health and age.
- We measure the amount of energy in food in kilojoules (kJ).
- The amount of energy you need depends on your age, sex and your job or lifestyle.

Questions

1. Which nutrients are essential for a balanced diet?

2. Which food gives the body the most energy?

3. Which disease is caused when there is not enough iron in the diet?

4. Place these activities in order of greatest energy need: weightlifting, sleeping, walking, reading a book.

5. The following statements describe some of the main parts of a balanced diet and why they are important. Fill in the missing words. The first letter of each word has been given to help you.

   a Glucose and starch are important examples of c_____. They are an important e_____ source in living organisms.

   b In many mammals, a layer of f_____ beneath the skin helps to insulate the body by stopping heat loss.

   c P_____ are body-building substances used in growth and r_____ of worn-out cells and tissues.

   d A_____ a_____ are the 'building blocks' of proteins.

   e W_____ is used for transporting things in cells and living systems.

   f R_____ is a deficiency disease caused by a lack of vitamin D and c_____ in the body.

6. Look at a selection of food packages. What are the countries of origin (the places where the food was grown)? Find these countries on a map. Calculate the 'food miles' those foods had to travel to reach your table. Invent the meal that travelled the farthest. Why are food miles harming the environment?

Systems in animals

11.2 The digestive system

▶ Objectives

After studying this topic you should be able to:
- explain the term digestion
- name the parts of the alimentary canal
- describe how food moves along the alimentary canal and is digested
- explain how digested food is absorbed.

In Topic 11.1, you learned about the types of food we eat and what we need for a balanced diet. What happens to the food we eat? It is digested in the body in the digestive tract, which is also called the **alimentary canal** or gut. The alimentary canal is a tube about 9 metres long, with the mouth at one end and the anus (back passage) at the other end. Food takes between 1 and 2 days to pass through the alimentary canal.

What is digestion?

We take food into our mouths in large pieces. Digestion begins by:
- breaking down food into smaller pieces by chewing it with our teeth (physical changes); and then
- big insoluble molecules in the food are broken down by chemical changes into smaller soluble molecules in different parts of the alimentary canal. The smaller molecules are absorbed (taken in) by the blood and carried to all the cells of the body where they are needed.

Enzymes: As the food passes along the alimentary canal, it is mixed with digestive juices. The digestive juices contain special proteins called **enzymes**. Enzymes help to speed up the breakdown of the large food molecules into smaller molecules. They work so fast that they can help to break down millions of molecules in a minute! The enzymes themselves are not used up or affected by these chemical reactions and can be used over and over again.

Look at Figure 11.13. Enzymes not only help to break down big molecules into smaller molecules, but they can also help to build up big molecules from smaller molecules. They occur in all the living cells of the body as well as in the digestive juices. When the big molecules are broken down (helped by enzymes), energy is released for the body to use. When the big molecules are built up from small ones (helped by enzymes), energy is used up.

The body temperature of humans is about 36.7°C. This is the best temperature for the enzymes to work properly in the cells.

11.2 Systems in animals

Did you know?

In the liver cells, an enzyme called **catalase** can break down about 100 000 molecules of hydrogen peroxide (a poisonous chemical) into water and oxygen in one second.

breaking down a big molecule

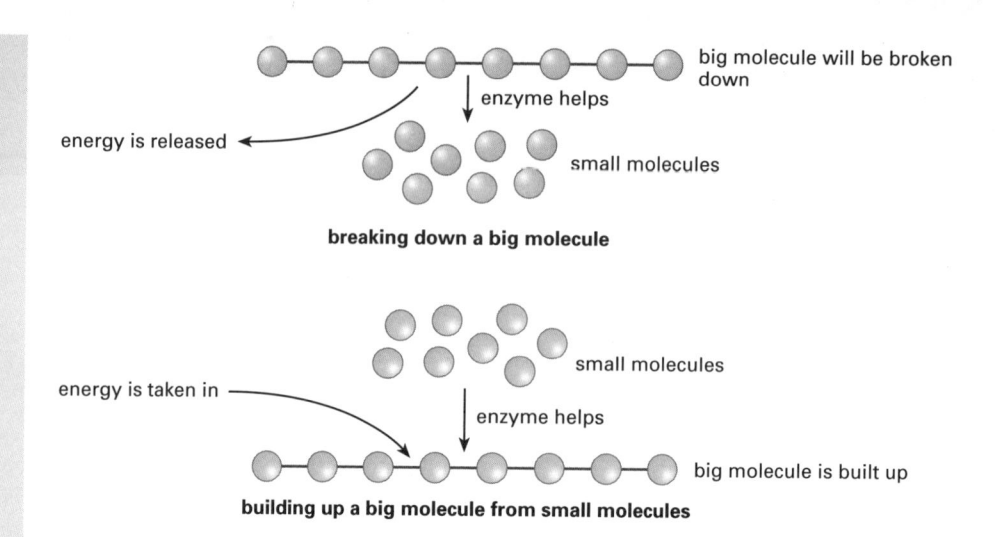

building up a big molecule from small molecules

Fig. 11.13 Enzymes help to break down big molecules into small ones. They also help to build up big molecules from small molecules.

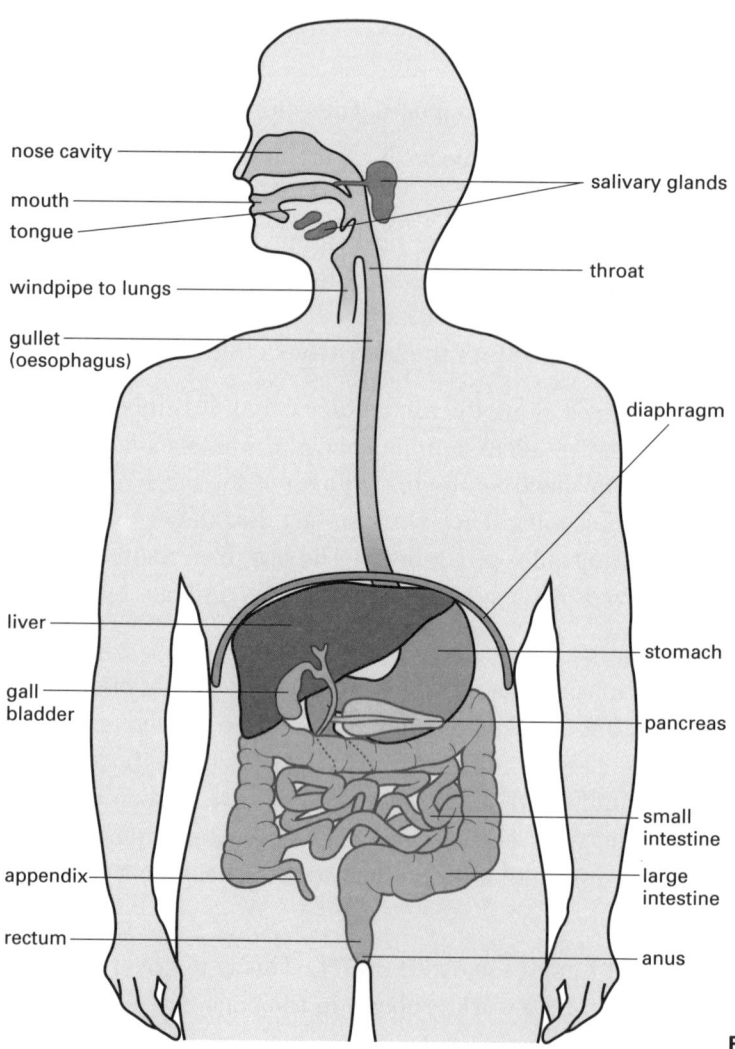

The alimentary canal

Study the drawing of the human alimentary canal (Fig. 11.14) as you find out what happens to the food as it passes along. Your teacher may be able to show you a dissection of a specially bred laboratory rat (or guinea pig).

Mouth: Digestion begins in the mouth. Food taken into the mouth cavity is chewed by the teeth. The tongue helps to mix the food with **saliva**, which is a digestive juice produced by the **salivary glands**. You can produce saliva in your mouth right now by imagining biting into something very sour such as a lemon! Did your mouth water? There is an enzyme in saliva called **amylase**. This breaks down large molecules of starch in the food into simpler sugar molecules called maltose. Maltose is an intemediate product in the breakdown of starch and is later broken down to release glucose.

Fig. 11.14 The human alimentary canal.

11.2 The digestive system

➲ Activity Have a chew!

Note: This activity should only be done under strict supervision of the teacher.

Hygiene is important: wash your hands before and after the activity.

You will need
- a dry unsweetened biscuit (or cracker)

Method
1. Copy Table 11.7 into your exercise book.
2. Pop the biscuit into your mouth and chew it slowly and thoroughly for two or three minutes.
3. Concentrate on what is happening in your mouth and fill in the table as you enjoy your biscuit.

Table 11.7 What happens in your mouth when you eat a biscuit?

Changes in your mouth as you eat	Observations
What happens to your lips?	
What do your teeth do to the biscuit?	
What happens to your jaws?	
What happens to your tongue?	
Why is the biscuit wet?	
What shape is the biscuit when you are ready to swallow it?	

Discuss
1. Which changes are physical changes?
2. Which changes are chemical changes?
3. How does the well-chewed biscuit taste? How does this show that dry biscuits can be broken down into sugars?

➲ Activity How does amylase act on starch?

Note: Because of the dangers of catching hepatitis or HIV, it is no longer possible to use your own saliva for experiments at school. Instead, your teacher will give you a solution of amylase prepared specially in a laboratory.

You will need
- a test tube of amylase solution
- a test tube half-filled with a 4% **suspension** of cold boiled starch (Starch molecules are so large, they do not form a true solution and are suspended in the water – forming a suspension.)
- a stopwatch or clock with a second hand
- iodine solution
- a glass rod
- a dropper
- a white tile

11.2 Systems in animals

Method
1. Place 20 drops of iodine solution on the white tile in four neat rows of five (Fig. 11.15).
2. Wash the dropper thoroughly.
3. Add a drop of the starch suspension to the first drop of iodine on the tile. The brown iodine solution will turn blue-black.
4. Pour the amylase solution into the starch solution and mix by shaking the test tube very gently.
5. Immediately place a drop of the amylase/starch mixture on the second drop of iodine on the tile and stir with the glass rod. Make note of the colour. Wash and dry the glass rod.
6. Repeat step 5 at 30-second intervals until the twentieth drop of iodine has been used.

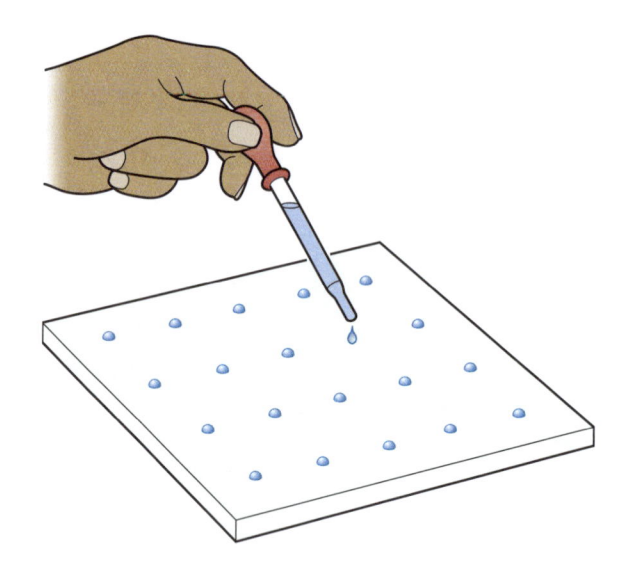

Fig. 11.15 Testing a starch/amylase mixture with iodine solution.

Discuss
1. How long did it take for the amylase to change starch into maltose?
2. When do you know that the starch has been digested?
3. Is the digestion of starch a physical or a chemical change?
4. Why is it important to chew our food and not bolt it down?

Swallowing and movement down the gullet: After the food has been chewed and mixed with saliva, it forms a ball known as a food bolus. This is swallowed and passes into a tube called the gullet or **oesophagus**. There are muscles along the gullet. The muscles behind the food contract (get smaller) and squeeze the food along. The muscles in front of the food relax and allow the food to move along the gullet and into the stomach.

The stomach: The stomach is a muscular organ and churns and mixes the food with **gastric juice**. Gastric juice contains enzymes that break down proteins. It also contains hydrochloric acid, which kills germs and creates the right pH for the enzymes to work. The food stays in the stomach for three or four hours and then passes into the small intestine in spurts through a ring of muscle. If the food you eat is bad, you feel ill and vomit.

The food is pushed back out through your gullet and mouth. Vomiting removes bad food from the digestive system quickly, before it does too much harm. Vomit often tastes acid with stomach juices. Clean your teeth at once, before the acid acts on them.

The small intestine, liver and pancreas: The small intestine is another tube; it is about six metres long. It produces **intestinal juice**, which contains a number of enzymes. The pancreas produces another digestive juice (also containing enzymes) that enters the small intestine through a tube. The digestion of carbohydrates, fats and proteins is completed in the small intestine. Look at Table 11.8, which is a summary of the digestion of food in the alimentary canal.

The liver produces a liquid called **bile**, which is stored in the gall bladder. It passes into the small intestine through a tube called the bile duct. Bile breaks up large drops of fat into smaller droplets so that the enzymes can work on the fat more quickly and easily.

Table 11.8 A summary of the digestion of food in the alimentary canal.

Class of food acted upon	Part of alimentary canal where it is digested	Soluble food product
Carbohydrates (starch and complex sugars)	Mouth and small intestine	Simple sugars
Proteins	Stomach and small intestine	Amino acids
Fats	Small intestine	Fatty acids and glycerol

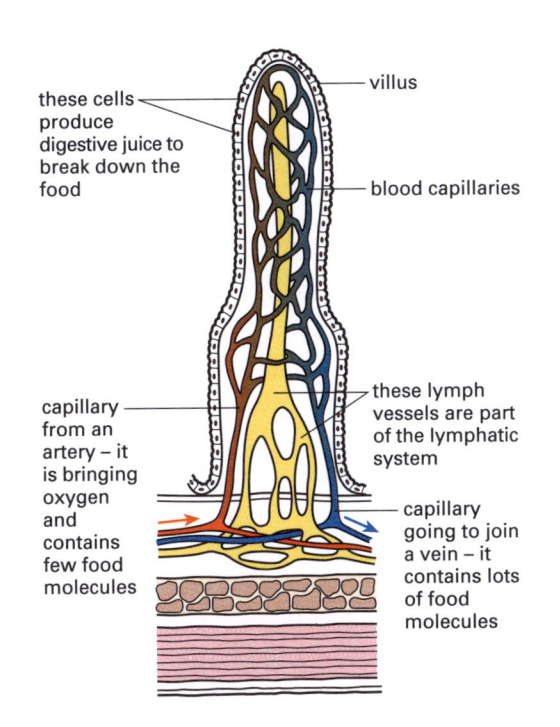

Absorption in the small intestine: Food is also absorbed in the small intestine. Even though the small intestine is very long, the surface area for absorbing food is increased even further because the inner surface is also folded inwards. These folds are called **villi** (see Figure 11.16). The small amino acid and sugar molecules (especially glucose) can pass through the cells of the small intestine and into the blood capillaries (the tiniest tubes that carry blood, see Topic 11.4). The blood then goes to the liver. In the liver, some of the food is stored and some waste is removed. The blood then flows into the main bloodstream to be carried all around the body.

Fig. 11.16 Part of the wall of the small intestine showing a close-up of the villi. The soluble food (small molecules) is absorbed by the blood capillaries (the smallest blood vessels) and the digested fats pass into the lymph vessels.

11.2 Systems in animals

The digested fats pass into the lymph capillaries. These are part of the **lymphatic system** (see Topic 11.4), which drains into the blood system near the neck.

➔ Activity Increasing surface area

What you need
- a ball of string
- a ruler
- a pair of scissors

Method

Work in pairs.

1. Unroll enough string to form a circle measuring about 30 cm across on your bench or table (Fig. 11.17).
2. Then cut the string, measure it in centimetres and again arrange it to form a circle.
3. Take the ball of string and make folds to represent villi as you unwind it inside the circle. Then cut the string.
4. Measure the piece of folded string.
5. Now you can work out how much longer it is than the string forming the circle. Divide the length of your folded piece of string by the length of the string that formed the circle. If, for example, your answer is 5, the inner surface is five times longer.

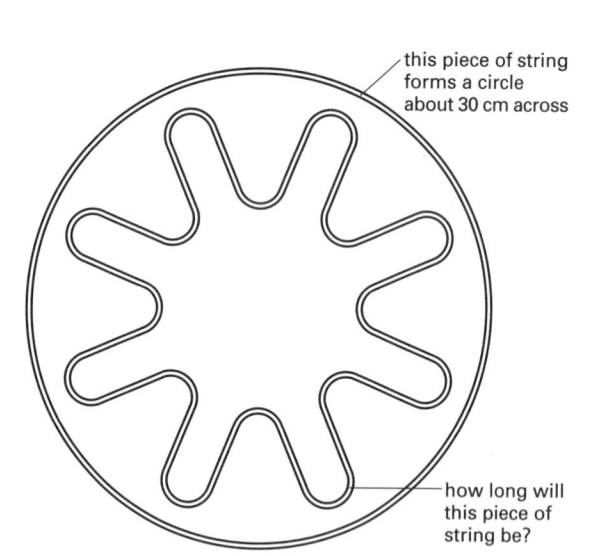

Fig 11.17 The surface area of the small intestine is increased by the villi.

The large intestine, appendix, rectum and anus: Undigested food passes into the large intestine and is made up of plant fibres that you cannot digest. Water is absorbed in the large intestine and the waste food becomes solid (known as **faeces**) and is stored in the rectum. It passes out of the body by **egestion** through the anus from time to time.

The **appendix** has no use in humans. In herbivores (plant-eating animals) like rabbits, it contains bacteria that can digest plant fibres. The appendix in humans sometimes becomes diseased and causes appendicitis. It has to be removed by having an operation.

What is diarrhoea?

Diarrhoea may be caused by germs or even stress. The faeces passed are very watery. Not enough water has been absorbed by the large intestine. If diarrhoea continues for more than a couple of days, the body loses too much water and this leads to **dehydration** (not enough water and salts in the body). If it continues, you should get medical help.

What is constipation?

You are constipated when you are unable to pass faeces regularly and when you do, they are very hard and painful to pass. Constipation can be prevented by increasing the amount of roughage in your diet, for example, by eating fruit, cereals and vegetables. These foods are rich in plant fibres.

What you should know

- Food is needed for energy, growth and repair.
- Food is digested in the alimentary canal (gut).
- Food is broken down into smaller pieces in the mouth by the teeth (physical changes).
- Big insoluble molecules in the food are broken down by chemical changes into smaller soluble molecules.
- Large carbohydrate molecules such as starch are broken down into smaller molecules such as glucose; proteins are broken down into amino acids; fats and oils are broken down into fatty acids and glycerol.
- Enzymes help to speed up the breakdown of the large food molecules into smaller molecules.
- Digestion begins in the mouth and is completed in the small intestine.
- Food is absorbed by blood capillaries (amino acids and glucose) and the lymphatic capillaries (fatty acids and glycerol) in the small intestine.
- The surface area for digestion and absorption in the small intestine is increased by the villi.
- Water is absorbed in the large intestine.
- Undigested food passes out through the anus as faeces.

Questions

1 What is an enzyme?

2 The following statements describe the process of digestion in the mouth. Fill in the missing words. The first letter of each word has been given to help you.

   a Food in the mouth is broken into smaller portions by the t_____.

   b This is a p_____ change.

   c The large carbohydrate molecules of s_____ are broken down in the mouth into m_____.

   d The enzyme in saliva is called a_____.

   e This is an example of a c_____ change.

11.2 Systems in animals

3 Give one example of a digestive juice.

4 Where in the gut does absorption of soluble food take place?

5 Explain what is meant by the terms: (a) constipation; (b) diarrhoea.

6 Research treatments for indigestion. Look carefully at the contents listed on the packets. What are the common ingredients? How do they work? Relate this to what you have already learnt about acidity and alkalinity. Devise your own advertising for an 'indigestion cure'. What will it say?

Systems in animals

11.3 Teeth

▶ Objectives

After studying this topic you should be able to:
- list the different types of human teeth
- explain the functions of each type of tooth
- explain that humans have milk teeth and permanent teeth
- describe the internal structure of a tooth
- explain that cleaning your teeth is essential to avoid decay, gum disease and loss of teeth.

In Book 1, Topic 2.6, you learned that mammals had different types of teeth and in Topic 11.2 that mammals chew their food. But the teeth of animals like the crocodile (a reptile) and the shark (a fish) all look the same. These animals swallow their food whole or in large chunks.

▶ Activity Looking at your teeth

You will need
- a small hand mirror

Method
1. Look at the picture of the teeth of the crocodile (Fig. 11.18).
2. Now examine your own teeth in the mirror. Remember to open your mouth wide and look at the teeth on the inside.

Fig. 11.18 A crocodile's teeth are all the same shape.

Discuss
1. Do your teeth look like those of the crocodile?
2. What are the differences between your teeth and the crocodile's teeth?
3. The teeth of sharks and crocodiles are constantly being replaced. How is that different from your teeth?

Comparing the teeth of mammals

Look at the pictures of the skulls and teeth of a dog, a rabbit and a human (Figs 11.19, 11.20 and 11.21). Which animal's teeth are most pointed?

11.3 Systems in animals

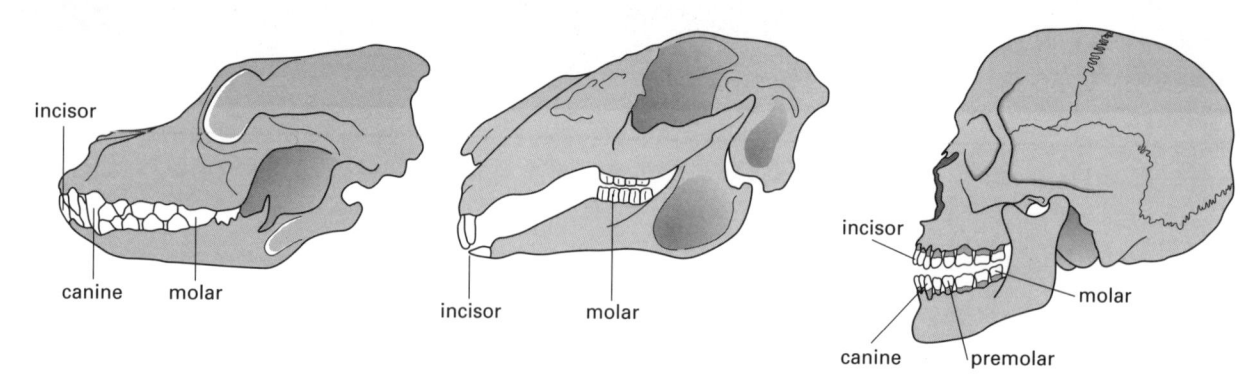

Fig. 11.19 A dog skull. A dog is a carnivore.

Fig. 11.20 A rabbit skull. A rabbit is a herbivore. Notice that there are no teeth between the incisors and the molars. Which teeth are missing? Why don't rabbits need these teeth?

Fig. 11.21 A human skull. A human is an omnivore.

? Finding out

Carnivores, herbivores and omnivores

Lions and tigers are examples of carnivores. Sheep, goats and horses are examples of herbivores. A pig is an omnivore. Find out what these animals eat and discuss how their teeth are related to the type of food they eat.

You can see from the pictures that there are four types of teeth. Feel your own teeth with your tongue as you learn about each type and look at them in a mirror.

The teeth at the front of the mouth are sharp and shaped rather like a chisel. These are the **incisors**. They are used for biting off pieces of food. The teeth next to the incisors are pointed and sharp. These are the **canines** and are used for tearing and ripping food – especially meat. Next to the incisors, towards the back of the mouth are the **premolars** and then finally, the **molars**. Premolars and molars are used for grinding food.

Look at the pictures of the skulls and teeth again. Do rabbits have all of the teeth that were described? Which ones are missing? Can you link the types of teeth that an animal has with its diet?

Dogs eat meat; rabbits eat plants; humans eat both meat and plants. Dogs are **carnivores** and their teeth are suited for tearing flesh off bones. The incisors are pointed, the canine teeth are very large and so are the molars for crushing bones. Rabbits are **herbivores** and eat plant material. Rabbits do not have canines to tear meat. They have incisors for biting and premolars and molars for chewing. Humans are **omnivores**, eating both meat and plant material. They have all four types of teeth.

➔ Activity Teeth and food

Organize a class discussion about animals' teeth and the food they eat.

Teeth 11.3

We have two sets of teeth

Adults usually have 32 teeth altogether. Can you remember some of your teeth wobbling and then falling out when you were younger? These were your first teeth, called **milk teeth**. You don't have any molars with your first set of teeth. What happened in the gaps that were left? The new second teeth or **permanent teeth** grew through your gums. You may not have 32 teeth yet. Some of your molars at the back of your mouth may not grow through until you are about 20 or even older. These are often called 'wisdom teeth'. Figure 11.22 shows the side view of a child's mouth. The permanent teeth are ready to grow down through the gums and will push the milk teeth out.

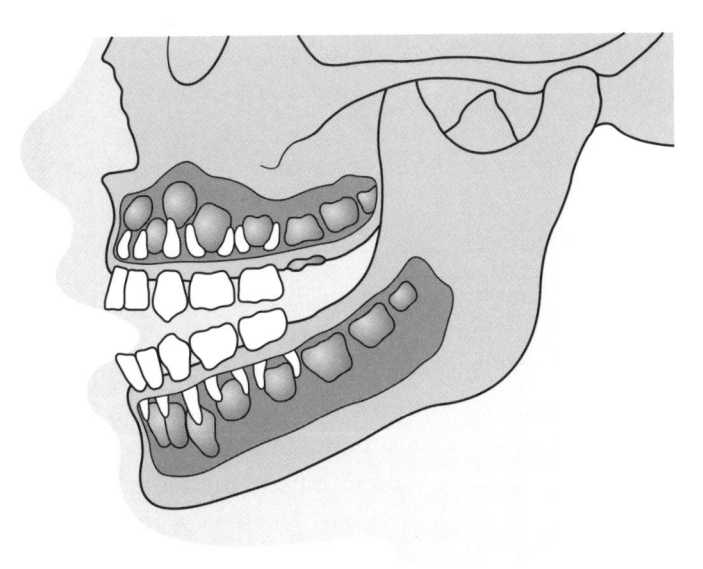

Fig. 11.22 Which type of tooth is already pushing down into the mouth in the top jaw?

Tooth structure

What do teeth look like outside and inside?

➔ Activity Looking at the outside of a tooth

Hygiene: Make sure you wash your hands before and after you have handled the teeth.

You will need
- some examples of animal teeth (your teacher will get these from the butcher)
- a model of a human tooth if your school has one

Method

1. Your teacher will show you a sample of an animal's tooth. Examine the outside of the tooth. You should see three distinct regions. The top of the tooth that lies above the gum is the crown. The part of the tooth that lies embedded in the jaw is the root. The part of the tooth that is in line with the gum is the neck. Use Figure 11.23 to help you.

2. Draw and label the parts of the tooth.

3. Count the number of teeth in your mouth.

4. Now draw Figure 11.22, showing the milk teeth and the permanent teeth and add as many labels as you can. Ask your teacher to check your work.

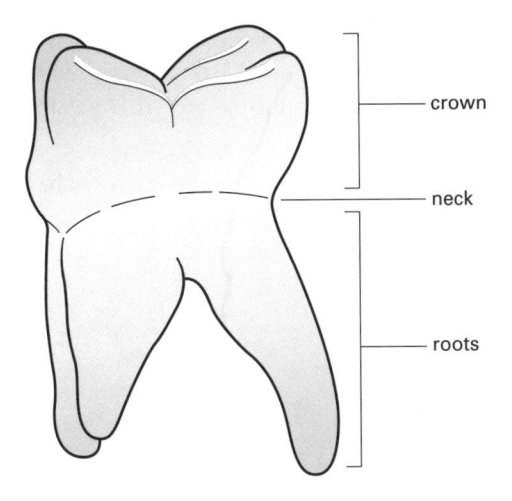

Fig. 11.23 The outside of a tooth.

Discuss

How many teeth should the following persons have in a healthy mouth?
a a newborn baby
b a 16-year-old
c a 30-year-old
d Why may an older person have fewer teeth? Explain some of the ways these missing teeth can be replaced.

The **crown** is covered by a very tough white material called **enamel**. Below the enamel is another strong material, the **dentine**. The dentine continues into the root of the tooth. The root is firmly held in a socket in the jawbone by tiny fibres. The root is protected on the outside by a thin layer of cement. Blood vessels and nerves are found in the centre of the dentine. This is called the **pulp cavity**. This inner part of the tooth is alive. The blood supplies the tooth with food and oxygen. The nerves mean that you will feel pain if the tooth is damaged.

Activity Looking at the inside of teeth

You will need
- animal teeth obtained by your teacher from the butcher, who will have sliced them in half lengthways.

Method
1 Figure 11.24 shows you what the inside of a tooth looks like. The parts are labelled. Compare it with the section of the tooth from the butcher.
2 Copy Figure 11.25 and add labels to help you learn the names of the parts inside a tooth. Ask your teacher to check your work.

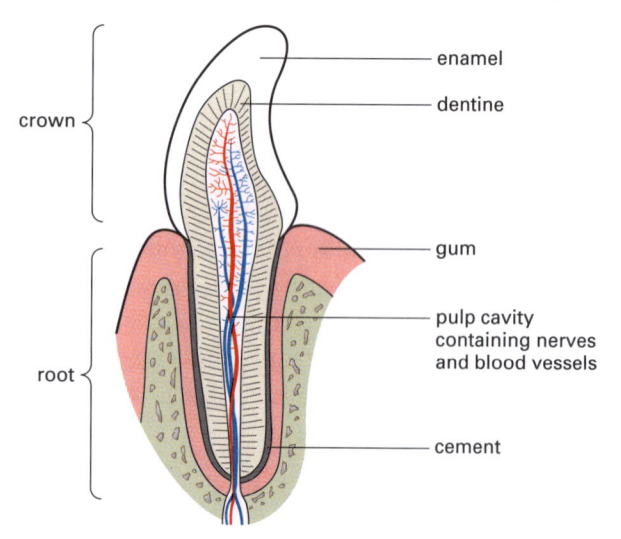

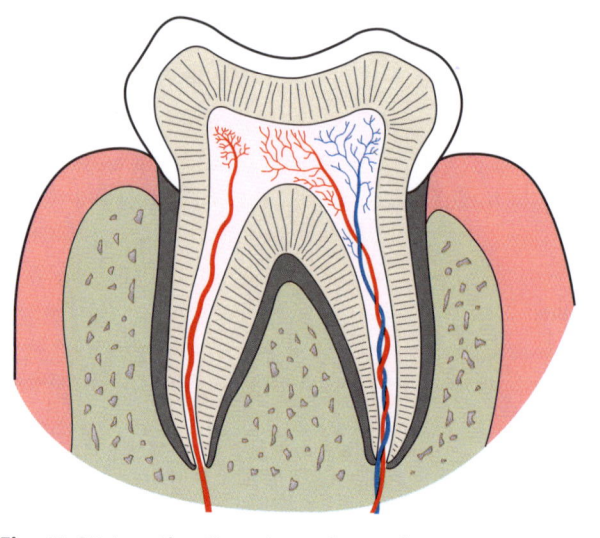

Fig. 11.24 A section through an incisor tooth.

Fig. 11.25 A section through a molar tooth.

Teeth 11.3

Calcium and vitamin D are important for healthy teeth and bones. Can you remember which foods are rich in calcium and vitamins from Topic 11.1?

Taking care of your teeth and gums

Have you ever had a bad toothache? What happened? If you do not look after your teeth, then they will decay. You will no longer have a healthy mouth with good teeth and gums like the person in Figure 11.26a. The nerves of the teeth will become exposed and will react to hot and cold food and drinks, sweet sugary food and to touch. All you feel is dreadful pain! You could eventually have teeth like the person in Figure 11.26b.

Fig. 11.26a A healthy mouth.

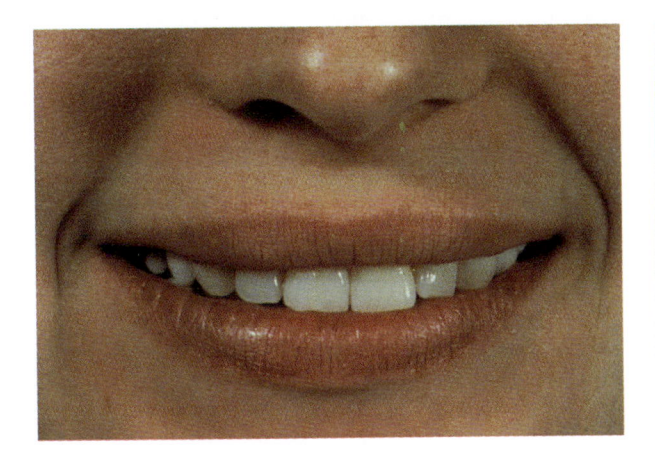

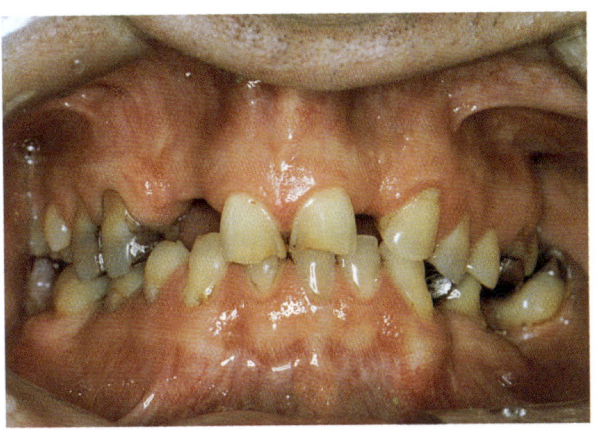

Fig. 11.26b An unhealthy mouth with decaying teeth and diseased gums.

Brushing your teeth is very important. You need to brush away food particles from the spaces between the teeth and from the surface of your teeth. Brush your teeth up and down and don't forget to brush your back teeth. You must also brush your gums to prevent diseases and to help the blood flow. Try to visit the dentist from time to time to have your teeth checked.

If food is left on teeth surfaces and between the teeth for a long period of time, bacteria that live in the mouth will get their own meal! The furry covering that develops on the teeth is called **plaque**. Bacteria digest this food, forming acids that attack the enamel of the teeth. This will lead to brown marks on your teeth – then cavities (holes) – then toothache! Eventually the entire tooth becomes rotten and the tooth is lost. Unhealthy gums cause teeth to become loose in the socket and they can fall out. Do your teeth feel furry now? If so, clean them as soon as you can!

It may not be convenient to brush your teeth after every meal, but you can rinse your mouth thoroughly after you have eaten. This will loosen any particles of food in the mouth, and they can be got rid of. Remember that eating sweet, sticky foods without brushing afterwards will eventually damage your teeth.

11.3 Systems in animals

Fluoride is added to the water supplies in many countries, and many brands of toothpaste contain fluoride. This substance helps to strengthen the teeth and prevents the formation of cavities.

▶ Activity Is your diet good for your teeth?

Method

Make a list of all the food you ate yesterday. Then write the words 'harmful' or 'harmless' against each type of food.

Discuss

1 If you wrote down 'harmful' against your food, how could you improve your diet?
2 How many sweet, sticky foods did you eat yesterday?
3 Did you clean your teeth after meals and before you went to bed?
4 Dentists recommend that you eat sweet foods in one go and then immediately clean your teeth. Why is this?

◯ What you should know

- Humans are omnivores and have four types of teeth: incisors, canines, premolars and molars.
- Incisors are used for biting food; canines are used for tearing meat; premolars and molars are used for crushing and grinding.
- Carnivores eat meat; herbivores eat plant material; omnivores eat meat and plant material.
- Humans have milk teeth and permanent teeth.
- The tooth is covered by a hard substance called enamel.
- The dentine lies below the enamel and the pulp cavity contains nerves and blood vessels.
- Teeth are held in the socket by tiny fibres.
- Poor care of the teeth can cause the teeth to decay.
- Poor care of the gums may lead to gum diseases and loss of teeth.

ⓠ Questions

1 Draw and label a section through a healthy tooth.

2 Which of these animals has teeth that all look the same?

    a horse   c rabbit

    b crocodile   d human

3 The following statements describe the structure inside a tooth. Fill in the missing words. The first letter of each word has been given to help you.

  a The outer covering of the crown of a tooth is a tough white material called e_____.

  b Beneath this layer is another strong material, the d_____.

  c The root of a tooth is firmly held in a socket in the jawbone by tiny f_____.

  d Blood vessels and nerves are found in the p_____ c_____.

  e C_____ is important in the diet for healthy teeth and bones.

4 Which of the following teeth are used for crushing and grinding food?

  a incisors

  b molars

  c canines

  d premolars

5 List three ways in which teeth can be protected against decay.

6 Research 'orthodontics'. Why is it especially important to your age group? What does an orthodontist do?

7 Look up tooth care on the internet. Enter the names of toothbrush and toothpaste manufacturers.

Systems in animals

11.4 Blood and the circulatory system

▶ Objectives

After studying this topic you should be able to:
- describe the structure and functions of the blood
- describe the structure and functions of the blood vessels
- describe the structure of the heart and blood system
- explain how blood flows through the heart and circulates around the body
- describe some common disorders of the blood, heart and circulation.

What is blood?

Blood is a living red fluid or liquid that travels around the body in special tubes called **blood vessels**. The blood vessels supply blood to and collect blood from all the cells of the body. The heart pumps the blood and keeps it circulating around, ensuring that every cell in the body has a continuous supply of fresh blood. The blood carries digested food, oxygen, waste materials, heat and so on around the body. This why the blood system is described as a transport system.

➔ Activity Examining blood

Note: It is no longer safe to make blood slides or smears with samples of our own blood at school because of the risks of catching hepatitis or HIV.

red blood cell, with no nucleus

platelets

lymphocyte, with large nucleus

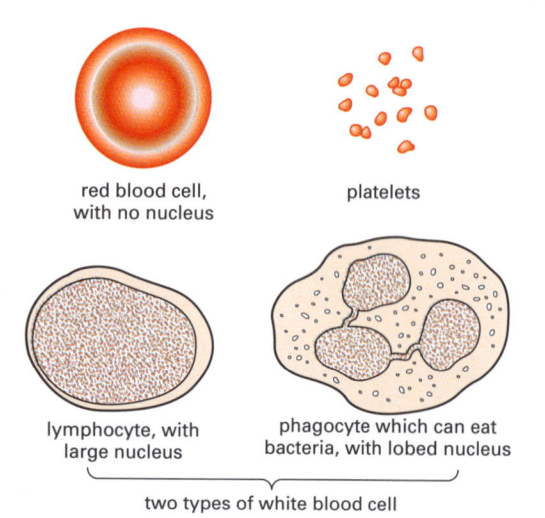

phagocyte which can eat bacteria, with lobed nucleus

two types of white blood cell

Fig. 11.27 Human blood cells.

You will need
- a prepared and stained slide of human blood cells
- a microscope

Method

1. Figure 11.27 will help you to identify the cells. Look carefully at the slide through the microscope. Most of the cells you will see are red blood cells. They are round with a hollowed-out middle part. You may also observe a few cells with an irregular shape and a few cells with a round nucleus. These are the white blood cells. They may be stained purple so that you can see them more easily.

2. Draw a few cells using Figure 11.27 to help you label them.

Blood and the circulatory system 11.4

The **red blood cells** transport oxygen around the body. They contain a red pigment called **haemoglobin**. When there is a lot of oxygen, as in the lungs, haemoglobin readily joins up with oxygen to form oxyhaemoglobin.

oxygen + haemoglobin → oxyhaemoglobin

Oxygen is carried around the body as oxyhaemoglobin in the red blood cells. When the cells reach an area that is low in oxygen, as in the body's cells, the oxyhaemoglobin releases the oxygen.

oxyhaemoglobin → oxygen + haemoglobin

Red blood cells are unusual in that they do not have a nucleus. This means that they can contain more haemoglobin and are therefore very efficient at carrying oxygen.

Did you know?

- A person of average size and weight has about 5 litres of blood in their body.
- There are about 7000 red blood cells for every white blood cell.
- Over two million red blood cells are made in our bone marrow every second.

There are fewer **white blood cells**. They help to defend the body against disease-causing germs. The white cells with the oddly shaped nuclei are called **phagocytes**. They attack germs by eating them. If you cut yourself, germs can get into your body. The phagocytes come to your rescue and rush to the wound. They start eating and killing the germs (Fig. 11.28). They are usually killed themselves and this is what causes pus (a yellow-coloured material) to form in a cut or wound.

The white blood cells with round nuclei are called **lymphocytes** (Fig. 11.29). They also protect us from germs that get inside our bodies by producing special proteins called **antibodies**. Antibodies attack the surface proteins on the germs and this kills them.

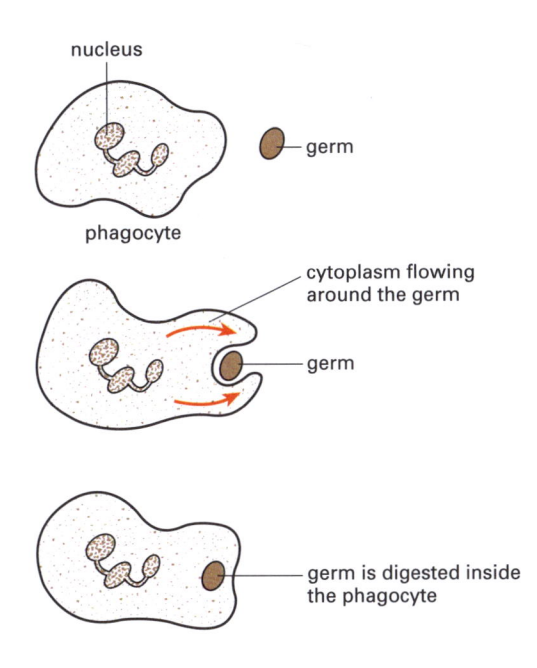

Fig. 11.28 White cells killing germs.

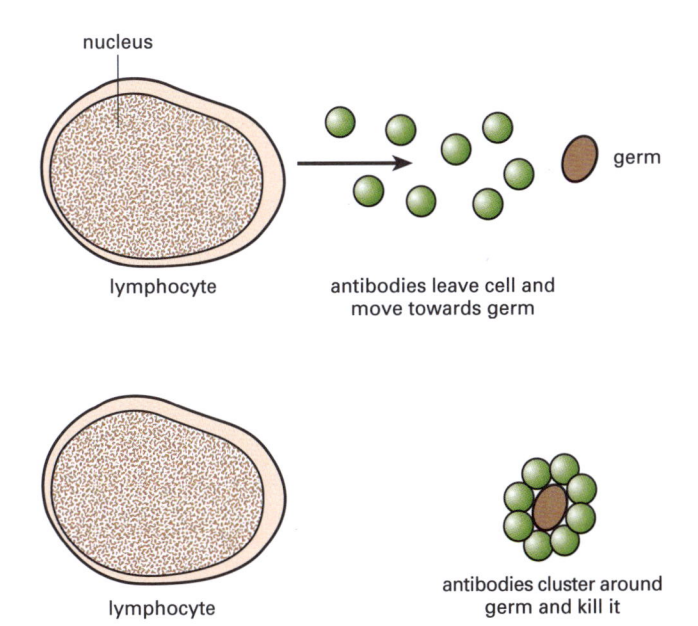

Fig. 11.29 Antibodies killing germs.

11.4 Systems in animals

❓ Finding out

Organ transplants

Organ transplants have saved many lives. Organs usually come from people who have been killed in accidents. People may have already given their permission to give their bodies for transplants or medical research beforehand. Sometimes relatives at a hospital are asked to give their permission for a person's organs to be used after a tragedy. Sometimes, close relatives can donate a body tissue or, for example, a kidney to a sick person. Some people think that organ transplants are wrong. What do you think? Find out about organ and tissue donation from your local clinic and/or hospital, and from newspapers, books and the internet.

If something gets into the body that the white blood cells recognize as being 'foreign' to the body they go on the attack. This causes problems for modern medicine when someone is given a heart transplant or a kidney transplant, for example. The body's natural defences don't like it! In the early days, the body rejected the new heart or kidneys. Doctors have tried to overcome these problems by treating the person with drugs and only using organs from people with a similar body chemistry. The person who gives the organ or tissue is known as the donor.

The red and white blood cells are carried in the **plasma**, which is a watery fluid. It contains 90% water. It also carries dissolved food, carbon dioxide, hormones (which you will learn about in Book 3, Topic 16.2), waste substances, salts, heat and **platelets**. Platelets are tiny pieces of blood cells and play a part in the clotting of the blood.

When we cut ourselves, the cut bleeds for a while and then stops. A network of tiny protein fibres forms in the cut, traps the blood cells and platelets and a clot forms. This dries up to form a scab, preventing germs from entering. The skin heals beneath the wound and the scab falls off. Usually, after a few weeks, we can no longer see where the cut was. Sometimes, if the wound is very deep, it leaves a scar.

The blood vessels

The blood is carried at high pressure to all the cells of the body in the blood vessels. There are three types of blood vessels: **arteries**, **veins** and **capillaries** (see Figure 11.30).

Arteries carry blood to the body organs. They divide up and branch into smaller and smaller tubes, ending in blood capillaries, which are the smallest blood vessels of all. Food and oxygen pass out from the capillaries into the cells. Carbon dioxide and other waste substances pass from the cells into the capillaries. The capillaries then join up and form the veins, which carry blood away from the organ, back to the heart.

The blood circulates through all the body organs. The circulation is maintained by the pumping action of the heart.

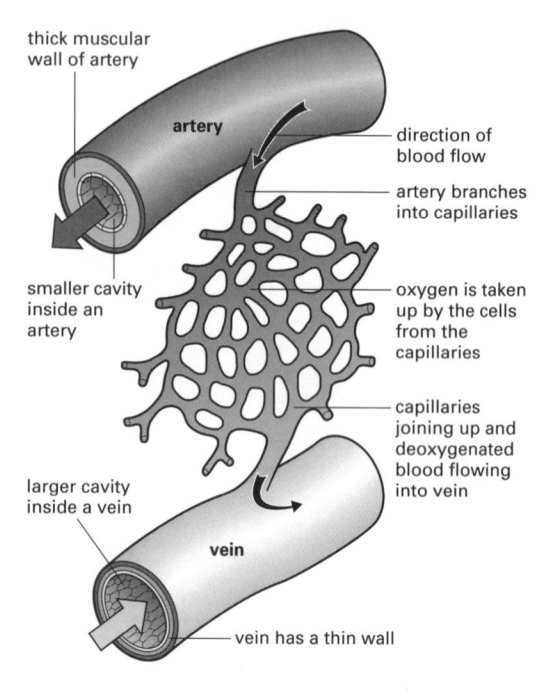

Fig. 11.30 Arteries divide into capillaries; capillaries join up to form veins.

Blood and the circulatory system   11.4

The heart and the circulation

Study Figures 11.31 and 11.32 as you read this section.

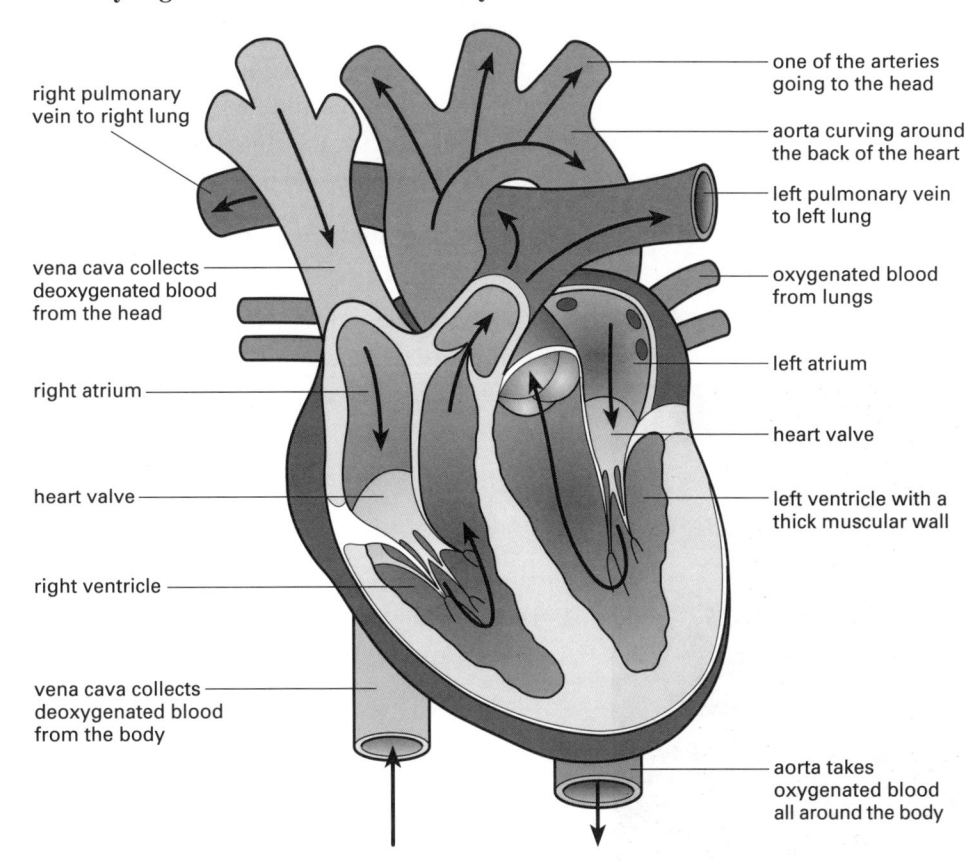

Labels on Fig. 11.31:
- right pulmonary vein to right lung
- vena cava collects deoxygenated blood from the head
- right atrium
- heart valve
- right ventricle
- vena cava collects deoxygenated blood from the body
- one of the arteries going to the head
- aorta curving around the back of the heart
- left pulmonary vein to left lung
- oxygenated blood from lungs
- left atrium
- heart valve
- left ventricle with a thick muscular wall
- aorta takes oxygenated blood all around the body

Fig. 11.31 Section through the heart showing the circulation of the blood. Note that the right side of the heart is shown on the left of the diagram – it is drawn as though you are lying face up on the page.

Labels on Fig. 11.32:
- deoxygenated blood is carried to the lungs
- air sac in lung
- oxygen diffuses into blood
- oxygenated blood returns to the heart
- oxygenated blood is carried to all cells in the body
- deoxygenated blood is returned to the heart in the veins
- oxygen passes from the blood to the body cells

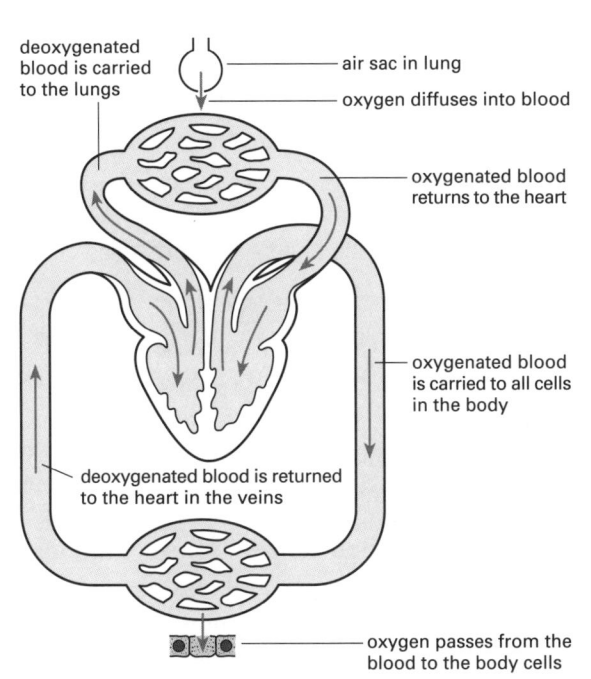

Fig. 11.32 A plan of the heart and the blood circulation.

The heart is a muscular pump in your chest beneath your ribs. Its pumping action is your heartbeat. The heart has four hollow parts or chambers: the right **atrium**, which leads into the right **ventricle**; and the left atrium, which leads into the left ventricle.

The veins in the body join up to form two very large veins called the **venae cavae** (singular: **vena cava**). They contain blood collected from all the body organs. The venae cavae carry blood into the right atrium. The blood has given up much of its oxygen to the cells and is described as deoxygenated blood. The deoxygenated blood then flows into the right ventricle and is pumped through the **pulmonary arteries** into the lungs, where the red blood cells pick up oxygen. The oxygenated blood is carried

95

11.4 Systems in animals

back from the lungs in the **pulmonary veins** to the left atrium. The blood then flows into the left ventricle. The left ventricle, which is the biggest, most muscular chamber, pumps the oxygenated blood at high pressure into the **aorta**, which is the biggest artery. All the other arteries branch off the aorta and take oxygenated blood all around the body. Have you noticed that the blood passes through the heart twice with each complete circuit around the body? Of course, the heart beats as a whole, so blood is pumped around both circuits at the same time.

There are valves in the heart to stop the blood flowing backwards.

➔ Activity Looking at a heart

Hygiene: Make sure you wash your hands thoroughly after handling the heart.

You will need
- A sheep's heart. Your teacher will get one from the butcher.

Method
1. Look carefully at the sheep's heart. Does it look the same as a human heart (Fig. 11.33)?
2. Identify each of the four chambers. Press the atria and then the ventricles.
3. It may be difficult to identify the blood vessels as the butcher may have trimmed them, but your teacher will help you.
4. Your teacher will then cut a vertical section (from top to bottom) through the heart to show you the heart valves.

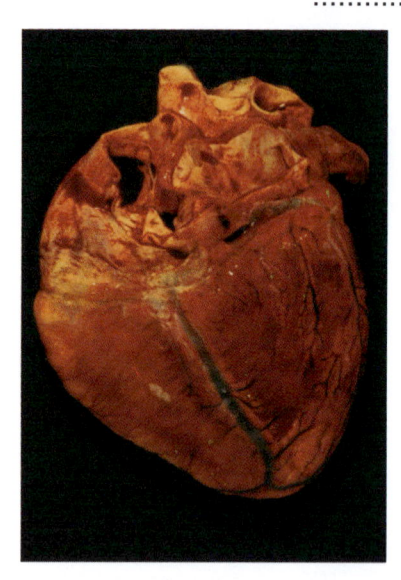

Fig. 11.33 The outside of a human heart.

Discuss
1. How did the ventricles and atria compare in terms of size and muscle?
2. Which arteries and veins could you identify?
3. Why does the heart have valves?
4. Follow the route of blood flow into and out of the heart – on both sides.

Arteries carry blood *away* from the heart. They usually carry oxygenated blood. The pulmonary arteries are exceptions because they carry deoxygenated blood (to the lungs). Veins carry blood *to* the heart. They usually carry deoxygenated blood. The pulmonary veins are exceptions because they carry oxygenated blood (from the lungs back to the heart).

Arteries have thicker, more muscular walls than veins because of the high pressure of blood from the heart. Veins have thinner and less muscular walls because there is less pressure pushing the blood along. They also have valves (Fig. 11.34). The valves are flaps that push open as the blood flows through and move back to stop the blood flowing backwards.

Blood and the circulatory system 11.4

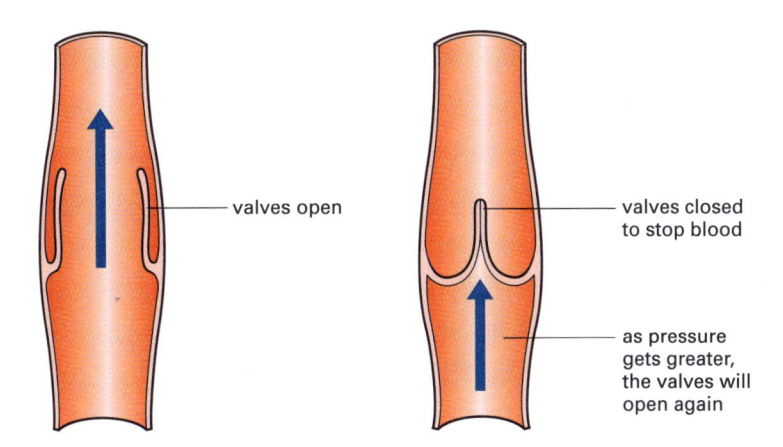

Fig. 11.34 Veins have valves to stop blood flowing backwards.

- valves open
- valves closed to stop blood
- as pressure gets greater, the valves will open again

→ Activity Arteries and veins

Method
Copy Table 11.9 into your exercise book, read through the text and fill in the spaces.

Table 11.9 Differences between arteries and veins.

Arteries	Veins
Carry blood away from the heart to all the organs of the body	
_____	Carry deoxygenated blood
_____	Have thinner, less muscular walls
Carry blood under high pressure	_____
Do not have valves	_____
The pulmonary arteries are unusual because they carry _____ blood to the heart from the _____	The pulmonary veins are unusual because they carry _____ blood from the _____ to the heart

→ Activity How fast is my heart beating?

You will need
- a stop clock or stopwatch with a second hand

Method
1. Sit quietly and study Figure 11.35.

    You are going to measure what your average heart rate is when you are not active – your **resting heart rate**.

2. Find your pulse on the inside of your left wrist using the fingertips of your right hand. You should feel your pulse throbbing. Do not use your thumb!

11.4 Systems in animals

Did you know?

If your heart was removed from your body it would continue to beat for a while. This is because it has its own 'pacemaker', which is a special group of cells that send out tiny electrical signals to the heart muscles.

If the pacemaker in someone's heart fails to work, doctors can fit an artificial pacemaker to their chest. This sends electrical signals to the heart muscles to make their heart beat.

3 Your partner will time one minute, telling you when to start and stop counting. Record the number of beats in one minute.

4 Repeat this twice and work out your average heartbeat by adding the three numbers together and dividing by 3.

5 Swap and let your partner find out his/her average heartbeat when at rest.

Discuss

1 How did your heart rate compare with those of the rest of the class?

2 Has anyone ever taken your pulse and why?

3 When have you noticed changes to your heart rate? What caused them?

4 A slow heart rate is one sign of physical fitness. Can you think why?

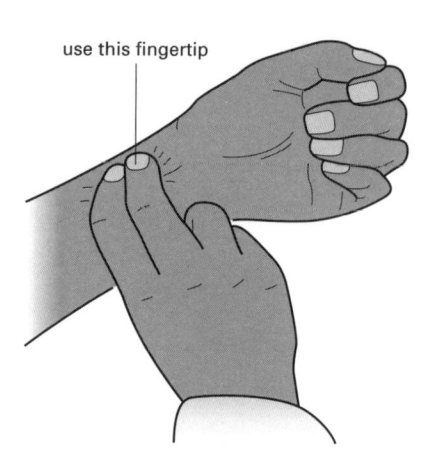

Fig. 11.35 How to take your pulse.

Disorders of the blood system

There are many disorders and diseases of the blood and blood system. These are some of the common ones.

Malaria: This is caused by a small germ (micro-organism) called *Plasmodium*, which attacks and destroys red blood cells. Mosquitoes carry the organism and spread malaria when they bite and suck blood from people. A person with malaria has a severe headache, loss of appetite, and fever. Malaria can be treated with drugs. The spread of the disease can be prevented by draining swamps and marshes where mosquitoes breed and using insecticides to kill the mosquitoes. Window screens and mosquito nets can be used to prevent people being bitten at night.

Anaemia: This is a condition in which there may be too few red blood cells or not enough haemoglobin. It is caused by insufficient iron in the diet to make haemoglobin. The person becomes tired very easily as not enough oxygen gets to the cells. Treatment includes eating food rich in iron (red meat) or taking iron tablets.

Sickle-cell anaemia: About one in ten people in the Caribbean have sickle-cell trait. If both parents have sickle-cell trait, there is a one in four chance of the children being born with sickle-cell anaemia. The disease has this name because the red blood cells have an abnormal shape resembling a sickle and do not have enough haemoglobin. The person with this disease becomes anaemic and has painful joints. People with sickle-cell trait have been found to be more resistant to malaria than other people!

Haemophilia: The blood lacks one of the factors important for clotting and so it is difficult to stop bleeding. A small cut could be very dangerous for someone with haemophilia. This is a disease passed on from parents to their children. It can be treated by giving people the missing clotting factor.

Leukaemia: This occurs when abnormal white blood cells are produced in large numbers. They stop the normal white cells from working and protecting the body from diseases. It is a form of cancer and is a very serious illness. It is treated by **radiotherapy** (with machines that direct radiation at the cells) or **chemotherapy** (treatment with special drugs).

Varicose veins: In older people especially, the walls of the veins of the legs stretch and become misshapen. Sometimes clots form or ulcers (sore regions) develop. Treatment can include wearing support stockings and taking exercise to help the circulation and avoid clotting. Very stretched veins can either be removed or cleaned out (called stripping) by having an operation in hospital.

High blood pressure: Our blood pressure increases when we take exercise or when we are angry or frightened, but some people have very high blood pressure all the time. This puts a lot of strain on the heart and could even cause a blood vessel to burst. If a blood vessel in the brain bursts, this damages and kills the cells nearby. This is known as having a stroke. If the brain is damaged, it may paralyse the limbs and affect the speech of a person. A severe stroke can result in death. The cause is not known for certain, but many doctors think that stress, smoking, eating too much and drinking too much alcohol are causes.

Atherosclerosis (hardening of the arteries): Cholesterol is a fat-like substance in the body. It is needed for many reasons, but if there is too much cholesterol in the diet, it can be deposited in the walls of the arteries. This causes them to block up and the blood flow slows down. It can lead to blood clots that can lodge in the heart, brain or lungs, for example, or can cause severe chest pain. High cholesterol levels in the body can be avoided by not eating too many animal fats in the diet (a source of cholesterol). It can be treated with drugs, or an operation can be carried out to bypass and avoid the diseased artery.

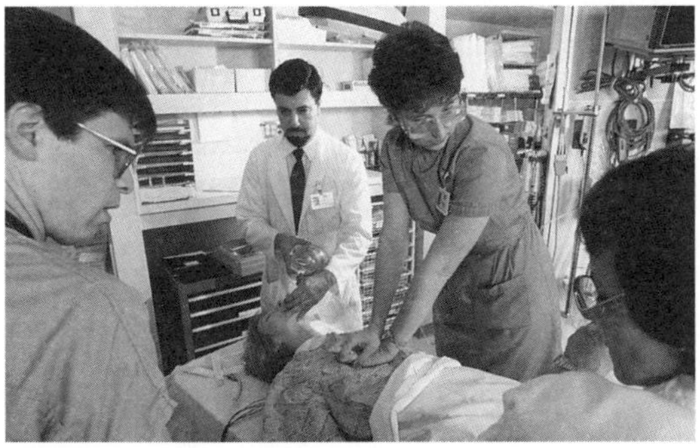

Fig. 11.36 This person is being given cardiac massage in the emergency room of a hospital.

Heart attack: The heart has its own blood supply. The blood vessels are the **coronary arteries** and veins. If a clot forms in one of the coronary arteries, this causes the person to have a heart attack. The heart is starved of oxygen and stops beating. Sometimes, the damage to the heart is not great. If cardiac massage is given straight away (Fig. 11.36) a person can survive.

11.4 Systems in animals

Fig. 11.37 A blood transfusion can be life-saving.

Sometimes someone loses a lot of blood, for example, in an accident. This results in low blood pressure and the person becomes unconscious. The person can be treated by being given a blood transfusion in hospital. Blood transfusions are also used to treat people with sickle-cell anaemia (Fig. 11.37). People volunteer to donate (give) their blood to hospitals, where it is stored in blood banks for transfusions. They are called blood donors.

The lymphatic system protects the body

When blood reaches the cells in the capillaries, the blood cells and big molecules stay behind, but the small molecules and fluid are squeezed out. Some of this fluid passes into the cells, but some stays outside the cells and is called **tissue fluid**. The waste from the cells passes into the tissue fluid, which is then collected in tiny lymph capillaries. These join up to form the lymphatic system, which rejoins the blood system in the veins in the neck.

Have you ever felt ill and had swollen glands in your neck? These are not proper glands, but are little swellings on your lymph capillaries called **lymph nodes**.

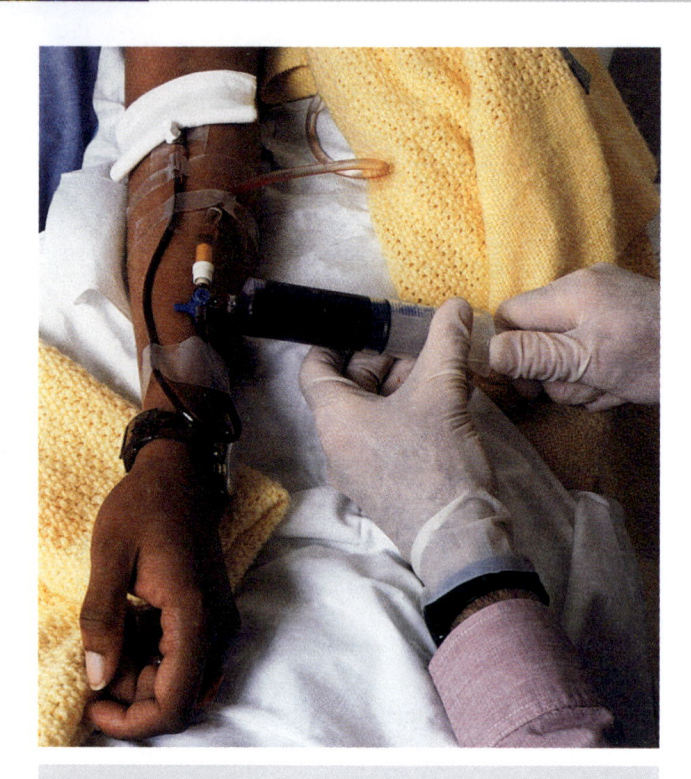

Did you know?

Dr Charles Drew was an African-American doctor who discovered a method to preserve blood plasma. He invented blood banks, and his discoveries saved thousands of lives during World War II. One night, in 1950, Dr Drew was involved in a car accident in North Carolina where racial segregation was practised at the time. Because of his race, the local hospital did not admit him. He died before he could get the blood transfusion he needed.

What do you think about Dr Drew's story? What does this story tell you about access to technology?

Discuss this story with your class. What other factors may prevent people from getting the benefits of technology?

Finding out

Human blood groups

Not everyone's blood is suitable to give to everyone else. Blood is grouped according to the ABO system, which has four blood groups: A, B, AB and O. If a person is given blood from the wrong blood group, the person's red blood cells will clot and the person could die. Find out about blood groups from your local clinic/ hospital, books and the internet.

? Finding out

Common blood disorders in my community

1. Draw up a questionnaire and tactfully ask your friends, neighbours and family (not strangers) if any of them or their family have suffered from any of the blood disorders. Do not force them to answer your questions. Your teacher will also help you to obtain information about community statistics from your local clinic and/or hospital.
2. Organize a discussion group to pool your answers.
3. As a class, draw a bar chart that will show how many of these disorders you are aware of in your community and which ones are the most common.
4. What patterns do you see? What conclusions can you draw?

They make special white cells to fight diseases. They sometimes swell up when you are unwell and fighting a disease. Other lymph nodes are found in your groin and armpits. The special white cells are also produced in the tonsils and adenoids in your throat. So if you get tonsillitis and your throat feels very sore and swollen, remember that this is a sign that these special cells are helping your body to fight disease.

→ Activity Protecting your heart and blood

1. Read the section on disorders of the blood system carefully and discuss what you can do in your everyday life to help protect yourself from some of these disorders.
2. Design a poster to explain to people in your community how a change in their lifestyle can help them to avoid high blood pressure, stroke, hardening of the arteries and heart attack.

◘ What you should know

- Blood consists of red blood cells, white blood cells, plasma and platelets.
- Red blood cells carry oxygen around the body; white blood cells help to fight against diseases; platelets help with blood clotting; plasma transports carbon dioxide, dissolved food and waste.
- Blood circulates around the body in arteries, veins and capillaries.
- Blood is pumped around the body by the heart.
- The blood passes through the heart twice with each circuit around the body.
- The heart is divided into four chambers: left and right atria and left and right ventricles.
- Common blood disorders include: malaria, anaemia, sickle-cell anaemia, haemophilia, leukaemia, varicose veins, high blood pressure and atherosclerosis (hardening of the arteries).
- The lymphatic system produces white blood cells to fight diseases.

11.4 Systems in animals

Questions

1. What are the functions of:
   a the red blood cells;
   b the white blood cells;
   c the blood plasma?

2. Describe the pathway a red blood cell takes from a vein in your arm to an artery in your leg.

3. In the form of a table, list the differences between an artery and a vein.

4. Which of the following diseases is caused by a germ?
   a malaria
   b heart attack
   c varicose veins
   d high blood pressure

5. Which of the following diseases cannot be protected against by having a healthy diet?
   a heart attack
   b haemophilia
   c anaemia
   d high blood pressure

6. Research sickle-cell anaemia. Who does it affect? What is known about it?

7. Research malaria. You can take drugs to prevent the illness. How do they work?

Systems in animals

11.5 Breathing and respiration in humans

▶ Objectives

After studying this topic you should be able to:

- explain how air is inhaled and exhaled (breathing)
- describe gaseous exchange in the cells
- briefly explain the process of respiration in the cells
- distinguish between respiration and breathing.

The human breathing system

Figure 11.38 shows the breathing system in humans. The lungs are the organs of the breathing system. They are found in the chest cavity and are protected by the ribs. You can breathe in through your mouth or your nose. The air then passes to the back of your throat and into your main air passage called the windpipe (**trachea**). At the top of the windpipe is the voice box (**larynx**). The windpipe divides into two narrower tubes going to the left and right lungs. Each of these tubes is called a **bronchus**. Each bronchus then divides into smaller and even narrower tubes, forming a network of air passages through the lungs. These tubes finally end in air sacs (**alveoli**). The air sacs are surrounded by blood capillaries. The air passages are always open to the air. They are kept open by C-shaped hoops of a hard tissue called **cartilage**. At the bottom of the chest cavity is the **diaphragm**. This is a sheet of muscle that separates the chest cavity from the abdomen.

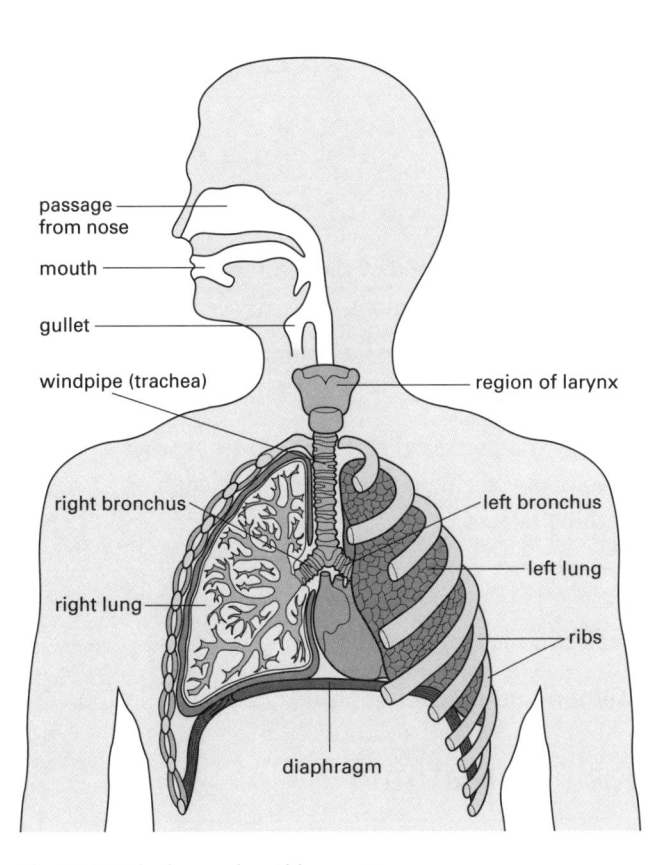

Fig. 11.38 The human breathing system.

The gullet, through which food passes from the mouth to the stomach, is found just behind the windpipe. A little flap closes over the entrance to the windpipe when you swallow food to stop your food 'going down the wrong way'. Has this ever happened to you? It makes you cough and choke and is very unpleasant. So – you cannot breathe in and swallow food at the same time. Choking and then coughing the food up are reflex actions to clear the air passages.

11.5 Systems in animals

The air is cleaned as it passes in through the nose. Hairs in the nose trap dust particles. Also, the nose and all the air passages are lined with a layer of specialized cells that produce a slimy fluid called **mucus** and also have tiny microscopic hairs (called cilia) that beat in a rhythm. The mucus makes the air moist and also helps to trap dust particles. The microscopic hairs move dust particles trapped in the mucus one way only – out towards the nose and mouth. Can you think why this is a good thing?

Activity Looking at a pig's lungs

Hygiene: Make sure you wash your hands thoroughly after handling the lungs.

You will need
- your teacher will get from the butcher some pig's lungs with the windpipe and voice box still attached
- a long hollow glass tube

Method
1. Feel the lungs with your fingertips.
2. Run your fingertips along the windpipe.
3. Your teacher (not you) will then place the end of the long glass tube into the trachea and bronchi and blow to expand the lungs.
4. He or she will then press gently on them to expel the air.

Discuss
1. Did the lungs feel spongy when you pressed them? Can you think why?
2. What could you feel when you ran your fingertips along the windpipe?
3. How are speaking and breathing related?

Breathing movements

Breathing in is called inhalation and breathing out is called exhalation.

Activity Investigating breathing

Method
1. Stand up and place your hands on your ribs.
2. Take a deep breath. In which directions did your ribs move? Repeat a few times to make sure.
3. Breathe in, hold your breath and then place your hands on your ribs as you breathe out slowly. In which directions did your ribs move? Again, repeat a few times to make sure.
4. Repeat step 2, but this time, place your hand on your stomach. Can you feel it moving? In which direction?

Breathing and respiration in humans 11.5

Breathing in: Look back at Figure 11.38 to remind yourself where the sheet of muscle called the diaphragm is. The diaphragm bulges up into the chest cavity. When you breathe air in, the diaphragm flattens out. The ribs move upwards and outwards. This increases the size (volume) of the chest cavity and decreases the pressure. Air rushes in through the nose or mouth and air passages, filling the lungs with air. Did you notice in the activity that when you breathe in, your stomach pushes out slightly? When the diaphragm flattens, it pushes on the liver and stomach beneath.

Breathing out: Your diaphragm goes back to its original position. The volume of the chest cavity decreases, increasing the pressure and so forcing the air out. You will have noticed that your ribs move downwards and inwards as you breathe out, back to their original position.

What happens in the air sacs?

In Topic 10.1, you learned that air is a mixture of gases and is a resource for living organisms. Air contains oxygen. So, every time you breathe air in, you take in oxygen. You breathe out carbon dioxide and water vapour.

Figure 11.39 shows you the blood capillaries and the air sacs. Notice that the oxygen passes from the air sacs into the blood capillaries where it combines (joins up) with the haemoglobin in the red blood cells. Figure 11.39 also shows that the carbon dioxide passes into the air sacs from the blood plasma. You have now learned that gases are exchanged between the blood and the air in the air sacs. This movement of gases is called **diffusion**.

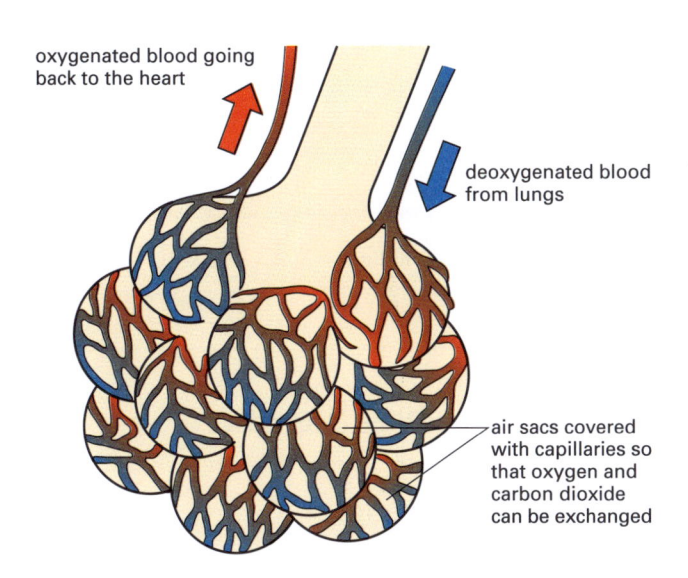

Fig. 11.39 Gases are exchanged between the capillaries and the air sacs.

Respiration takes place in the cells

The blood carries oxygen to all the cells, where respiration takes place.

The purpose of respiration is to release energy from the food for all the activities in the body. Remember that in digestion, large carbohydrate molecules are broken down into smaller molecules such as glucose. Glucose is used in respiration. This equation is a useful way of summing up what happens in respiration in the body cells:

glucose + oxygen → energy + carbon dioxide + water

The carbon dioxide and water are waste substances and are carried by the blood (in the plasma) to the lungs, where they are breathed out. The water is breathed out as water vapour.

Activity How does exercise affect my breathing?

You will need
- a stopwatch or stop clock with a second hand

Method
1. Your partner will tell you when to start and stop counting.
2. Sit quietly for a few minutes, then count the number of times you breathe in and out (your breathing rate) in one minute. Try to breathe normally!
3. Run on the spot for one minute (your partner will time you) and then sit down and count the number of times you breathe in and out in one minute.

Discuss
1. By how much did your breathing rate increase after you exercised?
2. What type of food is used up in the muscle cells of your legs when you exercise and need energy?
3. Which gas is used up when respiration takes place in your muscle cells?
4. Which gases are breathed out in the air you exhale?
5. Which types of food would you advise athletes to have in their diet? Why?

Activity What is in the air I breathe out?

Fig. 11.40 Investigating what is in the air we breathe out: left, breathing out on to a cold mirror; right, blowing into a test tube of lime water.

11.5 Breathing and respiration in humans

You will need
- a cold mirror
- a test tube containing some lime water (irritant)
- a drinking straw

Method
1 Breathe out onto the cold mirror (Fig. 11.40a).
2 Blow air bubbles gently into the lime water through the straw (Fig. 11.40b). Watch what happens to the lime water. (Look back to Topic 9.9 if you cannot remember what this tells you!)

Discuss
1 What in your breath makes the mirror become misty?
2 How long does it take for the lime water to turn milky? What does this tell you?
3 Would this change be quicker or slower after exercise?

Activity Comparing inhaled and exhaled air

Table 11.10 shows the percentages of gases in the air you breathe in and the air you breathe out.

Table 11.10 Comparing the gases in inhaled air and exhaled air.

Name of gas	Percentage of gas in inhaled air from the atmosphere	Percentage of gas in exhaled air from the lungs
Oxygen	20.97	16.4
Carbon dioxide	0.03	4.1
Nitrogen	79	79

Discuss
1 Why is there less oxygen in the air you breathe out?
2 Why is there more carbon dioxide in the air you breathe out?
3 Why is there the same amount of nitrogen in the air you breathe in as in the air you breathe out?

11.5 Systems in animals

Some common lung diseases

- **Colds** and **influenza (flu)** are infectious diseases caused by tiny germs called viruses. When you cough or sneeze, little droplets of moisture containing the germs pass into the air and can be breathed in by other people, who also catch the virus and get infected.
- **Pneumonia** is a serious lung infection caused by bacteria. It can stop you breathing and can kill.
- **Tuberculosis (TB)**, **whooping cough** and **diphtheria** are caused by bacteria. They are air-borne diseases and are very infectious.
- **Bronchitis** is inflammation of the bronchi (the tubes that lead from the windpipe to the lungs). It can be caused by bacteria. Chronic bronchitis is often caused by smoking. A person with chronic bronchitis has a permanent cough.
- **Lung cancer** is a serious disease most commonly caused by smoking tobacco. Smoking tobacco causes tar to be deposited in your lungs, which may cause cancer. Tobacco also contains nicotine, which is an addictive substance. This means that when you start smoking, your body wants more nicotine, which means you keep on smoking to get it. This makes it difficult for smokers to give up the habit. You will find out more about smoking in Topic 11.7.
- **Asthma** is not infectious. It is caused by allergies of different kinds. People can be allergic to feathers, pollen, fungal spores and certain food. When people are having an asthma attack, they cough and wheeze and find it very difficult to breathe because their airways become much narrower. In a serious asthma attack, the bronchi can become very narrow. Asthma is treated with drugs that help to open up the airways. These drugs are often given using an inhaler so that the drug goes directly to the lungs.

? Finding out

How do other animals breathe?

Some animals live in water, such as fish. They do not have lungs. They breathe dissolved oxygen from the water through gills. Find out about breathing and respiration in fish, using books and encyclopedias. If you have time, find out about breathing and respiration in other animals too.

? Finding out

Common lung diseases in my community

1. Draw up a questionnaire and tactfully ask your friends, neighbours and family (not strangers) if any of them or their family have suffered from any of the lung diseases described. Do not force them to answer your questions. Your teacher will also help you to obtain information from your local health centre.
2. Organize a discussion group to pool your answers.
3. As a class, draw a bar chart to show how many of these diseases you are aware of in your community and which are the most common.

Breathing and respiration in humans 11.5

◯ What you should know

- Breathing is the inhalation and exhalation of air.
- The lungs are the breathing organs of the body.
- Inhaled and exhaled air travels along air passages to and from the air sacs in the lungs.
- The air sacs have a good blood supply and this is where gases are exchanged.
- Oxygen is then transported in the blood to the body cells.
- Respiration (a chemical process) takes place in the body cells.
- Glucose in the cells is broken down with the help of oxygen, and energy is released for all the activities in the cells.
- Carbon dioxide and water (the waste products of respiration) are then carried from the cells to the lungs by the blood and are breathed out.
- Exhaled air contains more carbon dioxide and less oxygen than inhaled air.

◯ Questions

1. Which is the correct pathway taken by the air to get into the lungs?
   a. mouth/nose, air sac, bronchus, windpipe
   b. air sac, bronchus, mouth/nose, windpipe
   c. windpipe, bronchus, air sac, mouth/nose
   d. mouth/nose, windpipe, bronchus, air sac

2. Explain what happens when you choke on some food.

3. How are dust particles in the air prevented from entering the lungs?

4. Explain the difference between breathing and respiration.

5. Research asthma. Why is it becoming increasingly common among young children? How can it be treated? How do many young people overcome it to live normal lives?

Systems in animals

11.6 Excretion: getting rid of waste materials

▶ Objectives

After studying this topic you should be able to:

- explain that excretion is the elimination of waste substances from the body
- explain that the lungs are organs of excretion as well as breathing
- explain that the skin is an excretory organ as well as a sense organ
- describe the human excretory system and the excretion of urine
- describe how the kidneys also control the amount of salts and water in the body.

Examples of excretion

In Book 1, Topic 2.1 you learned that **excretion** means getting rid of waste substances formed by chemical reactions in the body. You have already learned that carbon dioxide and water vapour produced as a result of respiration are breathed out. So although the lungs are mainly known as respiratory organs, they can also be thought of as excretory organs if we think about getting rid of carbon dioxide and water vapour.

We sweat when doing heavy work or vigorous exercise or on a hot day. Water and salts from the blood capillaries around the sweat gland are collected in the sweat gland (Fig. 11.41). The sweat passes along the sweat duct onto the surface of the skin. When the sweat evaporates from the surface of the skin, this cools the body down. Sweat is a watery solution that contains salts and a substance called urea. In cold weather, very little sweat is produced.

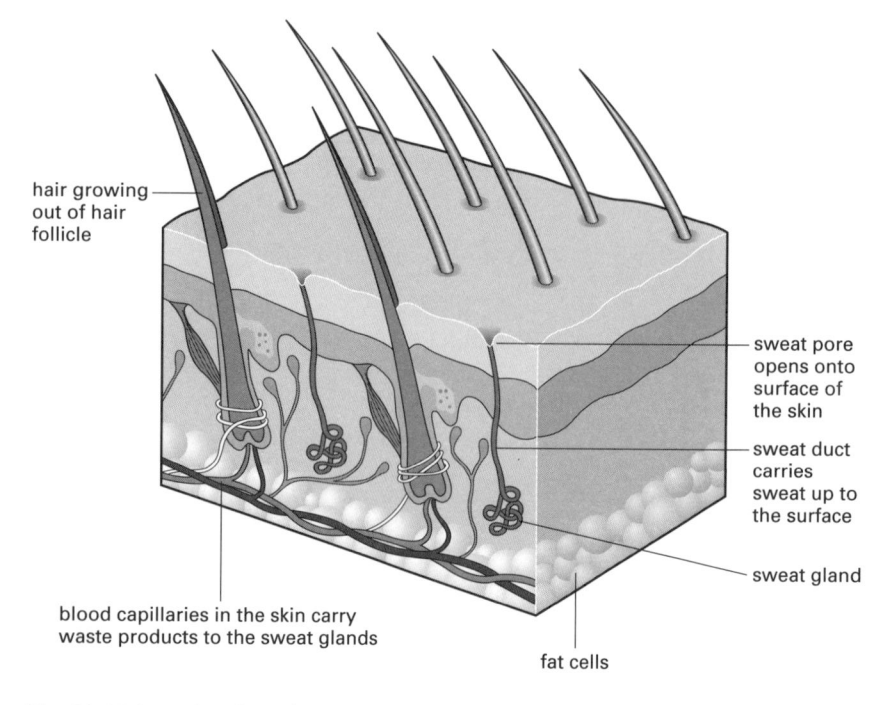

Fig. 11.41 A section through human skin.

Excretion: getting rid of waste materials 11.6

What happens to extra proteins in the body?

Unlike fats and carbohydrates, proteins cannot be stored in the body. So, we have to get rid of extra proteins otherwise they would harm the body. You have already learned that proteins are digested in the alimentary canal. They are broken down by enzymes into amino acids, absorbed in the intestine and taken by the blood to the liver. An amino acid molecule has a carbohydrate part and a part that contains nitrogen (Fig. 11.42). The carbohydrate part is used to provide the body with energy. The part of the molecule containing nitrogen is separated from the rest of the molecule and changed into a substance called urea. Urea is poisonous and cannot be stored. It is carried in the blood to the **kidneys**. Urea dissolves in water to form a watery liquid called urine. This is the main excretory product of the body.

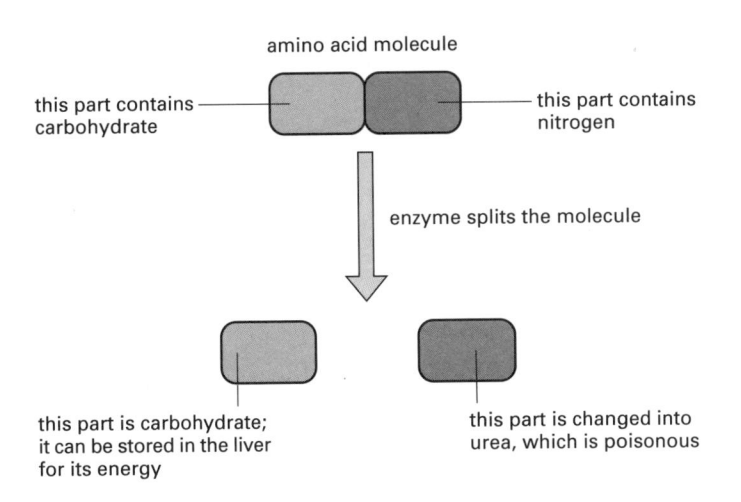

Fig. 11.42 The parts of an amino acid.

The human excretory system

The two (left and right) kidneys are excretory organs (Fig. 11.43) because they get rid of waste. They are found quite high up in the abdomen towards the back. A long tube called a **ureter** travels down from each kidney to the bladder. The bladder is an elastic muscular bag which stores urine. Another tube, called the **urethra**, carries the urine from the bladder to the outside. In males the urethra is in the penis, opening to the outside at the tip. In females the urethra opens just above the vagina.

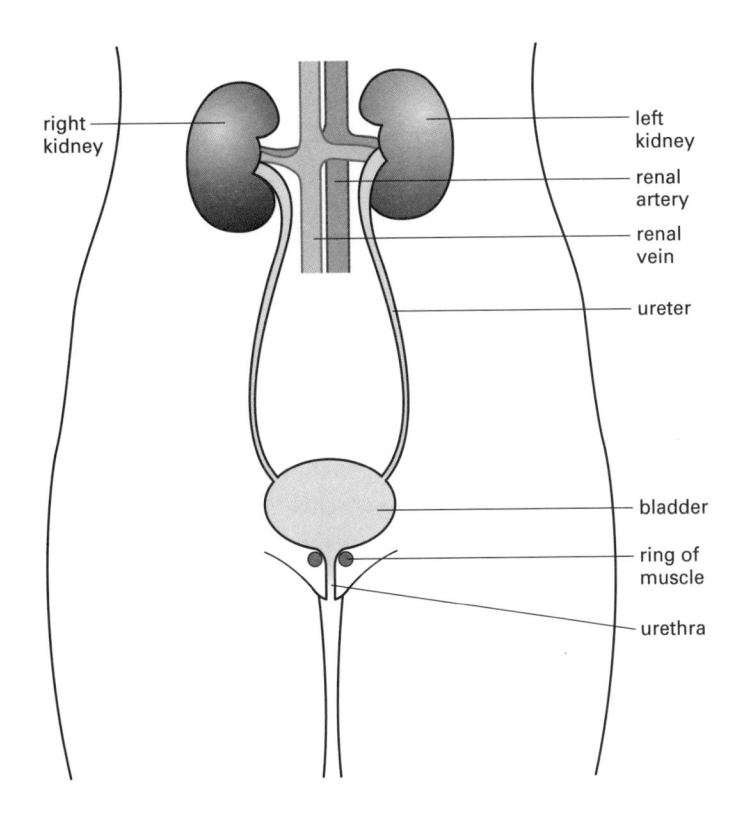

Fig. 11.43 The kidneys are excretory organs.

11.6 Systems in animals

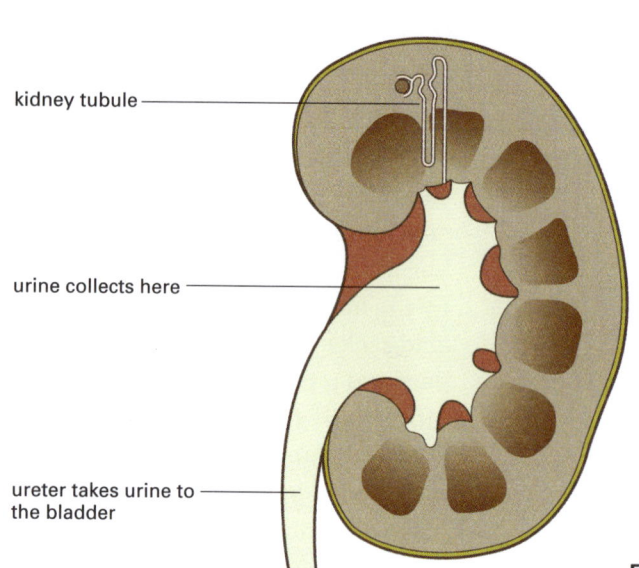

What happens in the kidneys?

The renal arteries supply the kidneys (Fig. 11.44) with blood, and the renal veins take the blood away. Inside the kidneys, the blood is cleaned by being filtered under pressure in tiny tubes called **kidney tubules**. Because of this pressure, smaller molecules such as water, salts and urea are forced out of thin blood capillaries into the kidney tubules. Remember that the urea and water form urine. The big molecules and the blood cells stay in the blood.

Labels on diagram: kidney tubule; urine collects here; ureter takes urine to the bladder

Fig. 11.44 A kidney cut in half to show the inside.

What happens in the bladder?

The urine and salts pass along the tiny tubes into the ureters and then into the bladder. Urine is stored in the bladder. The bladder has special muscles that relax as it fills. They can contract to expel the urine. The bladder stretches as more urine is collected. Between the bladder and urethra is a ring of muscle. It is usually closed. When we need to pass urine, we are well aware that we need to go to the lavatory, and this can feel quite uncomfortable! When we pass urine, the ring of muscle relaxes and the urine passes out of our bodies through the urethra. The urine we pass is a yellow liquid.

Babies wear nappies because they cannot yet control the ring of muscle leading from the bladder. Passing urine is a reflex action in a baby. A young child gradually learns to control the muscle and can then use the lavatory properly. Passing urine is then under the control of the will.

Have you noticed that in males, both sperm and urine pass out of the body through the urethra and penis? They cannot pass through at the same time. Urine cannot pass through an erect penis in sexual intercourse.

➲ Activity Looking at a kidney

Hygiene: Make sure you wash your hands thoroughly after handling the kidney.

You will need
- a fresh untrimmed pig's or sheep's kidney – your teacher will get one from the butcher

Excretion: getting rid of waste materials 11.6

Method
1 Look at the kidney and identify the renal artery and vein and the ureter.
2 Examine it again after your teacher has sliced the kidney in half.

Discuss
1 Why is the kidney reddish-brown in colour?
2 Why do we have two kidneys? What happens when a kidney is transplanted?

> **Did you know?**
>
> If one of your kidneys doesn't work properly and becomes diseased, the other kidney can take over its functions.

The kidneys control the amount of water and salts in our bodies

When the blood has been filtered in the kidney tubules, some water and salts are taken back into the tubules. They are reabsorbed. The amounts reabsorbed depend on the needs of the body at the time. For example, if you have lost a lot of water and salts on a hot day or after a lot of exercise, more water and salts will be reabsorbed in the kidneys. The urine will be darker yellow. If you have drunk a lot, the urine you pass will be paler yellow and more watery. Less water needs to be reabsorbed because the body has enough. This is just one example of the many ways in which the body regulates itself to keep conditions inside as constant as possible.

What happens if the kidneys are diseased?

The kidney machine: If the kidneys stop working, it is very serious because urea accumulates in the blood and the person could die. Modern technology has come up with a solution that has saved many lives. This is the invention and development of the kidney machine (Fig. 11.45).

The machine has a pump and a coiled tube made of a special thin membrane with tiny holes called pores. It also has a special solution of things that the body needs, such as glucose and salts. A vein in the person's arm is connected to the machine by a tube. As the blood flows into the machine, it is pumped through the membrane and cleaned and filtered. The unwanted substances such as urea are filtered out through the tiny pores into the solution, which has to be continuously changed to take the urea away. The blood then flows back into the person through another tube and into another part of the vein. The process is called **dialysis** (or

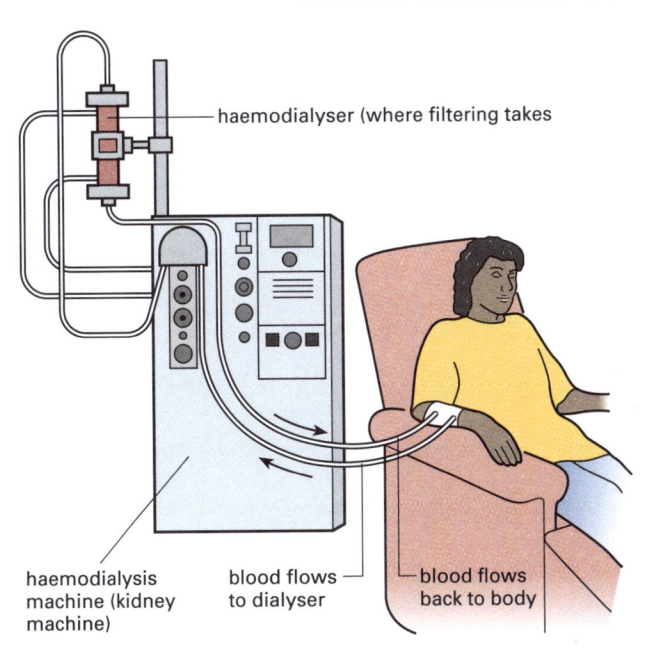

Fig. 11.45 This person is connected to a kidney machine. It filters out poisonous substances from the person's blood.

Labels: haemodialyser (where filtering takes [place]); haemodialysis machine (kidney machine); blood flows to dialyser; blood flows back to body

113

haemodialysis). Dialysis takes about five hours. A person usually has to have treatment three times a week.

People can be connected to these machines in hospital, but there are portable ones that a person can have at home. These machines are very expensive and are in short supply.

Kidney transplant: Sometimes, a person may receive a new kidney from a dead person's body. Some people give permission for their body organs to be used for transplants should they be killed in an accident, for example. One problem with transplants is that the body reacts to 'foreign' tissue in the same way that it fights diseases. The new kidney may cause the body to react against it and destroy the cells. This is called rejection. Drugs can be used to help stop this rejection. Close relatives have been known to donate a kidney to a sick person if their body chemistry matches closely.

What you should know

- The kidneys, lungs and skin are excretory organs.
- Urea is formed when excess proteins are broken down in the liver. It is poisonous and the body has to get rid of it.
- Urea and water form urine.
- The kidneys clean and filter the blood.
- Urine is stored in the bladder and is passed out of the body at intervals.
- The kidneys also control the amount of water and salts in the body.
- People with kidney failure can be given dialysis or a transplant.

Questions

1 Which other body organs carry out excretion as well as the kidneys?
2 What is the name of the poisonous substance the kidneys remove that comes from breaking down amino acids?
3 Explain what happens when the blood is cleaned and filtered in the kidney tubules.
4 Name the tube that carries urine to the bladder.
5 Which substances are reabsorbed (taken back into the body) by the kidneys?
6 What stops urine flowing out of the bladder continuously?

Systems in animals

11.7 The effects of drug abuse

▶ Objectives

After studying this topic, you should be able to:
- explain the meaning of the term 'drug'
- explain that drugs can be used to treat illnesses, but when taken for other reasons can have harmful effects
- describe the three main groups of drugs
- describe the effects of drug abuse on the body (including alcohol abuse and smoking)
- explain that drug abuse harms the addicts and the society in which they live
- communicate to others that you should always say 'No' to drugs.

A drug is a medicine or other substance that affects the body in some way. Many drugs are used to treat or prevent disease. Many familiar medicines we take are drugs, for example, we take aspirin and codeine for headaches or toothache or when we have the flu or a cold. People are prescribed drugs by the doctor to lift them out of their depression. If you suffer a torn ligament whilst playing sports, the doctor will prescribe drugs to help the healing process. **Antibiotics** are also drugs.

Some people take recreational drugs – to improve their mood or change their level of consciousness. Examples of these drugs are nicotine in tobacco, ethanol in alcoholic drinks, and caffeine in tea and coffee. Some recreational drugs are illegal, for example cannabis. So all of us in some way or another take drugs!

Drugs can help sick people, but they can also be dangerous. They can affect your brain either by slowing down the time you take to react to things around you, making you drowsy or sleepy, or they can make you more alert by speeding up the brain. They can also be poisonous. Because of the powerful effect that they have on the body, people who take them have to be carefully supervised by the doctor. They have to take the correct dose at the correct times.

Many drugs affect the brain. These can be divided into three main groups. Notice that in these three groups there are drugs that doctors use to treat patients who are ill, drugs we use in everyday life and the drugs we usually associate with drug abuse.

- **Depressants:** These include **sedatives** (also called **tranquillizers**). Valium and barbiturates are examples. They slow the brain down, making people feel calm. They are given to people to treat feelings of anxiety. Alcohol is also a sedative because it makes people feel more relaxed. The second group of depressants are painkillers (also called **analgesics**), for example, aspirin. As well as reducing pain, the stronger painkillers such as morphine and heroin have a greater effect on slowing the brain down. Morphine is used to treat people who are in severe pain.

- **Stimulants:** These make people more alert, for example, amphetamines and cocaine. These are used less frequently for medicinal purposes these days but are often used recreationally (even though this is illegal). Caffeine and nicotine are also stimulants.
- **Hallucinogens:** These make us see, hear and feel things that are not actually there. Such things are not real and are called **hallucinations**. The hallucinations can be terrifying for the people experiencing them. An example of a hallucinogen is the drug LSD.

You may have heard the word 'narcotics' being applied to drugs – on television programmes, for example. Doctors used to use this term for the pain-killing drugs such as heroin and morphine. But these days, especially in the USA, the word is used to describe all illegal drugs.

Drug abuse

You have already learned (in Book 1, Topic 7.1) that people can become addicted to drugs and need to take more and more. This is called dependence. When people use the term 'drug abuse' they usually mean that someone is taking drugs, such as cannabis or heroin, often in larger and larger quantities, so that they become dependent. But drinking too much alcohol and tobacco smoking are also very harmful and people become dependent on them.

When people abuse drugs, they damage their bodies and their mental health. Once people are 'hooked' (dependent), they crave for a particular drug and keep wanting more and more. They become psychologically dependent. They also become physically dependent. Their body becomes used to the drug. It becomes tolerant and the person needs more of the drug to give them the same effect. If they cannot get the drug, they experience **withdrawal symptoms**, such as vomiting, feeling dizzy and having muscle cramps. Their 'habit' also affects their relationships with other people, especially their family and friends.

Recreational drugs are often described as either 'hard drugs' (e.g. heroin and cocaine) or 'soft drugs' (cannabis and LSD), but it isn't easy to see a borderline. The use and distribution of hard drugs is illegal in many countries. Some of them (e.g. morphine) can only be used by doctors to treat sick people. Soft drugs can also harm the user if taken in large doses and often. Many people believe that taking soft drugs leads on to taking hard drugs, and so is equally dangerous. Table 11.11 shows the main hard

The effects of drug abuse 11.7

and soft drugs, using the three groups we have already discussed. You will notice that many of these drugs have a variety of names. The table also shows you the effects and dangers of taking these drugs.

Table 11.11 Common hard and soft drugs taken for recreation.

Type of drug	Names of drugs (and other names)	Effects (what they do to the body) and dangers
Depressants	Heroin ('H', smack, 'horse') and opium	The person has feelings of euphoria (feeling very good and confident) followed by drowsiness **Dangers:** very addictive, dreadful withdrawal symptoms (sickness, vomiting, muscle cramps). Overdose causes respiratory failure
	Cannabis (marijuana, 'pot', 'grass', hashish, 'dope', 'weed')	Effects vary from one person to another. They include feeling drowsy and relaxed or feelings of euphoria **Dangers:** it can produce hallucinations although its main effects are drowsiness. The person becomes slow in reacting to things and suffers from lack of coordination (falling over and dropping things, for example)
Stimulants	Cocaine ('coke', charlie'), and cocaine hydrochloride ('crack', 'rocks', 'base', 'freebase')	The person feels very energetic, confident and alert **Dangers:** very addictive, the person feels uneasy and may think they are being watched. They become depressed and exhausted. Crack cocaine is even more addictive and makes the person feel very aggressive to everyone around
	Amphetamines ('speed', 'ice', 'glass', 'crystal', 'sulphate')	As with cocaine, the person feels very energetic, confident and alert **Dangers:** very addictive, the person feels panic and depression, becomes very uneasy and has feelings of being watched, cannot eat and feels constantly tired
	MDMA (ecstasy, 'E')	In low doses the person feels calm but very energetic and can hear sounds and see colours more intensely than usual **Dangers:** the person can get heatstroke if this drug is taken, for example, while dancing vigorously. It can cause sleeplessness, depression and the feeling of being watched
Hallucinogens	LSD ('acid', 'trips', mescaline)	The person can hear sounds and see colours more intensely than usual **Dangers:** the person becomes confused and has hallucinations, seeing things that are not really there. Behaviour becomes unpredictable and strange. Some people have had hallucinations in which they think they can fly and have been killed falling off high buildings. The hallucinations are much more extreme than those experienced with cannabis

11.7 Systems in animals

In Book 1, Topic 7.1 you learned about the effects of inhaling ('sniffing') the vapour from substances such as glues, cleaning fluids, petrol (gasoline), lighter fuel, paint thinners, nail varnish remover, etc. These substances are very addictive and the persons who inhale them become tolerant very quickly, needing more and more. These substances make people drowsy, and may give them hallucinations or make them unconscious. The brain, liver and kidneys can be seriously damaged. Tragic deaths have occurred by suffocation or by people choking to death on their own vomit.

Why these drugs are so dangerous: People take drugs by swallowing pills, sniffing powders or by injecting drugs straight into veins (Fig. 11.46). Many drug addicts share syringes for injection, which can spread HIV and hepatitis (blood to blood). As well as the harmful physical and mental effects on the health of people, there are other dangers too.

Drug addicts constantly need fresh supplies of drugs to feed their habit. The people who manufacture and supply drugs illegally make vast fortunes. The drugs are expensive to obtain, and many drug users commit crimes such as burglary and violent theft to get money to buy drugs. Some become prostitutes, having sex with strangers to get money. The drug habit has caused misery for millions of people, not only the drug users themselves, but people who have been robbed and beaten up and even killed for money. The police spend a great deal of their time trying to catch the people who manufacture and supply the drugs and the drug addicts themselves, many of whom become criminals to feed their habit.

Fig. 11.46 A drug addict preparing to inject drugs into a vein.

Treatment and prevention: Drug users can get treatment in hospitals or specialized drug units. They have to be helped to get over their withdrawal symptoms. As well as medical treatment, they need support and counselling from qualified medical staff. Once they leave the hospital or drug unit, they need more support from family and friends to prevent them from going back to their drug habit.

The police try to stop drugs getting into the country from elsewhere, and arrest drug manufacturers and suppliers. But the problem in many countries is a very big one. The only real way to stop drug abuse is *never to start taking drugs in the first place*! Once you know the misery that drugs can cause, the message is clear:

ALWAYS SAY NO TO DRUGS.

Alcohol abuse

In many countries, people consume alcoholic drinks, usually without it affecting their health. Alcohol usually acts as a depressant, making people feel relaxed and less anxious. In larger quantities it makes them feel drowsy. It can also affect the memory and people's judgement, so that they do things that they would not normally do. For example, they may drive recklessly and cause an accident.

Alcohol affects the body by widening the arteries, making people very warm. It also makes people urinate more often, making them dehydrated and thirsty. The dehydration contributes to a 'hangover' after heavy drinking, where the person feels tired and low spirited, often with a headache and nausea (feeling sick).

It is difficult to know exactly when drinking leads to addiction to alcohol (alcoholism). But there are certain warning signs:

- The person drinks alcohol regularly every day.
- The person can go without alcohol for only about 10 hours before needing a drink.
- When the person wakes up, they feel sick and shaky, noises seem very loud, they have itchy skin and often there is ringing in the ears.

The period of time it takes for someone to become an alcoholic varies. It can be after 10 or 15 years of heavy drinking, or it can be just two years. Many doctors believe that the body chemistry of certain people makes it more likely that they will become an alcoholic. Others can resist it, even if they drink heavily.

The effects of alcohol on the body: The effects include cirrhosis of the liver (Fig. 11.47). The liver cells are damaged and replaced by scar tissue. The pancreas, brain and heart muscle are also affected. Some alcoholics find it difficult to relate to people around them and feel they need a drink to help them to cope with life. If they cannot have alcohol, as with other drugs, they get withdrawal symptoms. They have muscle tremors (their hands shake uncontrollably, for example), they feel very anxious and in some cases have hallucinations.

In very severe cases, people ruin their lives and some drop out of society and live on the streets.

Treatment: There are a number of treatments. One is called aversion therapy in which the person is given the drug Antabuse. This makes them feel very sick and nauseous every time they have an alcoholic drink. The idea is that the person comes to associate unpleasant symptoms with drinking alcohol. At first, the important thing is that the person must admit to being an alcoholic. Many people try to cover up their habit. They drink in secret and hide the alcohol away, although, in many cases, their

11.7 Systems in animals

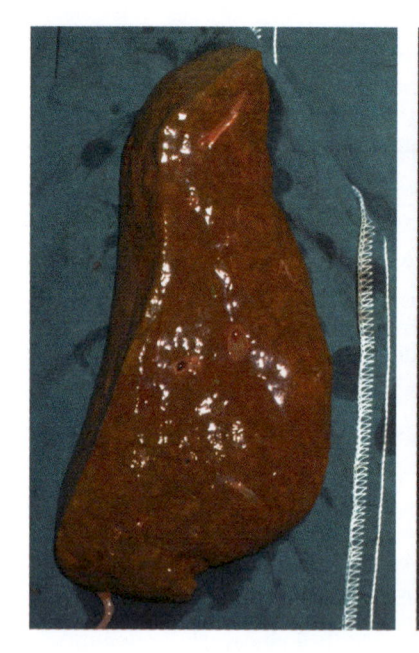

Fig. 11.47 Drinking too much alcohol affects the liver. Part of a healthy liver is shown on the left. The liver on the right has been damaged by cirrhosis.

behaviour may give people around them clues that something is wrong. Many doctors believe that if there are underlying problems in a person's life that can be resolved, this will help them to recover from the addiction. The fear is that the craving for alcohol will return when there are crises later on in that person's life. Some people join groups in which everyone is a recovering alcoholic so that they can support and help one another. The main cure is that the person must want to give up the habit, and resolve not to drink alcohol again.

When a person stops drinking, provided they have not got advanced cirrhosis of the liver, the liver will recover and they will feel healthier.

⊙ Activity The dangers of drugs and alcohol

1. Have a class discussion about the dangers of heavy drinking and taking drugs.
2. Find out if there are problems with people drinking too much alcohol or taking drugs in your community. Your teacher will help you and you may be able to get information from your local clinic.
3. Design posters to warn young people about the dangers of heavy drinking and taking drugs and pin them up in a prominent place.

Tobacco-related diseases

Doctors all over the world agree that cigarette smoking damages people's health and often results in death. The addictive drug is nicotine and the tobacco smoke also contains tar. Smoking damages the respiratory system and the heart and blood vessels.

The effects of drug abuse   11.7

Effects on the lungs: As you know, the cells lining the airways have microscopic hair-like projections called cilia that beat and waft dust particles out of the air passages (Topic 11.5). The hairs are damaged by the dark-coloured tar in the smoke (Fig. 11.48). Some of the cells die and are replaced by different flatter cells that can develop into **tumours**, causing lung cancer. Smoking can also cause cancer of the mouth, throat and gullet.

The cells lining the airways also produce mucus and when the tiny hairs stop beating, the mucus sticks in the chest and causes the person to cough ('smoker's cough'). The cells also become diseased more easily and the airways become inflamed, leading to chronic bronchitis. The person becomes breathless and as the disease progresses may even have to wear an oxygen mask. If the air sacs themselves break down, the person also becomes breathless and suffers from emphysema.

Effects on the heart: There is a greater risk of stroke and heart attack in people who smoke, mainly because nicotine raises the blood pressure and carbon monoxide reduces the ability of the blood to carry oxygen. This causes the heart to do more work and beat faster. The blood vessels in the legs are often damaged.

Pregnant mothers are advised not to smoke because it could damage the baby and is thought to cause miscarriages (the mother may lose her baby).

The best way of avoiding these diseases is *never to start smoking*. These days, smokers can be helped to stop in various ways. They can be given,

> **Did you know?**
>
> According to the World Health Organization, about 8% of the total number of deaths in the world are caused by smoking cigarettes.
>
> The risk of lung cancer is about 20 times greater in smokers than in non-smokers.

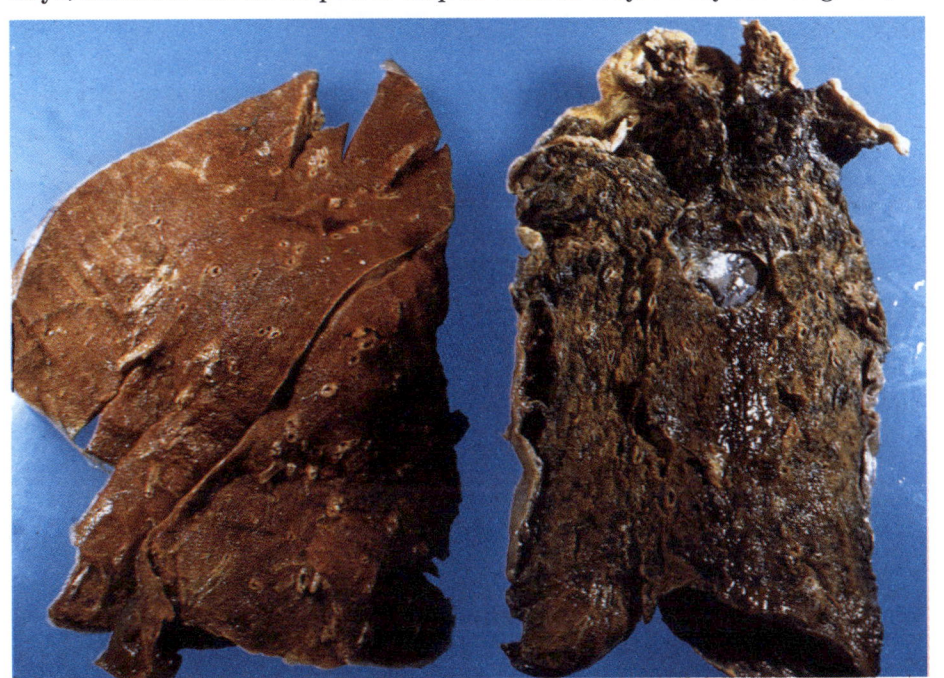

Fig. 11.48 Smoking affects the lungs. The lung on the left is healthy. The one on the right has been damaged by smoking.

for example, nicotine patches to stick on their arm (Fig. 11.49). This gives them a constant low dose of nicotine to help them with their withdrawal symptoms. These include feeling sick, shaking and feeling very irritable.

Lung cancer is not always caused by smoking. Some non-smokers can also get lung cancer. The exhaust from motor vehicles, dust, radioactive substances and smoke from industry can cause it. But statistics collected from around the world show that smoking is by far the main cause.

Fig. 11.49 Nicotine patches are used to help someone stop smoking.

Finding out

Campaigns against smoking

Many countries have launched campaigns to warn people of the dangers of smoking. Some governments have forced cigarette manufacturers to issue a health warning on the cigarette packets. Find out if your government or local health authority has a policy about cigarette smoking. Try to obtain information from your local health centre.

Activity Smoking damages your health

1. Discuss the disadvantages of smoking.
2. Do you think that people who smoke cigarettes smell nice? If not, why not?
3. Do you think that heavy smokers have nice white teeth? If not, why not?
4. Design a poster to discourage people from smoking cigarettes.

The effects of drug abuse 11.7

What you should know

- A drug is a medicine or other substance that affects the body in some way.
- Drugs can have powerful effects on the body.
- Drugs can be used to treat illnesses, but when taken for other reasons can have harmful effects.
- People can become dependent on recreational drugs.
- Drug abuse harms drug addicts and the society in which they live.
- Young people should always say 'No' to drugs.
- Smoking and alcohol abuse lead to serious health problems.

Questions

1. What are the names of the three classes of drugs?

2. Explain the meaning of these terms
   a. psychologically dependent
   b. physically dependent
   c. tolerant
   d. withdrawal symptoms
   e. 'habit'

3. Why is the statement 'All drugs are harmful' not true?

4. Research the effects that cigarette smoking has on people's general health – including skin tone and hair quality. Smoking is also linked to impotence (also called erectile dysfunction) in young men. Find out more.

Support and movement

12.1 Support and movement in humans

▶ Objectives

After studying this topic, you should be able to:

- explain why movement is necessary in animals
- describe the functions of the skeleton
- describe the arrangement of bones in the skeleton
- explain that movement takes place at the joints
- explain that movements are coordinated
- copy and practise some of the movements described
- describe some common injuries and diseases of the skeleton and muscles.

One of the characteristics of animals is that they move from one place to another. They move to search for food, to escape being eaten by predators and to search for a mate in order to reproduce. Because they move, they are described as motile organisms. There are exceptions of course. For example, corals, mussels, sea anemones and barnacles that live in the sea are attached to rocks. They do not move around. They feed on tiny organisms that float about in the water. Living organisms that don't move about but are fixed in one place are said to be sessile.

Humans and many other animals are supported by a skeleton inside their bodies. This is an **endoskeleton**. These animals are chiefly the **vertebrates**, so-called because they have a **vertebral column** (a backbone). Some of the **invertebrates** (animals without backbones), which you learned about in Book 1, Topics 2.3 and 2.4, have a skeleton on the outside of their bodies. This is an **exoskeleton**. Some invertebrates don't have a skeleton at all and are soft-bodied. You will learn more about them in Topic 12.2.

The human skeleton

The human skeleton is made up of lots of bones. It supports our weight against the force of gravity so that our body is raised above the surface of the ground. It also gives us our body shape. What do you think would happen if your skeleton suddenly vanished? The skeleton also enables us to move because it has joints. The muscles that bring about movement are attached to the skeleton. Your skeleton also protects the delicate organs of the body, such as the brain, some of the sense organs, the spinal cord, the heart and the lungs.

Support and movement in humans 12.1

→ Activity Looking at the human skeleton

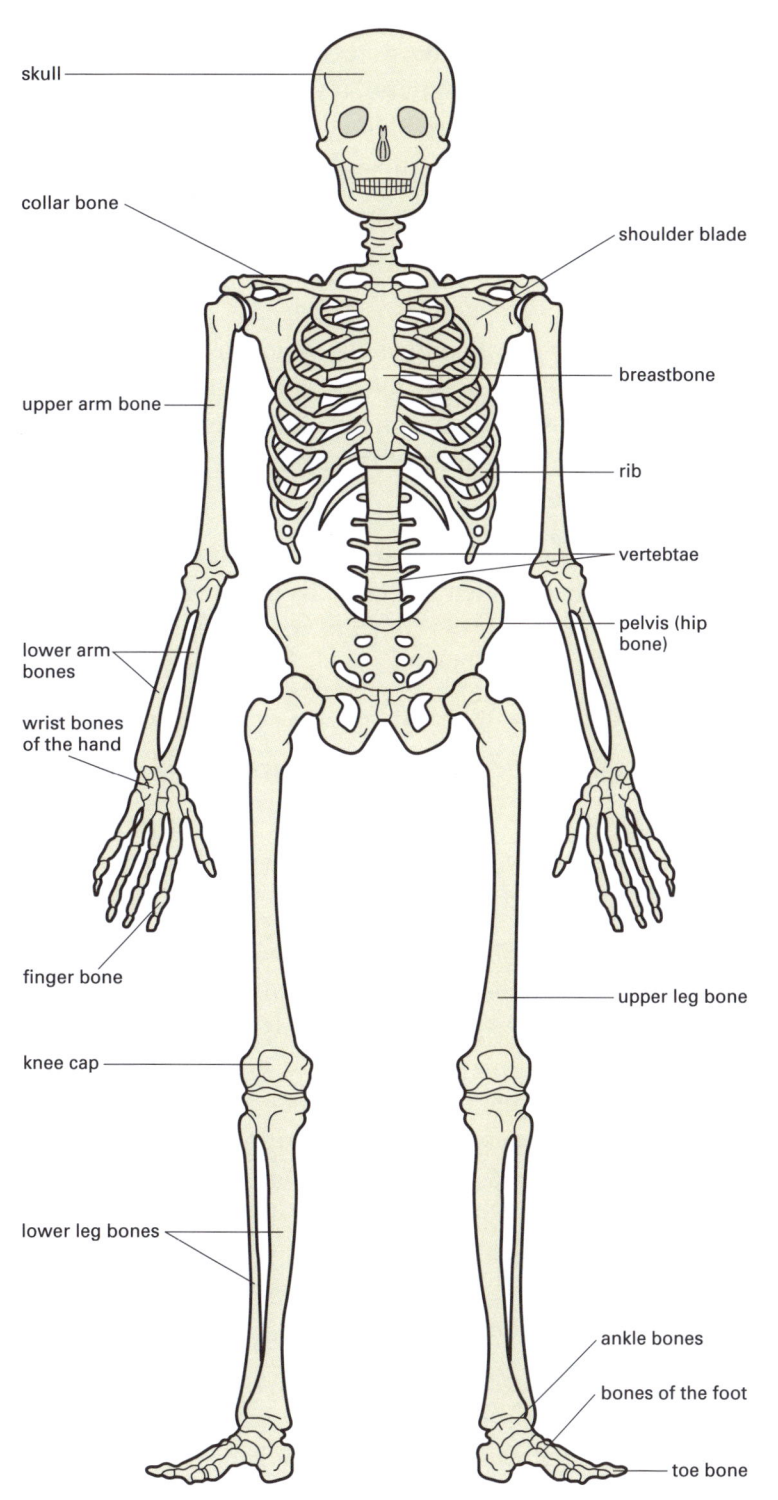

Fig. 12.1 The human skeleton.

Labels on figure:
- skull
- collar bone
- shoulder blade
- upper arm bone
- breastbone
- rib
- vertebtae
- pelvis (hip bone)
- lower arm bones
- wrist bones of the hand
- finger bone
- knee cap
- upper leg bone
- lower leg bones
- ankle bones
- bones of the foot
- toe bone

You will need
- a model of a human or other skeleton provided by your teacher

Method
Look carefully at Figure 12.1. Identify the bones on your model skeleton.

1. Look first for the skull and the upper and lower jaws.
2. Then look for the backbone (vertebral column). The individual bones of the vertebral column are the vertebrae.
3. Then look for the collar bone and shoulder blade.
4. You will see that the arms are suspended from the shoulder blade on each side.
5. Now look at the breastbone and ribs. They form the rib cage.
6. Next look for the pelvis or hip bone.
7. Look at each arm. Look for the upper arm bone, the elbow joint, the two lower arm bones, the wrist and the hands. The hands end in a thumb and four fingers. Notice that the upper arm bone fits into a socket in the shoulder blade.
8. Finally, look at each leg. Start by looking at the upper leg bone, the knee joint, the two lower leg bones, the ankle and the feet. Each foot ends in a big toe and four other toes. Notice that the upper leg bone fits into a socket in the hip bone.
9. Continue to observe the skeleton until you are sure that you are familiar with the parts. Make a sketch or label a diagram of a skeleton.

12.1 Support and movement

What is needed for movement to take place?

We need bones, muscles, **ligaments** and **tendons**.

Bone: Bone is a living tissue and is very hard. It contains mineral salts. The most important salt is calcium phosphate. In the centre of the bones of the limbs is the bone marrow, where red blood cells and some white blood cells are produced.

Muscles: Muscles are made up of muscle fibres, which can get shorter (contract) and relax again to reach their original size. Muscles *never* stretch and they cannot push.

Ligaments and tendons: Bones are held together by tough but elastic ligaments. They need to be elastic to allow the movement to take place. Tendons attach muscles to bones. They are made of tougher tissue than ligaments because they need to transmit the pull from the muscle to the bone without themselves stretching.

We need two other things: We need energy from food in our muscle cells so that they contract and relax. We also need signals (messages) from the brain to the muscles to stimulate them to contract and relax.

Where does movement take place?

Movement takes place at the **joints**. A joint is a place where two or more bones meet.

Movement at the elbow: the elbow joint is an example of a hinge joint. Straighten your arm and then bend it towards you. Feel your elbow joint.

Figure 12.2 shows you what a hinge joint is like inside. Another hard substance called cartilage covers the ends of the bones. Cartilage is not as hard as bone and is more elastic. It acts as a shock absorber by stopping the bones jarring together when there is movement. There is also a fluid inside the joint. This reduces friction (see Book 3, Topic 17.3) and allows the bones to slide over one another easily during movement.

Figure 12.3 shows you how movement takes place. Notice there are two muscles involved. When the arm bends, the biceps muscle contracts, getting shorter and fatter, and pulls the lower arm bones up. The triceps is longer and thinner because it has

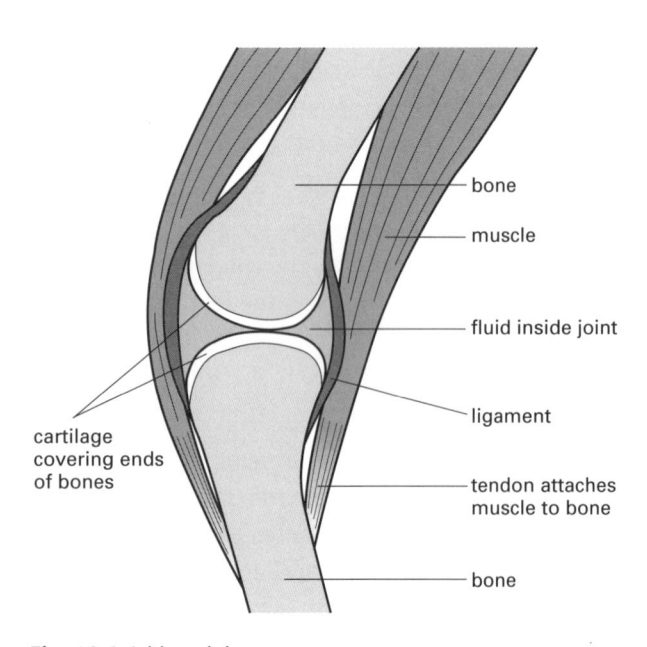

Fig. 12.2 A hinge joint.

Support and movement in humans 12.1

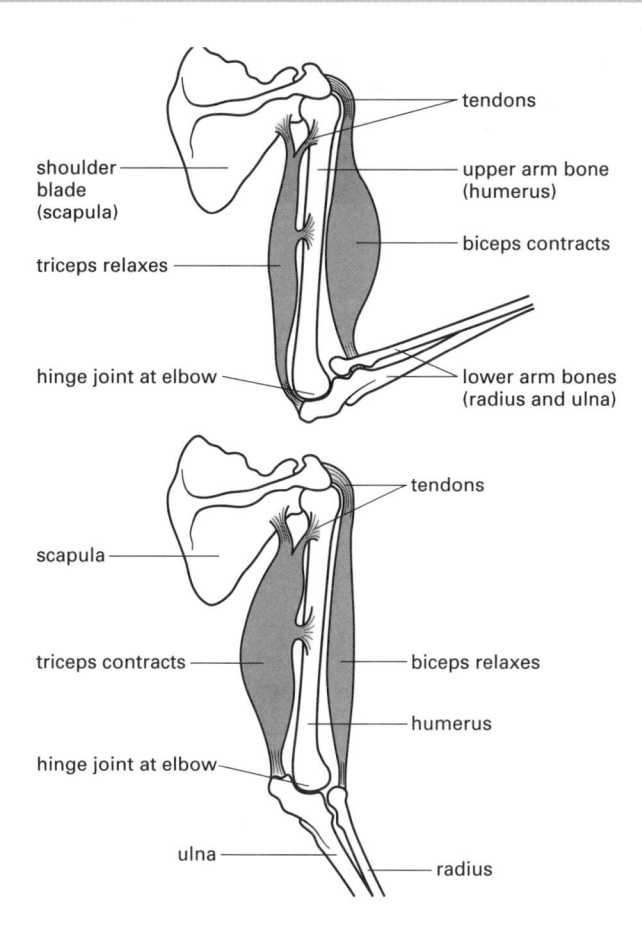

Fig. 12.3 Movement at the elbow joint. When the arm bends (flexes) (top) the biceps contracts and the triceps relaxes. When the arm straightens (extends) (bottom) the biceps relaxes and the triceps contracts.

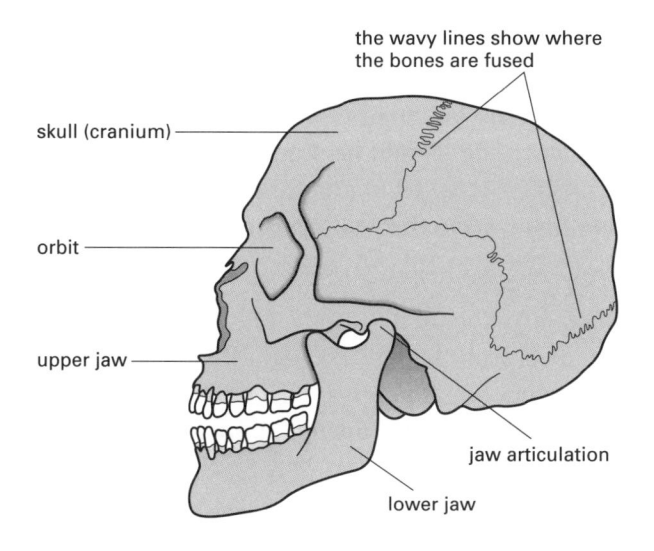

Fig. 12.4 The bones of the skull are fused so that there is no movement between them.

relaxed. When the arm straightens, the triceps contracts and pulls the arm bones down to straighten the arm. This time the biceps relaxes and looks longer and thinner. It goes back to its original shape. The two muscles act in opposite ways: when one muscle contracts, the other relaxes. This is how animals bring about movement.

➔ Activity Other joints in the body

You will need
- a model of a human or other skeleton provided by your teacher

Method

1. Look at the skull of the skeleton. Find where the bones are joined (Fig. 12.4).
2. Nod your head as if you are agreeing with someone. This is a joint between your skull and the first vertebra. Look at it on the skeleton.
3. Now move your head from side to side as if you are saying no. This movement is at the joint between the first and second vertebrae. It allows your head to pivot (turn from side to side). Look at it on the skeleton.
4. Do the rest of these movements outside where you have plenty of room. First, stand and bend your arms at the elbows. Then straighten them. Can you remember the name of the type of joint at the elbow?
5. Now stand up away from other people, giving yourself plenty of space. Move one of your arms at the shoulder in any way you can. Can you move it in front of you, to the back, out from the sides of your body and around in a circle? This is because the shoulder joint is an example of a ball-and-socket joint. It can allow

127

12.1 Support and movement

movement in more than one direction. Your hip joint is another example of this type of joint.

6 Try some more body movements (bending your knees and your fingers and toes) and try to identify the type of joint where the movement takes place.

7 The little bones in your wrists and ankles slide over one another, making them very flexible. These are gliding joints.

8 When you return indoors, look again at the skeleton and identify the joints you used to move. Did you notice that your backbone allowed you to bend and stretch? The joints between your vertebrae move only very slightly. But if you add up the amount of movement possible along the whole of your spine, you can see that it is very flexible.

Record
List all the movements you can do with your legs, then your arms and then your arms and legs together.

Discuss
Look at the picture of the skull again (Fig. 12.4). What type of joint is there between the upper and lower jaws? What movement does it allow?

Coordination

Your body movements are very precise. They are coordinated by your brain. For example, if you are waiting to catch a ball, your eyes are fixed on it. As soon as the ball leaves the thrower's hand, a message is sent from your eyes to your brain, which sends a message to the muscles in your arm. Your arm moves to where the brain thinks the ball might be when your hand is raised. When you practise catching, your brain gets better at predicting where the ball might be and where the best position for your hand should be. Look at the picture of the javelin thrower (Fig. 12.5) and think about the coordination involved to throw it accurately and as far as possible.

Human beings are able to do wonderfully precise things with their bodies, from ballet dancing, athletics and gymnastics, to very small precise movements such as sewing or piano playing or drawing. Many of the small

Fig. 12.5 The athlete is pushing against the ground with the feet. The force is transmitted through the legs, hips and vertebral column to the shoulder and then to the arm holding the javelin. The arm then moves forward at the shoulder joint and straightens at the elbow joint.

Support and movement in humans   12.1

precise movements are possible because humans have an opposable thumb that enables them to grip things, as well as the flexible hinge joints in their fingers and the gliding joints in their wrists. Standing on two legs and having your hands free has its advantages! Humans also have a highly developed brain to coordinate all these movements and the ability to learn and practise them.

What happens when my muscles get tired?

When we exercise, our muscles need oxygen for respiration to take place in the cells in order to produce energy from the glucose. But our blood circulation isn't fast enough to get all the oxygen we need to our muscles. So something else also happens in the cells. Some of the glucose produces lactic acid instead of carbon dioxide and water. In this chemical reaction, less energy is produced at one go, but it is extra energy and can be produced without oxygen. This is an example of anaerobic respiration in animals (respiration without oxygen). Lactic acid is poisonous and so we need to get rid of it when we stop exercising. So we breathe in and out very quickly and deeply. The oxygen can then get rid of the lactic acid. This is called the oxygen debt. When you breathe deeply and quickly for a while after stopping exercise you are 'paying off' this oxygen debt. Have you noticed that sprinters after running the 100 metres do a lot of puffing and panting (Fig. 12.6)? Now you know why!

Fig. 12.6 A sprinter breathes quickly and deeply at the end of a race to pay off the oxygen debt.

What happens when we run a long race, such as the 5000 metres or a marathon, for example? Have you noticed that when you run a long distance you begin to feel so tired that you think you can't go on any longer? (Some athletes refer to this as 'the wall'.) Then suddenly, you begin to feel better again. Well, lactic acid is produced and this is what makes you feel tired. Then your body adjusts and starts to break down the lactic acid as you go along.

➔ Activity Movements I use in my favourite sport

Method
Write about your favourite sport and describe some of the movements you do. Use some of these words to help you with your description: energy, muscles, bones, joints, hinge joint, ball-and-socket joint, oxygen, oxygen debt.

12.1 Support and movement

Discuss

1. Why is exercise good for you?
2. Some famous athletes have been accused of taking drugs to help them to perform better. They have been accused of cheating. Do you think taking drugs for these reasons is dangerous?
3. How can you improve your athletic performance safely? How does this work?

Sprains, fractures and dislocation

Sprains: Sometimes we fall awkwardly or stumble and sprain a wrist or ankle. This means that we have either torn a ligament or a tendon. It is very painful and we have to wait for the tissue to heal.

Fractures: When we have a fracture, we have broken the bone in some way. The bone may break without affecting the surrounding tissue. This is a simple fracture. A compound fracture is when the bone pokes through the skin after an accident and then there is a risk of germs getting into the body. Sometimes the bone breaks in more than one place, and sometimes the break is not right across the bone. The person's limb is straightened and enclosed in plaster to keep the ends of the bone together so that the bone can heal (Fig. 12.7). Bone cells then make new bone across the area of the fracture (Fig. 12.8). Broken bones take quite a long time to heal, much longer than a cut on your finger.

Dislocation: This happens when a bone comes out of its socket, for example, dislocation of the shoulder is common in sports injuries. A local

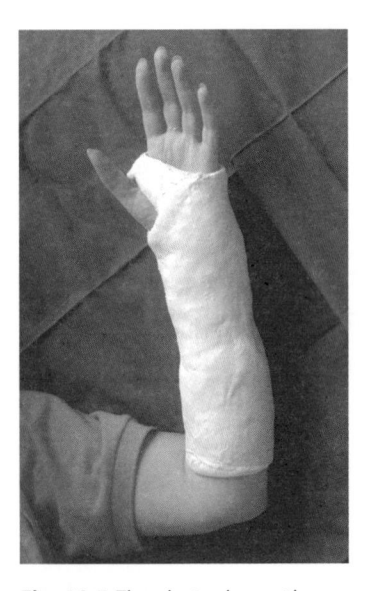

Fig. 12.7 The plaster keeps the limb straight and the ends of the broken bone together so that the fracture can heal.

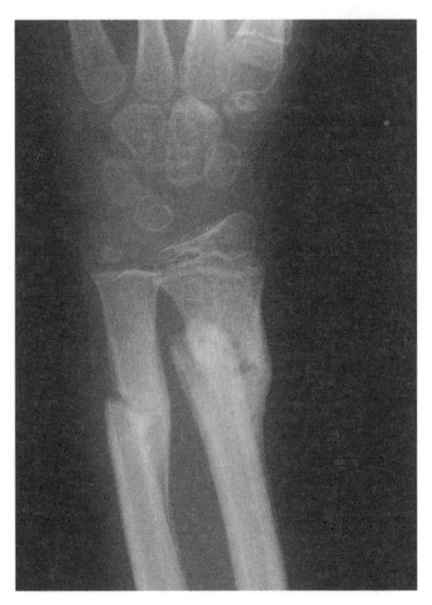

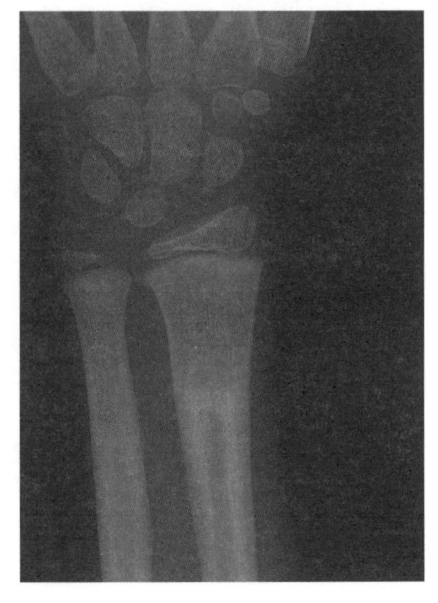

Fig. 12.8 The X-ray on the left shows that the bone in the arm is fractured. The X-ray on the right was taken months later and shows that the bones have now healed. New bone has formed between the broken ends of the bone.

or general anaesthetic relieves the pain while the bones are moved back into their normal position. In some people, the tendency of the hip to dislocate is an inherited condition.

Activity Common sports injuries

Ask your PE teachers for information about common sports injuries at school. You may have had some of these injuries yourself while playing sport. You may also know of some famous sports stars who have been injured. Choose one type of injury to write about in more detail. Find out: what caused the injury, which specific part(s) of the body was (were) injured, what first aid was given and details of any further treatment.

> **Did you know?**
>
> People with severe arthritis in their knees or hips can have an operation to replace the joints with artificial ones. Plastic, stainless steel and rare metals, like titanium, are used to make the new ones.

Diseases

Many diseases affect the bones, muscles and joints. Here are some examples. Rheumatism causes pain in the muscles and joints. In arthritis, the joints become inflamed and the cartilage is worn away. Movement becomes restricted and is painful. Another disease is osteoporosis, where the bones lack calcium salts and become very thin and fractures occur very easily. There are treatments for these diseases, but some are more successful than others.

What you should know

- Movement is necessary in animals to enable them to hunt for food, escape from predators and find a mate.
- Vertebrates have an endoskeleton.
- The skeleton gives the body a definite shape, supports the weight of the body, protects delicate internal organs, allows muscle attachment for movement and provides a system of joints and levers for movement to take place.
- Bones contain high levels of calcium; red blood cells and some white blood cells are produced in the bone marrow.
- Movement takes place at the joints.
- There are different kinds of joints, including hinge joints and ball-and-socket joints.
- The cartilage and fluid inside a joint act as a shock absorber and a lubricant.
- Muscles act in pairs or larger groups to enable a joint to move. Movements are coordinated by the nervous system.
- After vigorous exercise, there is an oxygen debt to be repaid.
- Common injuries of the muscles and skeleton include sprains, fractures and dislocations; common diseases include arthritis, rheumatism and osteoporosis.

12.1 Support and movement

Questions

1. Why do we have a skeleton?

2. Fill in the blank spaces in the following statements:
   a. Bones are held together by tough but elastic _____.
   b. Tendons attach _____ to bones.
   c. The elbow joint is a type of _____ joint.
   d. _____ covers the ends of the bones and acts as a shock _____.
   e. When the arm bends, the biceps muscle _____ and the triceps muscle _____.

3. What has happened inside your muscles when you pant after running a fast race?

4. Choose the correct answers to the questions below from this list of words:
   brain, eyes, heart, lungs, nose, sex organs, spinal cord
   a. Which parts of the body are protected by the skull?
   b. Which part of the body is protected by the vertebral column?
   6. Which parts of the body are protected by the rib cage?

5. Research joint replacement. Which body joints can be repaired? What materials are used for the artificial joints? Why are they not rejected by the body? How long do they last? Why do natural joints last longer?

Support and movement

12.2 Support and movement in animals

▶ Objectives

After studying this topic, you should be able to:
- describe movement in other land vertebrates
- explain how birds are adapted for flying
- explain how fish are adapted for swimming
- describe the functions of an exoskeleton
- describe how arthropods move
- explain how certain soft-bodied animals are supported and move.

Movement in other land vertebrates

Vertebrates that live on land can move by walking, running, hopping, leaping, crawling, gliding and climbing (Fig. 12.9). Their feet push against the ground to move the body forward. But have you noticed that animals with four legs do not move them all at once? The legs move at different times, but the whole movement is coordinated. When a dog walks along, its legs seem to be slightly out of phase, but it is perfectly balanced. If the dog sees a cat, it immediately speeds up to chase it, but again, is perfectly coordinated.

Some land vertebrates don't have any legs. These are the snakes (Fig. 12.10) and some lizards, such as slow worms. As these animals have adapted and changed over millions of years, their limbs have become less important and so do not develop.

Fig. 12.9 Two familiar examples of vertebrates with four legs.

Fig. 12.10 The snake glides along in search of its food.

▶ Activity Movement with four legs

Method
You can do this activity at school or at home. Look at any vertebrates with four legs and observe how they move. Here is a list of animals you could observe: dog, cat, frog, toad, lizard, horse, goat, cow, sheep, pig.

Record
Copy Table 12.1 and record your results. Write down the name of each animal you have observed and describe their movements. For example, some animals may be able to walk, run and climb.

12.2 Support and movement

Table 12.1 Recording movement in vertebrates with four legs.

Name of animal	Type(s) of movement
Cat	Walking, running, climbing

Discuss

Discuss your observations as a class and fill in any extra information on your table. Use photographs or slow-motion film to help your understanding.

Flight in birds

The only animals that can fly are birds, insects and bats. The two back limbs of birds are legs, which enable them to walk, run, hop and perch. The two front limbs are the wings that enable them to fly. The bodies of birds are also adapted to help them to fly. The overall shape of a bird is smooth and streamlined. This makes it easier for the bird to push through the air when it flies. Their bones have cavities filled with air to make them lighter and there are also special air sacs inside their body to assist breathing.

The wings are covered with feathers. The small soft down feathers help to keep them warm. You notice these when you see little chicks hatching from an egg (Fig. 12.11). Adult birds have down feathers to keep them warm, but they are covered by the large flight feathers (Fig. 12.12). These feathers are arranged so that they overlap.

Fig. 12.11 This one-day-old chick is covered with downy feathers.

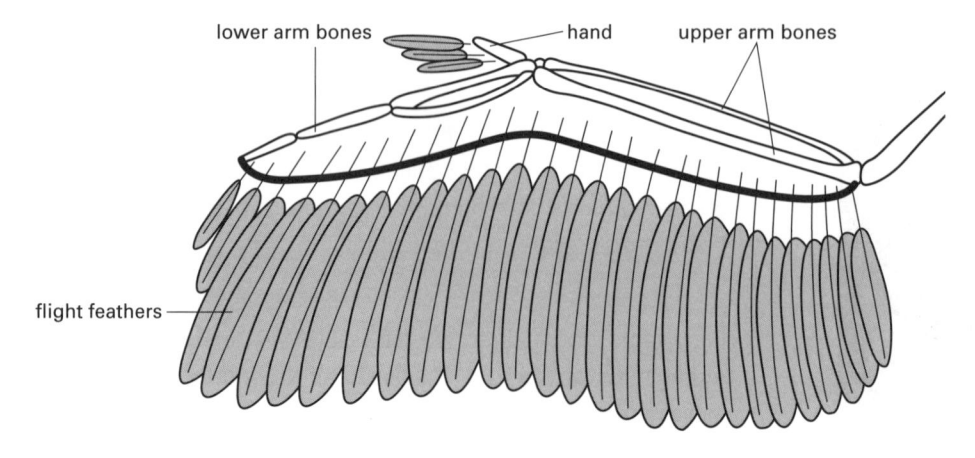

Fig. 12.12 A bird's wing showing the flight feathers.

When birds fly, they flap their wings up and down (Fig. 12.13). First, the wings beat down vertically against the air, causing the bird to move upwards. The wings then move forwards with the front edge tilted slightly upwards. When the wings are

Fig. 12.13 An albatross in flight.

Fig. 12.14 The ostrich is a flightless bird.

raised again, they bend and move upwards and backwards. This pushes the bird forwards. So, when the wings move down, this makes the bird move up, and when the wings move up, the body moves forwards.

Birds can use various tilting movements of their wings to change direction when flying. They also use their tail as a rudder (like a ship's rudder) to steer them along. Birds can also glide in the air, making use of the air currents. Vultures and albatrosses can glide for hours on end.

Not all birds can fly. These are described as the flightless birds, for example, the ostrich (Fig. 12.14).

Activity Observing birds

Method

1 Look around your home and school and find out which are the most common birds in your area. You can ask your teacher and your family and friends. You can also use books to help you to identify them. Look especially at the way they fly. For example, do they glide or do they flap their wings as they fly? Because you live in a tropical climate, you should be able to see some beautiful tropical birds. Collect any feathers you see on the ground.

2 Choose your favourite bird and make a careful drawing. Record the ways that it moves on the ground and in the air.

Swimming

Some mammals such as whales, dolphins and sea lions can swim. All fish can swim. They are expert swimmers (Fig. 12.15). Fish, like other vertebrates, have an endoskeleton. Most fish have a bony skeleton, for example, kingfish and marlin, but others like sharks and rays have skeletons made of cartilage. Fish also have fins to help them swim. Their

Did you know?

When penguins dive into water to catch fish, they continue to use their flight movements in the water! Ducks and other waterfowl can also do this.

Some falcons can dive down in the air towards their prey at speeds reaching almost 300 km per hour.

12.2 Support and movement

bodies have a streamlined shape to help them move through the water more easily.

Fish have two long sets or blocks of muscles on either side of their backbone. When the muscles on one side contract, the muscles on the other side relax. Then the opposite happens. The result is that the fish moves from side to side. The tail fin pushes the fish forwards in the water and the other fins can be moved at an angle to help the fish change direction (Fig. 12.16). The bony fish also have a swim bladder inside their bodies. It is filled with air to help them to float.

Fig. 12.15 Fish are expert swimmers.

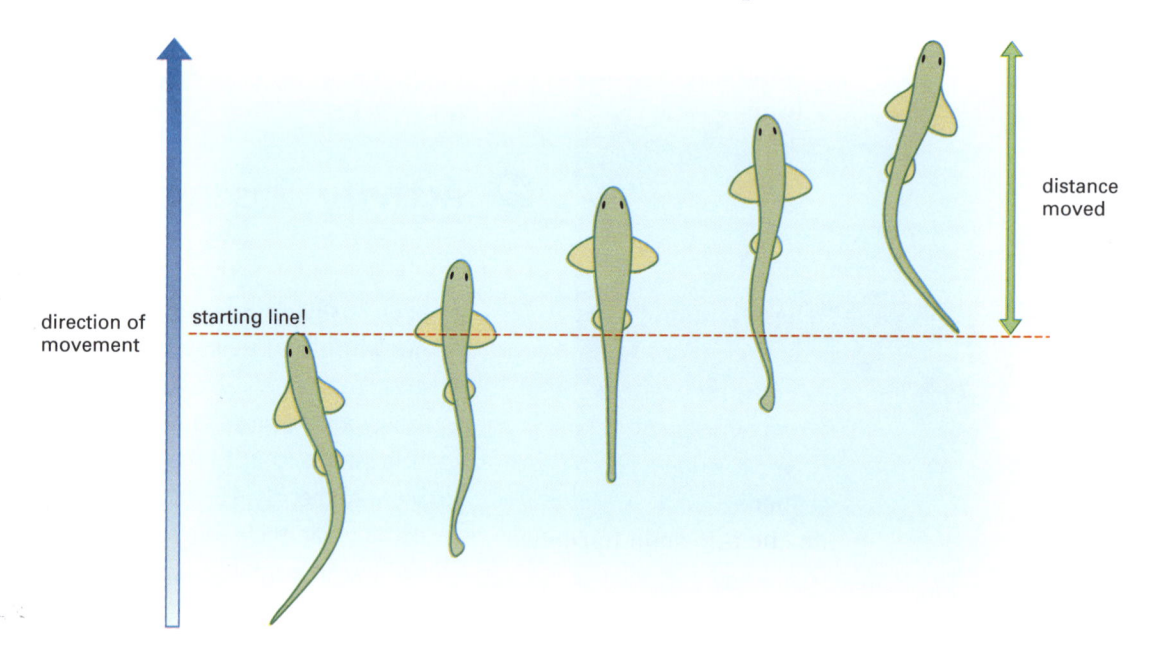

Fig. 12.16 The body of a fish moves from side to side as it pushes forwards through the water.

Activity Observing fish

Perhaps you have an aquarium at home or at school or perhaps there is an aquarium at your nearest seaside. If not, your teacher will show you some fish swimming in a tank. When you visit the seaside, you could also look for tiny fish in rock pools. Look carefully at their swimming movements.

Next time someone in your family at home prepares a fish for cooking, look at it carefully. The flesh running along the backbone on each side of the body consists of the muscles the fish used for swimming. Look also for small muscles at the base of the fins. The fins are used for balance and for turning.

Support and movement in animals 12.2

Animals with an exoskeleton

In Book 1, Topic 2.3, you learned that some invertebrates have a hard 'skin' or outer covering. These animals are the **arthropods**. Arthropods include the insects, spiders, crabs, prawns, centipedes, etc. These animals all have jointed legs. The 'skin' is a kind of skeleton. Because it is on the outside, it is called an exoskeleton. It supports and protects the body. The muscles that move the parts are attached to the inside of the exoskeleton.

The leg of an arthropod consists of a series of hollow tubes linked together, usually by hinge joints. Muscles inside the leg act in pairs to bend and straighten each joint. Although these animals have several pairs of legs, their leg movements are coordinated by the animal's nervous system, so that they work together effectively.

Crayfish (Fig. 12.17) show how legs can work well underwater. These arthropods live in freshwater streams and rivers. They have five pairs of walking legs, the front pair of which are equipped with pincer-like claws. Crayfish generally shuffle along the riverbed. However, they also have an escape mechanism, in which the abdomen and tail flap rapidly, causing the animal to shoot backwards through the water.

If these animals have a skeleton on the outside, how do they grow? Well, from time to time, the exoskeleton splits to expose the soft parts of the animal underneath, rather like the way we pull our arms out of the sleeves of a jacket. This is called moulting and happens several times until the animal grows to its full size. The animal is unprotected when this happens, but a new exoskeleton has already started to develop under the old one and soon hardens.

Did you know?

The arthropods (including the insects) account for four-fifths of all the animals on our planet. Scientists believe that their exoskeleton stops them from being even more successful. It stops them growing to a very large size. If they did grow larger, the exoskeleton would be like a heavy suit of armour and would make them very slow moving. They could then be easily attacked by predators. There are, however, a few really big ones. The Japanese spider crab has a leg span that measures 3.5 metres across!

Fig. 12.17 A crayfish.

12.2 Support and movement

Fig. 12.18 Some examples of arthropods; a woodlouse (top), a shrimp (middle) and a millipede (bottom).

Fig. 12.19 An earthworm.

➡ Activity Looking at arthropods

Treat the living animals with care and put them back where they were found after you have made your observations. Remember, that we must have respect for all living organisms and avoid hurting or damaging them by careless behaviour. Don't forget to wash your hands after the activity!

You will need
- some living examples of arthropods (Fig. 12.18), such as a millipede, a woodlouse or a shrimp, provided by your teacher
- a hand lens
- some glass dishes

Method
1. Leave the animals in their containers and look carefully at the way they walk. Use your hand lens to examine their jointed legs. Look up at them from below. Try to observe the legs straightening and flexing.
2. Find out where these animals live. Where did your teacher get them from?
3. Look up some pictures of arthropods in books and encyclopedias. Choose one example and make a careful drawing.

Animals with no legs

Some animals do not have a hard exoskeleton or legs. An example is the earthworm (Fig. 12.19). It is a soft-bodied animal that lives in the soil. Beneath its skin are two sets of muscles. One set are arranged in a circle (circular muscles) and the other set run along the length of the body (longitudinal muscles). When the earthworm burrows, its front end becomes long and thin. The circular muscles contract and squeeze the body into this shape. Then the longitudinal muscles contract and the body becomes short and fat again. These movements pass along the body (Fig. 12.20), moving the earthworm forwards.

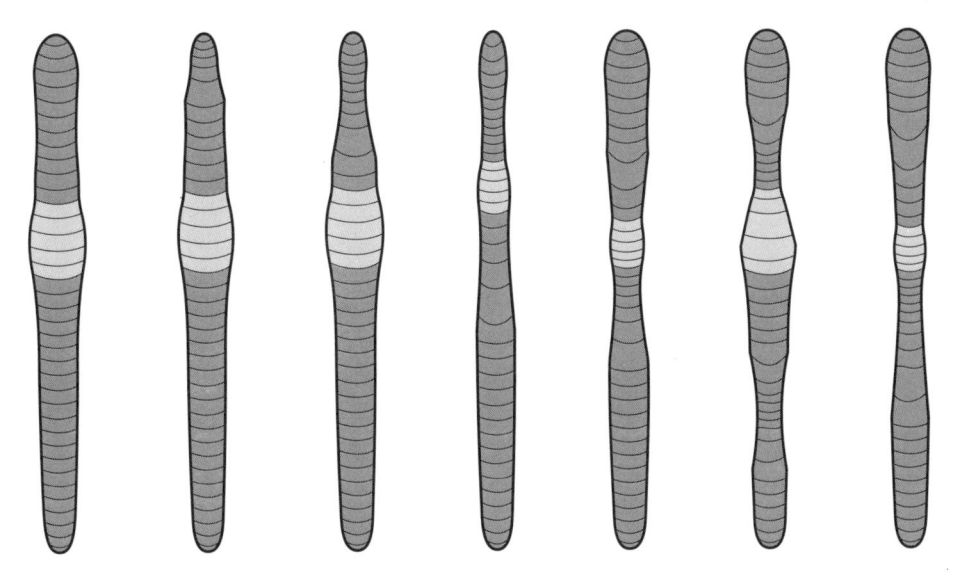

Fig. 12.20 Movement in an earthworm.

Inside the body of the earthworm is a cavity filled with fluid. The muscles press against the fluid and the fluid pushes against the muscles. This gives the body support and shape. It is a type of fluid skeleton. The cavity of fluid also protects the gut of the earthworm, which runs through the centre of the body from mouth to anus.

Activity Movement in earthworms

Hygiene: Make sure you wash your hands thoroughly after handling the worm.

You will need
- a living earthworm, which your teacher will provide
- a container
- a hand lens
- a piece of white paper

Method
1 Remove an earthworm from the container and very gently place it on a sheet of white paper.

2 Observe the way it moves. The muscles contracting and then relaxing will seem to pass along the body in waves.

3 Now keep very quiet and lift the piece of paper up near your ears. You should be able to hear tiny scratching sounds as the earthworm moves. The earthworm has tiny bristles underneath its body. It moves along on these bristles and uses them in the same way that we use crutches! It pokes them into the soil and then swings forward. Use your hand lens to look at the body closely. Find the bristles.

4 When you have finished, your teacher will return the earthworms to the soil.

12.2 Support and movement

What you should know

- Vertebrates that live on land move by walking, running, hopping, leaping, crawling, gliding and climbing.
- Many land vertebrates have four legs.
- Birds have wings to enable them to fly.
- The bodies of birds are adapted for flight by being streamlined, having air sacs and having air cavities in the bones.
- Fish are adapted for swimming by being streamlined, having two sets of strong muscles each side of the backbone, fins and muscular tails.
- Bony fish have a swim bladder filled with air to help them to float.
- Some animals have an exoskeleton that supports and protects the body and provides a system of joints for movement.
- Arthropods are animals with jointed legs.
- Some soft-bodied animals such as earthworms have a cavity of fluid that acts rather like a skeleton. The muscles press against it and it protects the gut.

Questions

1. What is the difference between an exoskeleton and an endoskeleton?

2. Fill in the blank spaces in these sentences.

   a. When the wings of a bird move downwards, this makes the bird move _____.

   b. When the wings move up, the body moves _____.

3. How are the bodies of fish adapted for swimming?

4. Why is the cavity filled with fluid inside the body of an earthworm thought to be a type of skeleton?

5. Find out how some other legless animals move, for example snails, slugs and jellyfish.

Electricity and magnetism

13.1 Using electricity

> **Objectives**
>
> After studying this topic you should be able to:
> - outline how a battery works
> - describe how mains electricity is produced and distributed
> - say how much electricity an appliance will use
> - know how amounts of electricity are measured and how to read an electric meter.

Fig. 13.1 At work with computers.

Fig. 13.2 Each of these batteries has two terminals. Can you spot the positive and negative terminals?

Electricity is very useful. At the flick of a switch, we can have lights shining brightly in the darkness. Refrigerators keep food and medicines cool so that they remain usable for longer. Turn on the radio or television and you receive pictures and sounds from around the world. Electricity is bringing **energy** to you. Electricity is a secondary energy source. You can't mine electricity, or pick it from trees. It has to be made – either by burning a fossil fuel or by using a renewable energy source to generate it (see Book 1, Unit 4). Electricity is convenient – it flows along wires to where it is needed. It does not need pipes or ducts, unlike other energy sources.

Electricity can carry something else. Think of the telephone. A small electric current carries your friend's voice along the wires to your ear. Computers are becoming increasingly important in everyday life (Fig. 13.1). Inside the computer are highly complex electrical circuits. Tiny electrical currents flowing through these circuits allow masses of information to be processed at high speed.

Sources of electricity

Batteries can be a useful source of electricity (Fig. 13.2). We use them in portable appliances like radios and personal stereos. Every battery has two terminals, labelled positive (+) and negative (–). If you connect a battery the wrong way round, you may damage the equipment you are trying to use.

13.1 Electricity and magnetism

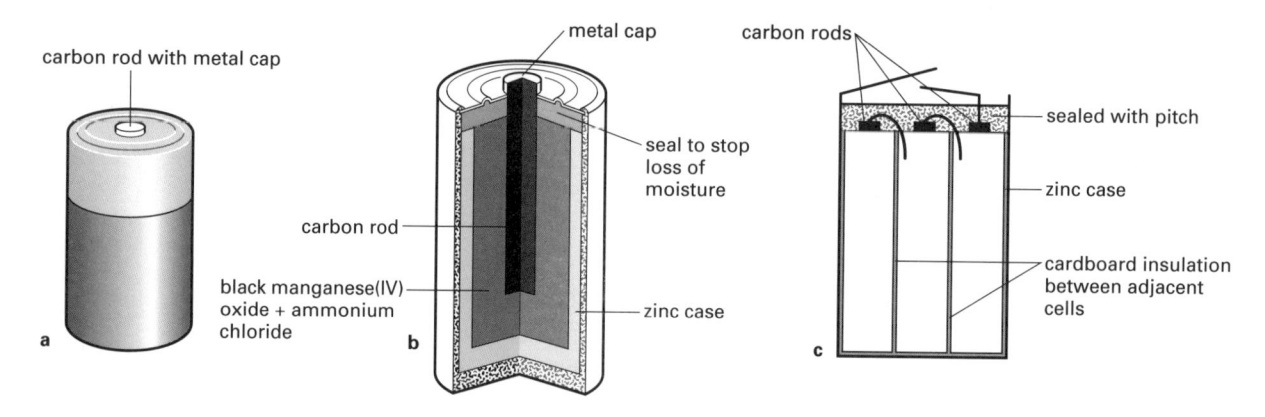

Fig. 13.3 (a) Outside and (b) inside a dry cell (a standard 1.5 V 'battery'). (c) Section through a battery of three cells.

A small 'battery', such as you would use in a radio, is in fact a single **cell**. This typically provides a voltage of 1.5 volts (or 1.5 V, using the symbol V for volts). Larger batteries, such as those used in powerful torches, are made up of two or more cells. For example, a 6 V **battery** is made up of four cells (Fig. 13.3).

How does a battery make a radio work? The chemicals inside a battery store energy. When you switch on the radio, a chemical reaction happens inside the battery and some of the chemical energy is released as electrical energy. It is carried around the circuits inside the radio by an electric current.

A car has a battery, which is needed to start the car. When the ignition key is turned, energy from the battery starts the engine turning.

➲ Activity Cells in a flashlight

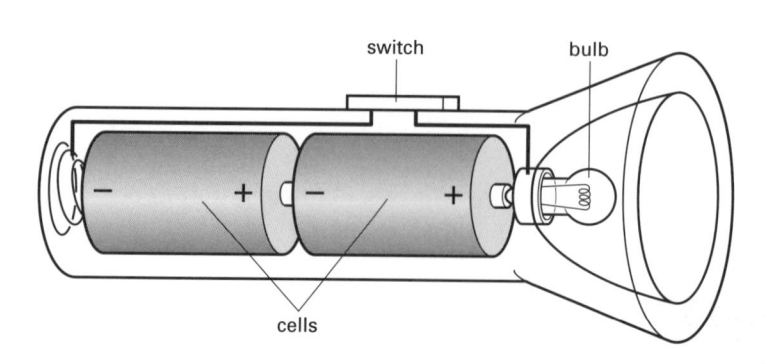

Fig. 13.4 Cells ('batteries') inside a flashlight.

You will need
- a flashlight
- dry cells ('batteries')

Discuss

1 Find out the correct way to put the cells in the flashlight (Fig. 13.4). Switch on – does it light up?

2 Try turning one or two cells round. Does the flashlight still light up? Try to explain your findings. Why is there a spring inside the flashlight?

3 Explain why a scientist would say that the flashlight works using 'cells' rather than 'batteries'.

Using electricity **13.1**

→ Activity Making a simple cell

You will need

- a beaker or glass jar
- two metal plates, one zinc and one copper
- dilute sulphuric acid
- an ammeter, connecting wires and clips

⚠ Danger!
Care needed when handling acid!

Eye protection must be worn

Method

1. Partly fill the beaker with acid.
2. Immerse the two metal plates in the acid. Make sure that they do not touch.
3. Connect the plates to the ammeter to see that electricity is being produced (Fig. 13.5).

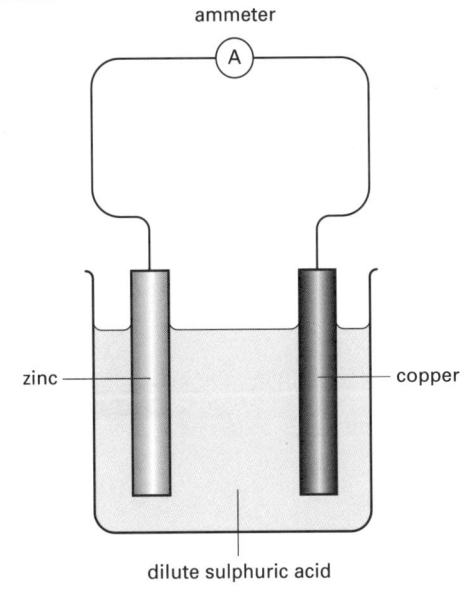

Fig. 13.5 A simple cell.

Discuss

You may notice small bubbles of gas forming on the copper plate. This is hydrogen, and it stops the cell from working well. Shake the plate gently to remove the bubbles.

It may surprise you to find that you can make electricity using a fruit such as an orange. Rinse the two metal plates and stick them into an orange. Is electricity produced? What is in the orange that makes this possible?

Mains electricity

Most of the electricity we use comes from power stations. It is usually cheaper to make large amounts of electricity in one place than to provide every house, school or other building with its own electricity generator.

The mains electricity supply to a house is usually at a voltage of 110 V or 220 V. In some Caribbean countries it is 240 V. This is a high enough voltage to work lights, heaters, televisions, washing machines and so on. But the power station produces electricity at a much higher voltage – perhaps 25 000 V (or put another way, 25 kilovolts, where the 'kilo' stands for 'thousand'; in short form this is written as 25 kV). This high-voltage electricity is transported around the country along thick wires or cables called power lines, carried on tall poles or pylons (Fig. 13.6). Before it reaches the homes where it will be used, the electricity passes through a local electricity substation. You may know of a substation near your home or school – it will have warning signs telling you to keep out.

Inside the substation are devices called transformers. These reduce the voltage of the electricity from 25 kV to 110 V (or the voltage used in your country) – a safer level.

Fig. 13.6 Tall pylons carry the cables through which electricity is distributed from a power station to supply local substations. At these substations, transformers reduce the voltage to the low voltages used in homes and offices.

Paying for electricity

The more electricity you use, the more you will have to pay. Some appliances use electricity much faster than others, so they cost a lot to run. You may be able to find out how quickly an appliance uses electricity by looking for the label that shows its **power rating**. This is usually marked in watts (W) or kilowatts (kW).

1 kilowatt = 1000 watts

or, written in short form:

1 kW = 1000 W

Table 13.1 gives the power ratings of some well-known household appliances. You can see that a microwave oven is much cheaper to run than an electric oven. Appliances that produce a lot of heat have high power ratings.

Table 13.1 Typical power ratings of some domestic appliances

Appliance	Power rating
Light bulb	40 W, 60 W, 100 W
Television set	100 W
Computer	100 W
Microwave oven	650 W
Heater	1 kW, 2 kW
Water heater	2 kW
Electric kettle	2 kW, 3 kW
Electric oven	4 kW

13.1 Using electricity

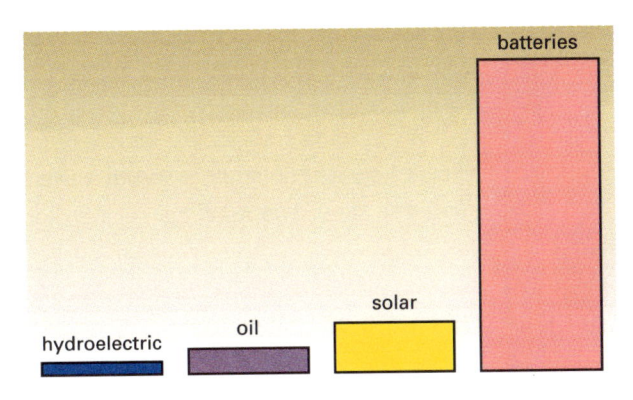

Fig. 13.7 The relative cost of electricity from different sources.

Comparing prices: Batteries are an expensive source of electricity, as you can see from the bar chart in Figure 13.7. We use them because they are convenient in certain situations – when we need only a little electricity, and for appliances we want to carry around.

Solar cells are expensive, so the electricity they produce is twice the price of electricity from a power station. However, the cost of solar cells is coming down rapidly as new methods of making them are developed.

Paying the price: An electricity meter records how much electricity has been used. There are two types:

- digital meters show the number of Units of electricity used directly;
- dial meters have a row of dials from which you can read off the number of Units used.

The electricity company or corporation reads the meter at regular intervals so that it can work out how many Units have been used.

It is useful to understand about Units of electrical energy. Suppose you have an iron that is rated at 1 kW and it is used for 2 hours. The number of Units of electrical energy used is:

Units used = 1 kW × 2 h = 2 kilowatt hours (kW h)

If a 2 kW heater is used for 6 hours:

Units used = 2 kW × 6 h = 12 kW h

A kilowatt hour is another name for a Unit of electrical energy. Here is how to do this calculation:

> Units used (kW h) = power rating (kW) × time (h)

The electricity company charges a certain amount of money for each Unit used, so you can then work out the cost of using any appliance.

● Activity Reading the electricity meter

A dial meter has a row of dials, representing thousands, hundreds, tens and units. For each dial, you look at the needle: which two numbers is it between? Note down the lower of the two. Take care! Sometimes the numbers go clockwise, sometimes anticlockwise.

13.1 Electricity and magnetism

This reading is 8900 Units

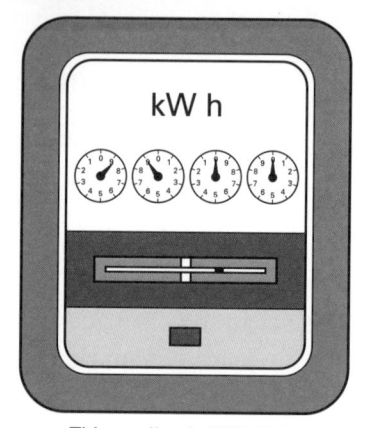

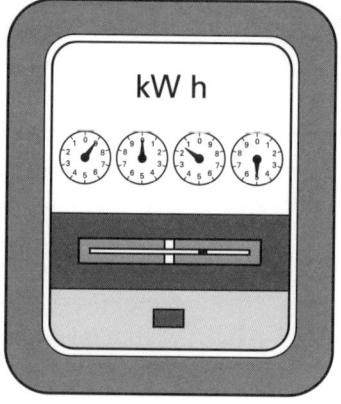

What is this reading?

Try the two examples shown in Figure 13.8 – the first one has been done for you.

Now calculate the number of Units used between these two readings.

Fig. 13.8 Reading the dials on an electricity meter.

⭕ What you should know

- Batteries are made up of cells, and release stored energy in the form of an electric current.
- Every battery has a positive terminal and a negative terminal.
- Mains electricity is produced in power stations.
- The high voltage of the mains electricity power lines is reduced by transformers to the low-voltage electricity used in the home.
- Amounts of electricity are measured in Units (or kilowatt hours, kW h).

❓ Questions

1 You are spending the evening at home. Calculate the number of Units of electricity that you use with each of the following:

  a an electric oven (4 kW) for 1 hour;
  b a computer (100 W) for 2 hours;
  c a light bulb (60 W) for 4 hours;
  d an electric fan (40 W) for 3 hours;
  e a television (100 W) for 2 hours.

  What is the total number of Units that you used?

2 You have to put three new batteries (cells) in a radio. They go end-to-end inside the case. Which of the following arrangements of their terminals is the correct one?

  a + − − + + −
  b + − + − − +
  c + − + − + −

3 You come across a gang of children near a power line. They are planning to fly a kite there. Explain how you would persuade them that this is dangerous.

Electricity and magnetism

13.2 Using electricity safely

> ### Objectives
>
> After studying this topic you should be able to:
>
> - name some features of electrical wiring that make electricity safer to use
> - describe how to connect an appliance to a three-pin plug.

Everyone knows that electricity can be dangerous. However, we can use batteries (cells) without fear because they do not push enough electricity through us to do us any harm. The mains electricity supply is different – 110 V or more can easily kill. But several features of the electricity supply in our homes are there to make things safer for us.

Near the electricity meter there is likely to be a **fuse** box (Fig. 13.9). This contains fuses, which will 'blow' if there is a fault. This prevents a big current from flowing through the wires and causing damage to the wires, the appliance or to the user. A fuse contains a thin piece of wire that gets hot and melts quickly when a big current flows. This breaks the circuit so that no current flows – a fuse is the weakest link in the chain. The fuse must be replaced when the fault has been put right.

Fig. 13.9 An electricity meter and fuse box.

Nowadays, these fuses may be replaced by **circuit breakers**; if a large current flows, the circuit breaker 'trips' and breaks the circuit. The switch can be easily reset when the problem has been sorted out. School laboratories and workshops often have circuit breakers.

Electric wires and many appliances have a coating or casing made of **insulating material**. This is a material, such as plastic or rubber, that does not allow electricity to pass through it. Insulating materials form a barrier between the electricity and any parts that someone might touch, whether on purpose or by accident. So, for example, you can touch the cable of an electric fan without getting a shock, because it is coated in insulating plastic. However, if insulating material is worn or cracked, it must be checked and repaired by an expert, such as an electrician, otherwise you could get a nasty shock!

A three-pin plug is designed as a safe way of connecting an appliance to the mains. There is one pin for each of the three wires inside a standard electric cable. These wires are called 'earth', 'live' and 'neutral'. Here are some of the safety features of the three-pin plug:

- Its case is made of strong insulating plastic, which electricity cannot pass through, and which does not break easily.

13.2 Electricity and magnetism

- It has an earth pin that is longer than the other two, so that the plug connects to earth before live.
- The cable (or flex) is held firmly by the cable grip.
- It has a fuse that protects the appliance from currents that are too big.
- The wires of the cable are colour coded so that each one is easily recognized and can be connected to the correct terminal.

The earth connection is important. It is attached to the metal case of an appliance, such as a washing machine or refrigerator. If the live wire accidentally touches the case inside the appliance, you may get a shock if you touch the appliance. However, with an earth connection, the current flows safely away into the ground.

Many modern appliances such as hairdriers and radios have plastic cases, and so they are well insulated. This is known as double insulation, and such appliances do not need an earth connection.

Fuses for use in plugs come in a range of values (Fig. 13.10). These are measured in **amps** (short for amperes, which are units of electrical current; the symbol for amps is 'A'). Common fuse values are 2 A, 5 A, 13 A and 30 A. A fuse with a value of 2 A will blow if the current rises above 2 A; a 5 A fuse will blow if the current goes above 5 A, and so on.

Fig. 13.10 A range of fuses used in electric plugs.

⊕ Activity Wiring a three-pin plug

Many appliances are sold with a plug already attached. However, it is still useful to know how to attach a new plug to an old appliance.

You will need
- pliers or wire cutters
- a screwdriver
- a plug
- a length of cable

⚠ Danger!

Care needed!

Never take apart electrical devices when they are plugged in.

Method

1. Carefully remove the outer insulation from about 3 cm of cable (Fig. 13.11a).
2. Carefully remove the insulation from the last few millimetres of each of the three wires (Fig. 13.11b).
3. In each wire, twist the strands of wire together (Fig. 13.11c). Trim any loose wires if necessary.
4. Wrap each wire clockwise around the correct single screw and tighten the nut (Fig. 13.11d). Make sure that you screw down on the bare wire, not the insulation.

Using electricity safely   13.2

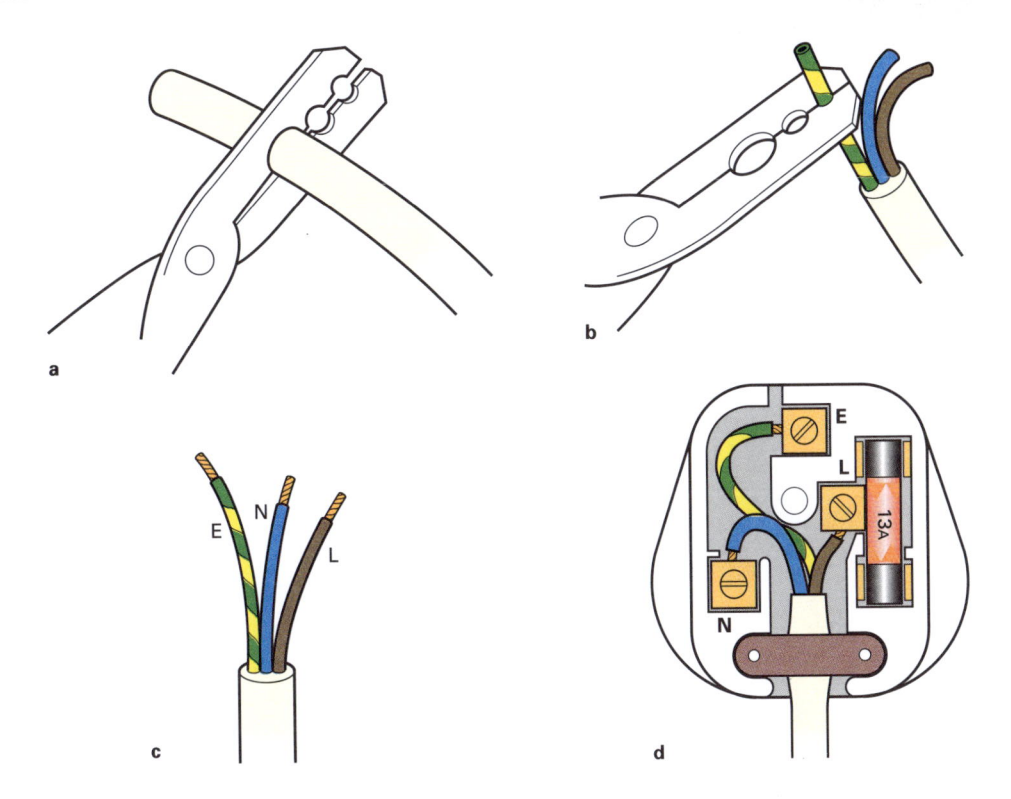

Fig. 13.11 How to connect a three-pin plug.

5 Screw down the cable grip. Tug on the cable to check that nothing is loose.
6 Replace the outer casing of the plug, making sure it fits correctly and is tight.

◘ What you should know

- Insulation materials are used to prevent dangerous leaks of electricity.
- Fuses protect appliances if too much current flows.
- A three-pin plug is the safe way to connect an appliance to the mains electricity.
- The earth wire carries electric current away if the metal case of an appliance becomes live.

◉ Questions

1 Match the descriptions below to items in the following list:

   transformer, fuse, battery

   a Made up of two or more cells
   b Changes the voltage of an electricity supply
   c Protects wiring and appliances from excess current

13.2 Electricity and magnetism

2 Look at the plugs in Figure 13.12. Each one has a fault. Which plug matches each of the descriptions below?

   a earth wire not connected
   b live and neutral wires swopped over
   c cable not held firmly by cable grip
   d case broken to expose live terminal
   e broken fuse replaced with aluminium foil

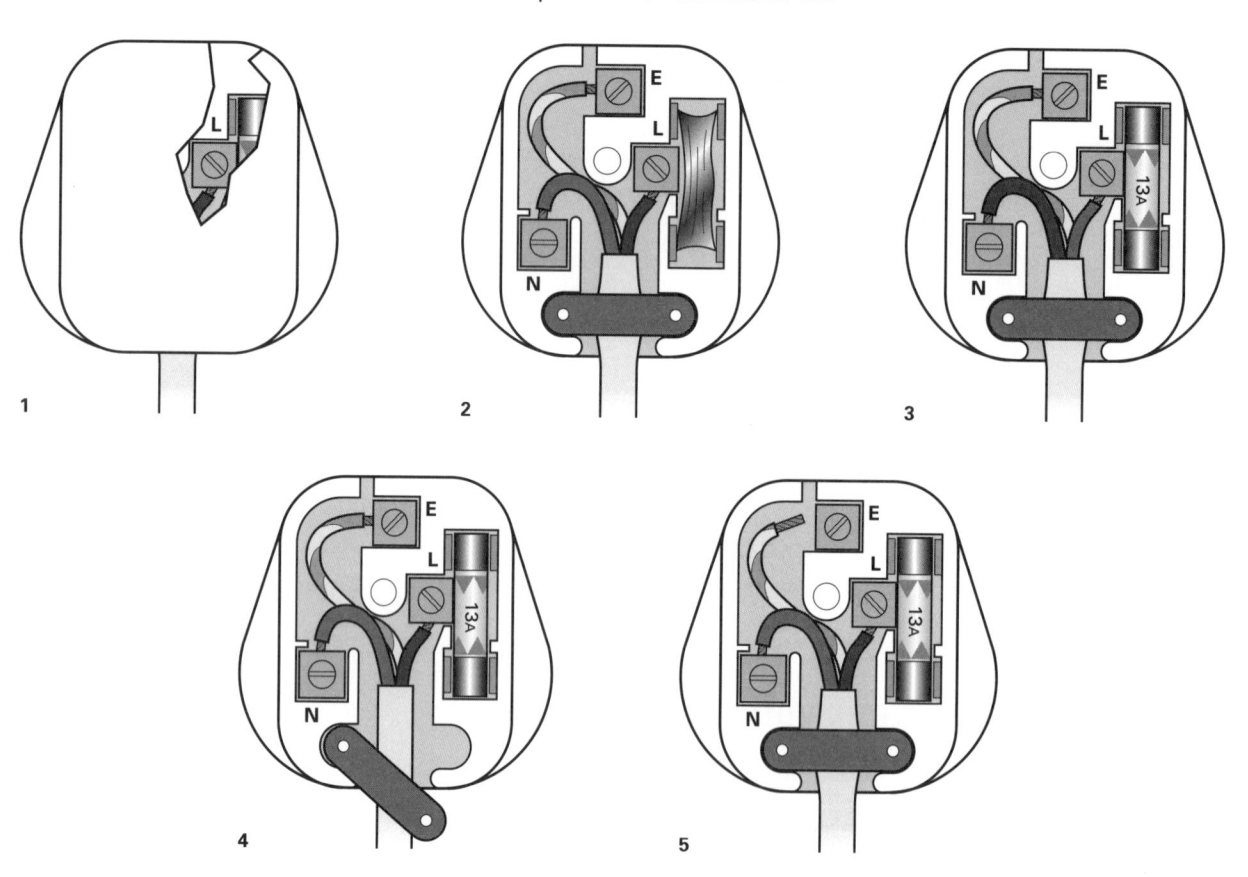

Fig. 13.12 Can you spot the faults in these electric plugs?

3 Devise a safety code for people using mains electricity devices. Give them positive rules like 'Plug in before you switch on'.

4 Make a list of instructions for wiring a plug correctly; write each one on a separate piece of paper. Shuffle the pieces of paper, and challenge a friend to put them in the correct order.

Electricity and magnetism

13.3 Electrical circuits

▶ Objectives

After studying this topic you should be able to:
- describe what happens in a simple electrical circuit
- say what is meant by current and voltage
- outline how we measure current and voltage.

We talk about 'electricity', and we also talk about 'electric current' and 'electrical energy'. What is the difference? It is easy to get mixed up between current and voltage.

In science, we have to use words very carefully, because they may have special meanings. In this topic, you will learn how to use technical words correctly to talk about electricity.

Round and round

You have probably made some simple electrical circuits. The one in Figure 13.13a has a cell, a bulb and a switch. When the switch is closed, the circuit is complete and the bulb lights up. There is a complete circuit of metal from one end of the cell to the other. Start at the positive (+) end of the battery and trace around the circuit to the negative end (−). (This is the way the electric current flows.)

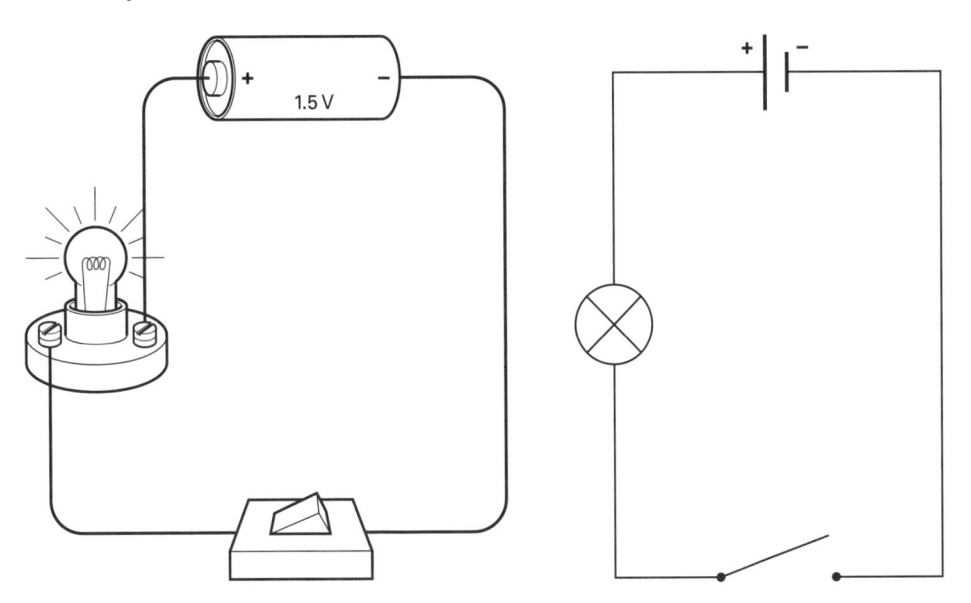

Fig. 13.13 A simple electrical circuit. How it looks in real life (left). How it looks in the form of a circuit diagram (right).

- When the switch is closed, two pieces of metal come into contact with each other.
- The filament of the bulb is a thin metal wire through which the electric current can flow.

13.3 Electricity and magnetism

It is much easier to draw a circuit diagram (Fig. 13.13b) to represent the circuit than a picture of each of the components. You will need to learn the circuit symbols for a cell, switch and lamp, as well as several other electrical components. These are shown in Figure 13.14.

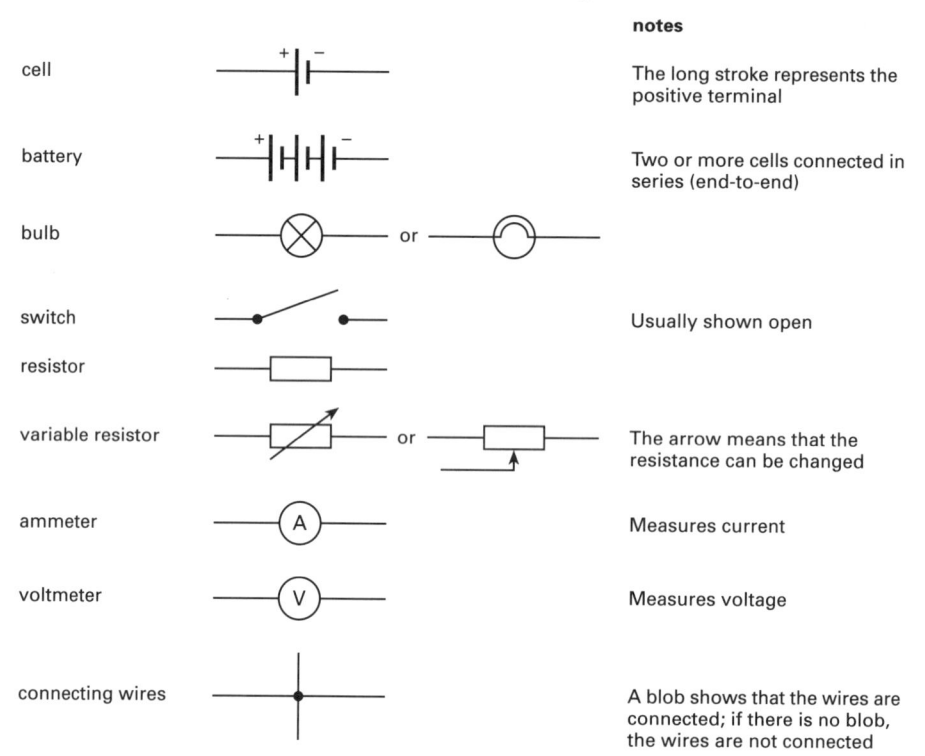

Component	Symbol	Notes
cell	—+|⊢—	The long stroke represents the positive terminal
battery	—+|H|H|⊢—	Two or more cells connected in series (end-to-end)
bulb	—⊗— or —◯—	
switch	—•╱•—	Usually shown open
resistor	—▭—	
variable resistor	—▱— or —▭↑—	The arrow means that the resistance can be changed
ammeter	—(A)—	Measures current
voltmeter	—(V)—	Measures voltage
connecting wires	—┼—	A blob shows that the wires are connected; if there is no blob, the wires are not connected

Fig. 13.14 Symbols used in simple electrical circuits.

● Activity Setting up circuits

You will need
- 3 V bulbs in holders
- 1.5 V cells
- connecting wires
- a switch

Method

The bulb shows when a current is flowing in a circuit – the bulb lights up.

1 Set up circuit 1 in Figure 13.15. Does the bulb light? Try unscrewing the bulb. Explain what happens.

2 Set up circuit 2 in Figure 13.15. How can you tell that a bigger current is flowing than in circuit 1? Why is the current bigger?

3 Set up circuit 3 in Figure 13.15. Close the switch. What can you say about the current flowing in this circuit? How could you change the circuit to make the current bigger? Test your idea. What will happen if you unscrew bulb 2 in circuit 3? Give a reason for your answer. Test your idea.

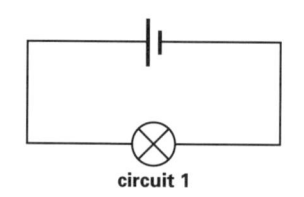

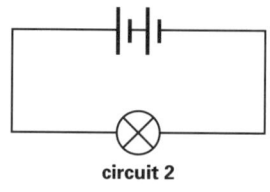

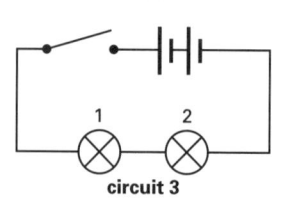

Fig. 13.15

Electric current

You cannot see an electric current, so you will need to make a mental picture of current flowing. We can think of the wires of a circuit as pipes with water flowing through them – that is why we talk of current 'flowing'. The current is pushed around the circuit by the cell or battery. We can picture the cell as a pump, pushing the water through the pipes.

If you have tried the circuit-building activity, you will know that we can use a bulb to show when a current flows. The more brightly the bulb lights up, the bigger the current that is flowing through it. A more scientific way to tell when a current is flowing is to use a meter called an **ammeter**. To add an ammeter to a circuit, we need to disconnect the circuit and add the ammeter end-to-end with the other components. We say that the ammeter has been connected in series. The ammeter measures the current flowing in **amperes** (symbol A). (In speech, we usually say 'amps'.) You can see from the circuit diagram (Fig. 13.16) that the current flows *through* the ammeter.

Fig. 13.16 The correct way to connect an ammeter in a circuit.

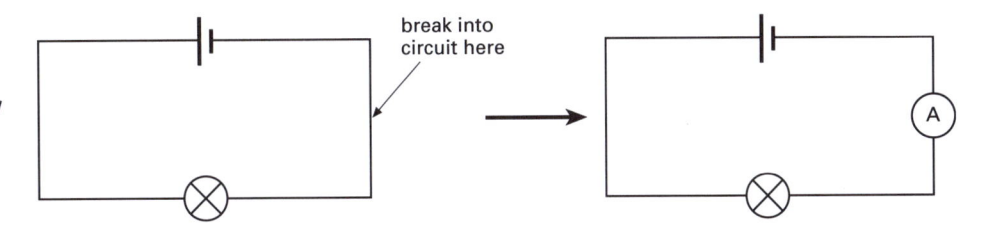

Did you know?

Remember how we said that electric current flows from positive to negative? In fact, if you could see inside the wires, you wouldn't see any 'current'. Instead, you would find tiny particles called electrons flowing. Electrons are very, very tiny – much smaller even than the atoms of which the metal wires are made. Scientists had the idea of current long before they found out about electrons.

In fact, electrons flow in the opposite direction to the current, from negative to positive. So, although we always talk about current flowing from positive (+) to negative (−), you should realize that this is only a model that scientists and engineers use to explain what happens in circuits. The electrons are actually flowing in the opposite direction (Fig. 13.17).

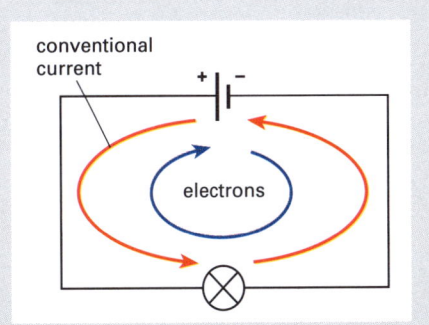

Fig. 13.17 Directions of current and electron flow.

13.3 Electricity and magnetism

Voltage and energy

Two cells connected end-to-end (in series) will light a bulb more brightly than a single cell. A 6 V battery will light a bulb more brightly than a 3 V battery. The bigger the voltage, the greater the current that flows around a circuit.

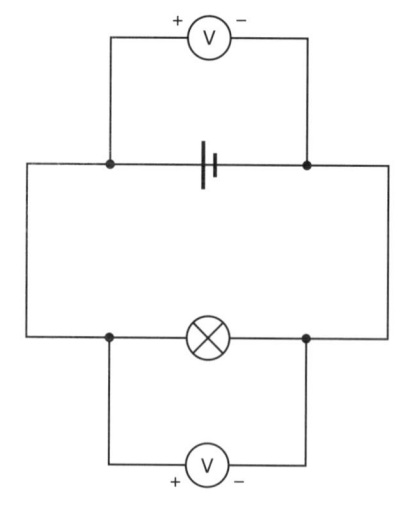

Fig. 13.18 The correct way to connect voltmeters in a circuit.

The **voltage** of a battery tells us about the 'push' it gives to make a current flow around a circuit. The greater the voltage, the greater the push and so the greater the current that flows. (A battery is like a pump, pushing water through pipes. The greater the voltage, the stronger is the push it gives so that the water flows faster through the pipes.)

Voltage is measured in **volts** (symbol V) using a **voltmeter**. This is connected in a different way to an ammeter. It is helpful always to think about the voltage between two points, for example between the two ends of a cell or battery. The two terminals of the voltmeter are connected to the two points. We say that the voltmeter measures the voltage *across* a component. In the circuit diagram shown in Figure 13.18, one of the voltmeters is measuring the voltage across the cell; the other is measuring the voltage across the bulb. The voltmeters are each connected in parallel, not in series like an ammeter.

- An ammeter measures the current flowing *through* a component in a circuit.
- A voltmeter measures the voltage *across* a component in a circuit.

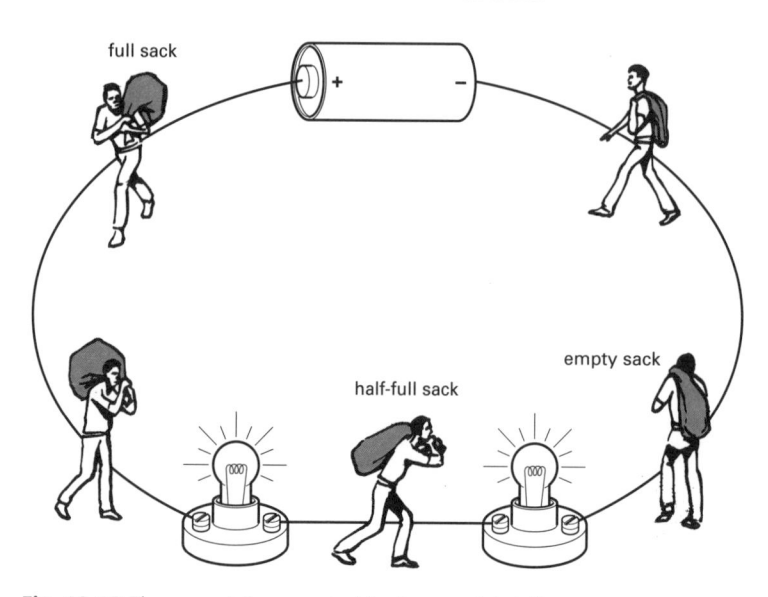

Fig. 13.19 The current (represented by the people) delivers energy (represented by the sacks of coal) from the battery around the circuit. In this case each light bulb receives half the energy travelling around the circuit.

In a circuit with a battery and a bulb, the battery is the source of energy. The electric current carries the energy from the battery to the bulb. The bulb converts the energy to light and heat. The drawing in Figure 13.19 shows how we can picture this. The people move around the circuit – they represent the current. The battery gives each person a sack of coal – this represents the energy. As each person passes through the first bulb, they deliver half of their coal. Then they deliver the second half to the second bulb. They then continue round to the battery to refill their sacks.

Now you can see why a complete circuit is necessary. The current delivers energy from the battery to the bulbs. The two bulbs share the energy equally – that is why they are equally bright. The current must flow back to the battery so that it can collect more energy to keep the bulbs glowing brightly.

Getting the voltage right

Electrical appliances, including bulbs, are often marked with the voltage they are designed to work with. It is important to match this to the voltage of the electricity supply. A bulb labelled 3 V will light brightly with a 3 V battery; it will be dim with a 1.5 V cell; and it will burn out with a 6 V battery.

If you look at a light bulb intended for the mains electricity you will see that it, too, is labelled with a voltage, perhaps 110 V or 240 V. You need to use bulbs that match the voltage of your local supply. In Trinidad, Barbados, Jamaica and parts of Guyana, the supply voltage is 110 V. In other Caribbean countries it is 220 V or 240 V. If you plug a 240 V appliance into a 110 V supply, it will not work properly because the voltage is not high enough. If you plug a 110 V appliance into a 240 V supply, it may be ruined.

➲ Activity Measuring voltages

You will need
- dry cells of different sizes
- a voltmeter
- connecting wires

Method
1. Measure the voltage across the terminals of each of the cells. Compare your measured values with those marked on the cells by the manufacturers.
2. Connect two dry cells in series. Do their voltages add up correctly?
3. Make a wet cell (see Topic 13.1, page 143) and measure the voltage it provides. Keep the voltmeter connected for a few minutes. Record what you observe, and try to explain your observations.

Discuss
1. How accurate are the values of voltage marked on a cell?
2. Why is a dry cell better than a wet cell? Give at least two reasons.

What you should know

- An electric current flows around a circuit. It carries electrical energy from the cell to the components in the circuit.
- Current is measured in amps (or amperes) using an ammeter connected in series.
- Voltage is a measure of the push that makes a current flow. The bigger the voltage, the bigger the current.
- Voltage is measured in volts using a voltmeter connected in parallel.
- Electrical appliances must be used with an electrical supply of the correct voltage.

Questions

1 Copy the circuit symbols shown in Figure 13.20 and label each with the name of the component it represents.

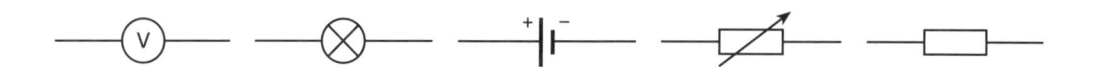

Fig. 13.20 Give these circuit symbols their correct labels.

2 Draw a circuit diagram to represent the following:
   a A bulb connected to a battery of two cells.
   b An ammeter is included in the circuit to measure the current flowing through the bulb.

3 Your younger brother's torch will not work. Explain all the checks you would make in trying to make the bulb light again.

4 Visit the Crocodile Clips site on the internet (http://www.crocodile-clips.co.uk) and explore some virtual electrical circuits.

Electricity and magnetism

13.4 Electrical resistance

▶ Objectives

After studying this topic you should be able to:

- say what a resistor does
- say how resistance is measured
- describe Ohm's law
- list some uses for variable resistors.

When making electrical circuits, you may have noticed that some bulbs light up more brightly than others. You can buy different light bulbs to use at home; a 100 W bulb is much brighter than a 40 W bulb. Why is this?

A bright bulb lets through more electric current. We say that it has less electrical **resistance**. The greater the resistance of a component, the smaller the current that will flow through it when it is connected to a cell.

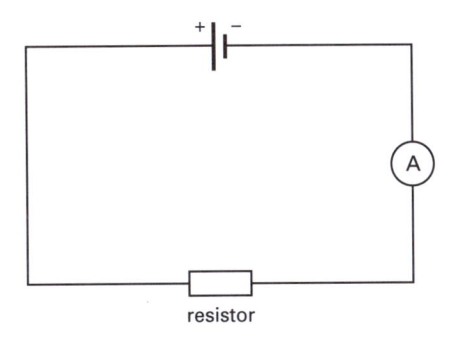

Fig. 13.21 Circuit diagram showing an ammeter connected to test how different resistors affect current flow.

We can control how much current flows around a circuit using special components called **resistors**. Resistors are made of materials through which it is difficult for an electric current to flow; in other words they 'resist' the current flow. The circuit diagram in Figure 13.21 shows how you can investigate the effect of different resistors on the flow of current around a circuit.

The resistance of a resistor is measured in **ohms** (symbol Ω, which is the Greek letter omega). Table 13.2 shows what happens if you try different resistors in the circuit shown in Figure 13.21. Find the pattern in these results.

The voltage is always the same (6 V). As the resistance is gradually increased, the current gradually decreases. This shows that more resistance means less current.

Table 13.2 Effect on current of different values of resistor.

Voltage (V)	Resistance (Ω)	Current (A)
6	10	0.60
6	20	0.30
6	30	0.20
6	50	0.12
6	100	0.06

We can say more than this. We can see that doubling the resistance (from 10 Ω to 20 Ω) causes the current to halve. Ten times the resistance gives one-tenth of the current. We can calculate resistance if we know the current that flows through a component and the voltage that is pushing it, using the following equation:

$$\text{resistance } (\Omega) = \frac{\text{voltage (V)}}{\text{current (A)}}$$

Check this using the figures from the first row of the table:

resistance = 6 V/0.6 A = 10 Ω

We can think of the resistance of a component as the voltage needed to make a current of 1 A flow through it. For example, it takes 10 V to make 1 A flow through a 10 Ω resistor, but it takes 20 V to make 1 A flow through a 20 Ω resistor.

Ohm's law

A German scientist called Georg Ohm made a detailed study of electrical resistance, which he published in 1826. He didn't have convenient ammeters and voltmeters to work with, so it was a great triumph to make his discoveries. You can repeat his investigations with the circuit shown in Figure 13.22.

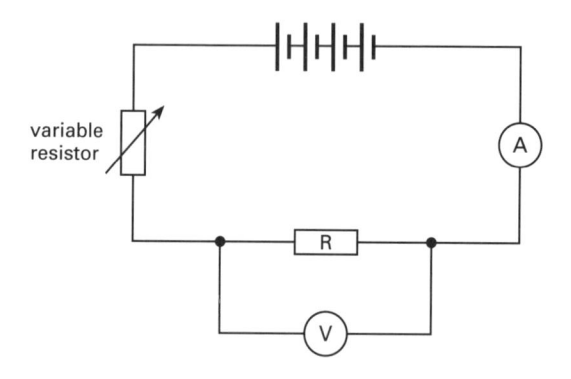

Fig. 13.22 Circuit for investigating Ohm's law.

The circuit includes a variable resistor. This can be adjusted to alter the current flowing through the fixed resistor R. Ohm looked at how the current flowing through R changed as he changed the voltage across it. He found that double the voltage made double the current flow; three times the voltage gave three times the current, and so on. In other words, the current that flowed through the resistor was proportional to the voltage across it. He also found that this is only true if the temperature remained constant. His result is known as **Ohm's law**.

Activity Looking at Ohm's law

You will need
- graph paper

Method

A group of students investigated a resistor. They changed the voltage across the resistor and recorded the current each time. Table 13.3 shows their results. Unfortunately, they are a bit jumbled up because they did not change the voltage in a systematic way. This makes it difficult to see the pattern in the results.

1 Copy Table 13.3, putting the rows in order with the lowest voltage first.

Table 13.3

Voltage (V)	Current (A)
1.3	0.52
0.5	0.20
3.0	1.20
1.8	0.72
0.9	0.36
2.4	0.96

13.4 Electrical resistance

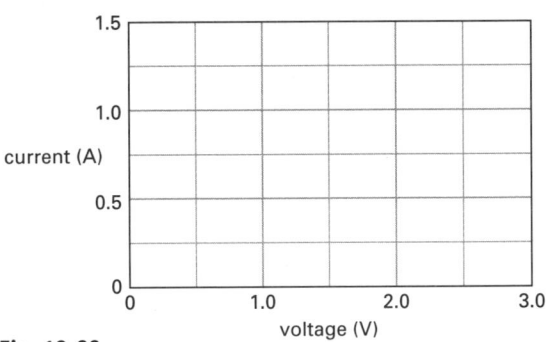

Fig. 13.23

2. Add an extra column to your table. For each row, calculate the resistance (= voltage/current), and record this in the new column. What do you notice? What should you write as the heading of this column?

3. Draw a graph of current against voltage, using axes like those shown in Figure 13.23. What shape is the graph?

Variable resistors

The Ohm's law experiment makes use of a variable resistor, also known as a **rheostat**. As you turn or slide the knob of a variable resistor, you are changing the length of resistance wire in the circuit (Fig. 13.24). Variable resistors have a number of applications:

- the volume control of a radio, TV set or stereo;
- the speed control on an electric sewing machine;
- the temperature control on an iron;
- the speed control of a toy electric train or racing car set;
- the dimmer control for lights in the theatre or cinema.

Fig. 13.24 A variable resistor (or rheostat). The current flows through the coil of resistance wire.

→ Activity Dimming the lights

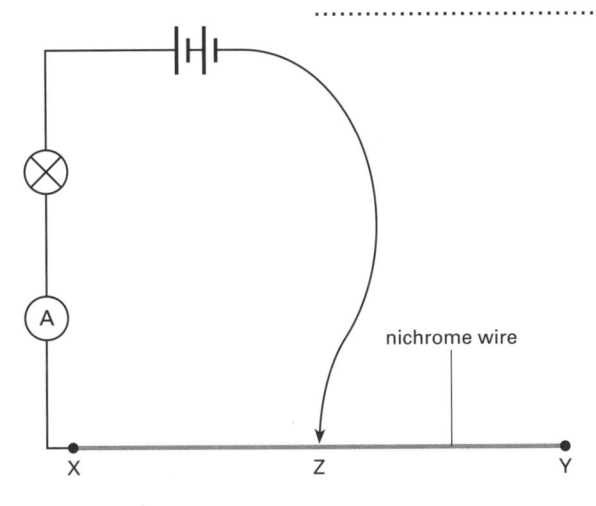

Fig. 13.25 Circuit showing the principle of a dimmer switch.

You will need
- a bulb in a holder
- an ammeter
- a dry cell
- nichrome wires of different thicknesses
- connecting wires and clips

(Nichrome wire is used for making electrical appliances such as hotplates, toasters and hairdriers.)

Method
1. Set up the circuit shown in Figure 13.25.
2. Slide the clip Z gradually from Y towards X along the wire.

Record

Record how the brightness of the bulb changes as the clip is moved nearer to X. In a table, record ammeter readings for different positions of the clip.

Discuss

1 How does the resistance in the circuit change as the clip is moved? Explain your answer.

2 How does the current change if you use different thicknesses of wire?

◯ What you should know

- Resistors control the amount of current flowing in a circuit.
- The resistance of a resistor is measured in ohms (symbol Ω).
- The flow of current through a resistor increases in proportion to the increase in voltage across it. This is Ohm's law.
- Resistance can be calculated as follows:

    resistance = voltage (V)/current (A)

@ Questions

1 Copy the sentences below, choosing the correct word from each pair.

   a A voltmeter can be connected in series/parallel with a resistor to measure the voltage across/through it.

   b The resistance of a component is measured in ohms/amps, and is calculated by multiplying/dividing the voltage by the current.

2 State whether each of the following statements is true or false.

   a Doubling the voltage across a resistor reduces the current by half.

   b Doubling the resistance with a fixed voltage reduces the current by half.

   c Halving the resistance with a fixed voltage reduces the current by half.

   d Increasing resistance ten times with a fixed voltage increases the current five times.

3 Research some everyday uses of rheostats – in the theatre, music and broadcasting industries, in electric vehicles, etc.

Electricity and magnetism

13.5 Series and parallel circuits

Objectives

After studying this topic you should be able to:
- describe how voltage is shared in a series circuit
- describe how current is shared in a parallel circuit.

You may have noticed that there are two ways of connecting two bulbs in a circuit. These are shown in Figure 13.26.

One way is to connect the bulbs in series (end-to-end) (Fig. 13.26a): the current flows through one bulb and then the other. There is more resistance in the circuit, because the current has to push through both bulbs, so they light up dimly.

The other way is to connect the bulbs in parallel (side-by-side) (Fig. 13.26b): the bulbs are brighter, because each bulb feels the full push of the battery. A large current flows around the circuit; it splits in half at point X, and the two halves recombine at point Y.

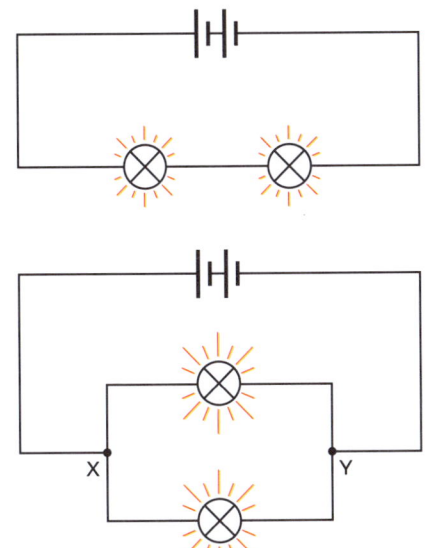

Fig. 13.26 Circuits showing bulbs connected in series (top) and in parallel (bottom).

Numerical examples

What exactly happens to the voltage and the current when bulbs or other components are connected in series and in parallel? We can tell better if we connect resistors of different known resistances, and then measure the voltage across each one, and also the current flowing through them.

Series circuits: Look at Figure 13.27. The resistors are connected in series.

- The current is the same all the way around the circuit.
- The voltages across the three resistors add up to the same as the voltage of the battery:

$$1\,V + 2\,V + 3\,V = 6\,V$$

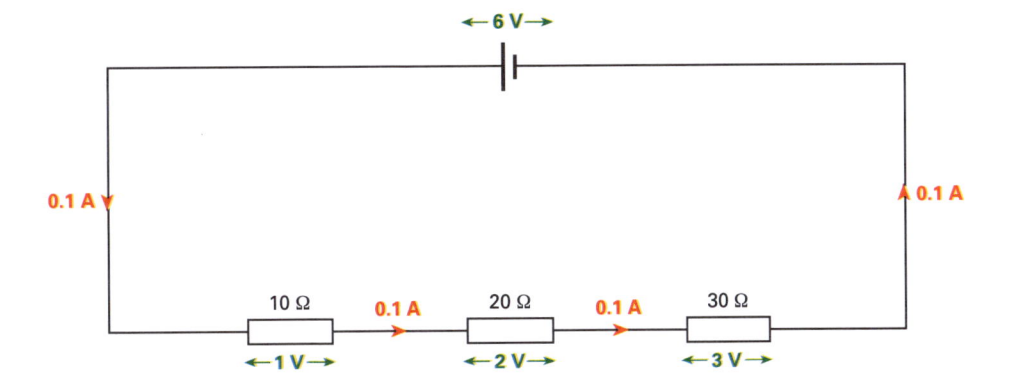

Fig. 13.27 Resistors connected in series.

161

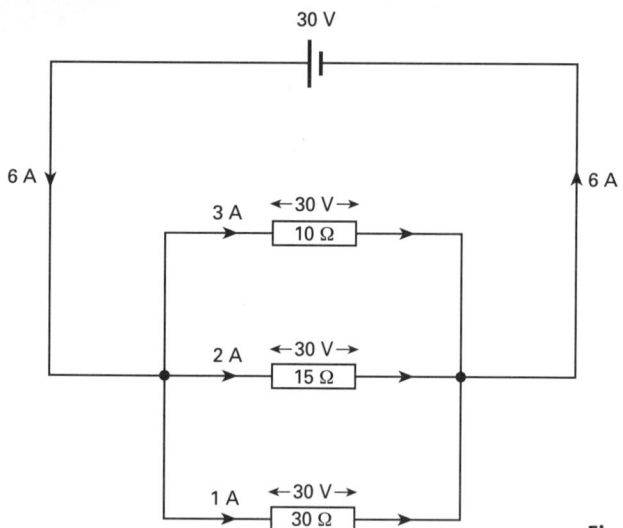

13.5 Electricity and magnetism

Parallel circuits: Now look at Figure 13.28. These resistors are connected in parallel.

- The voltage is the same across each resistor.
- The currents through the three resistors add up to the same as the current flowing from the battery:

$$1 \text{ A} + 2 \text{ A} + 3 \text{ A} = 6 \text{ A}$$

Fig. 13.28 Resistors connected in parallel.

○ What you should know

- Components in a series circuit have the same current flowing through them; the voltage of the supply is shared between them.
- Components in a parallel circuit have the same voltage across them; the current from the supply is shared between them.

ⓠ Questions

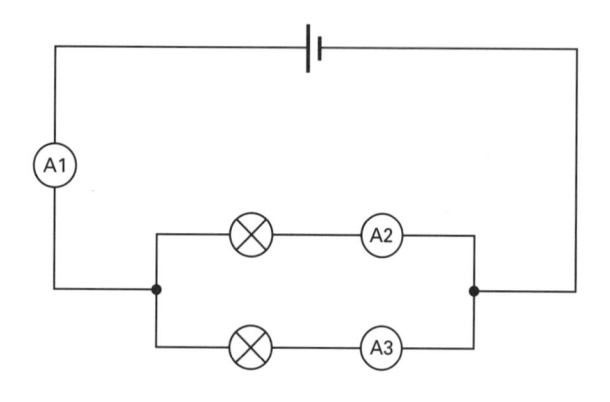

Fig. 13.29 Parallel circuit with bulbs.

1. Look at the circuit in Figure 13.29. It contains two identical bulbs connected in parallel, and three ammeters, labelled A1, A2 and A3.

   a If the reading on A1 is 0.2 A, what will be the readings on A2 and A3?

   b If the bulb next to A2 blows, the reading on A1 drops to 0.1 A. Why is this? What will be the reading on A3?

2. Two identical bulbs are connected in series with a battery. Three ammeters are added to the circuit, to measure the current before and after each bulb. Each ammeter reads 0.5 A.

   a Draw a circuit diagram to represent the circuit.

   b Explain why all three ammeters show the same reading.

   c If one bulb blows, how will each ammeter reading change? Explain your answer.

Electricity and magnetism

13.6 Static electricity

▶ Objectives

After studying this topic you should be able to:
- describe how things become charged with static electricity
- describe how positive and negative charges behave with one another
- outline the properties of insulators and conductors.

In the previous topics you studied circuits in which electricity moves around – a cell or battery makes an electric current flow. Now we can look at some effects of electricity at rest, which we call **static electricity**.

Perhaps you have noticed some effects of static electricity (Fig. 13.30). You may have discovered that you can rub a balloon on your clothes and that it will then stick to the wall or ceiling. If you wear clothes made of synthetic fibres such as polyester or nylon, you may notice a faint crackling coming from them when you take them off. In the dark, you may even see small sparks. This is static electricity; it works best on a dry day, when the humidity is low.

Fig. 13.30 Lightning is an effect of static electricity. When a thundercloud becomes highly charged, a bolt of lightning leaps between the cloud and the ground.

▶ Activity Charging up

You will need
- a plastic rod or ballpoint pen
- woollen, cotton and nylon cloths
- small scraps of paper
- access to a tap

Method
1. Rub the plastic rod or pen with a cloth.
2. Hold the rod near some scraps of paper (Fig. 13.31). Does the rod attract the paper? Which cloth gives the biggest effect? Does the whole rod attract paper, or just the end?
3. Turn on the tap so that a gentle stream of water runs into the sink.
4. Rub a rod with a cloth then bring it close to the water (Fig. 13.32). What happens? Try bringing the cloth close to the water.

13.6 Electricity and magnetism

Fig. 13.31 What happens when you move the charged rods towards the paper?

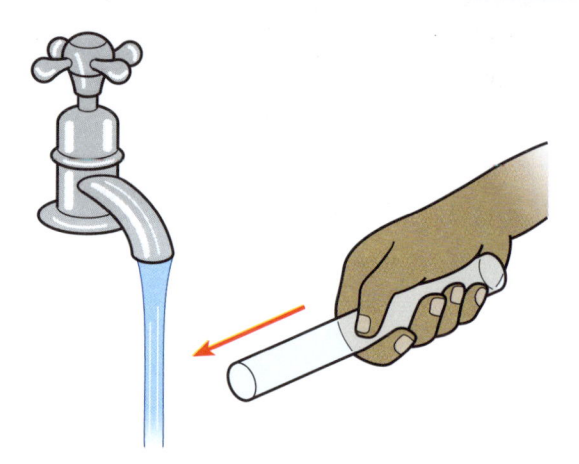

Fig. 13.32 What happens when you move a charged rod close to a water stream?

Charging by friction

When you rub a plastic rod with a cloth, you can feel the force of friction as you rub. This force causes the rod to become charged up with static electricity. At the same time, the cloth also becomes charged.

A charged rod behaves rather like a magnet, but it is not the same as a magnet. A magnet will not attract paper or water. The rod is charged up along its length; a magnet only attracts things to its ends.

The plastic materials you have been charging up are electrical insulators. If you tried charging up a metal rod in the same way, the static electricity would escape immediately, because metals are electrical conductors.

➲ Activity Attraction and repulsion

You will need
- plastic rods
- cloths for rubbing
- a watchglass

Method

1. Rub one end of a plastic rod to charge it up. Balance it on an upturned watchglass.

2. Rub another rod in the same way. Bring its charged end close to the charged end of the first rod (Fig. 13.33). What do you observe?

3. Now bring the charging cloth towards the balanced rod. What do you observe?

If you have rods of different materials, such as polythene and acrylic (Perspex), you may find that they behave differently. Explore their behaviour.

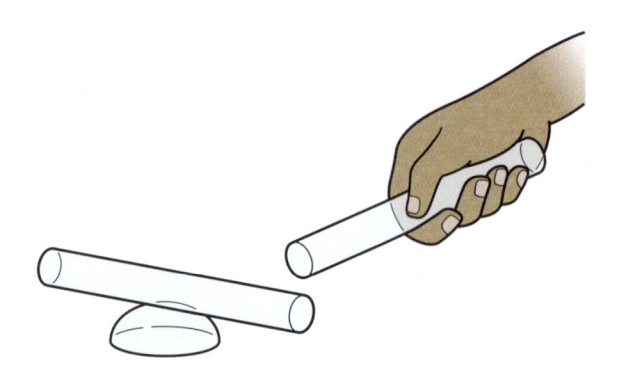

Fig. 13.33 Rods charged in the same way repel one another.

Static electricity 13.6

Electrons on the move

Static electricity can produce both attraction and repulsion. This suggests that there are two types of static electricity, which we call 'positive charge' and 'negative charge'. So, what happens when you use a cloth to charge up a plastic rod?

At first, both are uncharged or neutral. The force of friction rubs tiny charged particles called **electrons** from one material to the other. (These are the same particles that move through a metal when an electric current flows.) Electrons have a negative electric charge – that is why they flow around a circuit towards the positive terminal of a cell.

- The material that gains electrons becomes negatively charged.
- The material that loses electrons becomes positively charged.

For example, if you rub a polythene rod with a nylon cloth, electrons are transferred from the cloth to the rod. The polythene becomes negatively charged, the nylon becomes positively charged.

If you bring two negatively charged rods close together, they will repel each other. A negative rod and a positive cloth will attract each other. We can say:

- opposite charges (positive and negative) attract;
- like charges (negative and negative, or positive and positive) repel (Fig. 13.34).

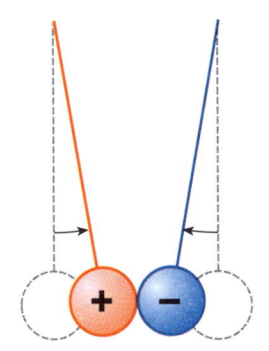

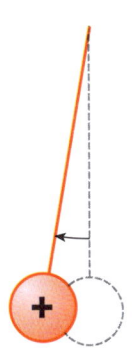

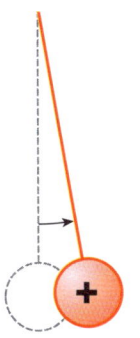

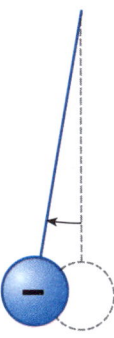

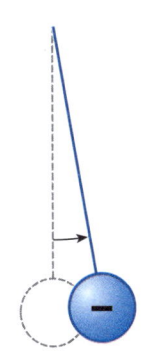

Fig. 13.34 Opposite charges attract; like charges repel.

13.6 Electricity and magnetism

Did you know?

A van de Graaff generator can produce very high voltages, sometimes up to 5 million volts. It was invented by the US physicist Robert van de Graaff in 1931. Scientists use it to accelerate electrons or other particles, but it can be used on people too. In Figure 13.35, the girl's body has been charged up to about 1 million volts. Her hair stands on end because each hair repels its neighbours. This is not dangerous because although the voltage is high, only a tiny current flows.

Fig. 13.35 Being charged with static electricity by a van de Graaff generator can produce a hair-raising experience!

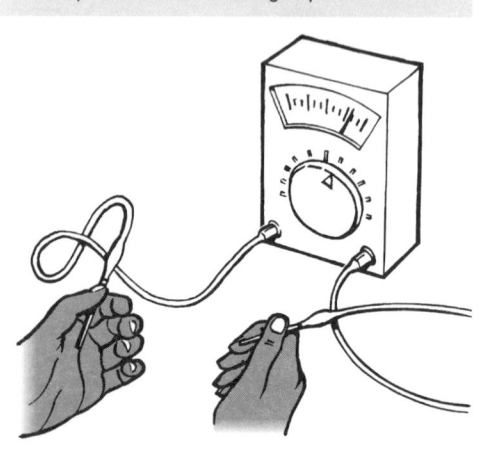

Conductors and insulators

We have seen that only insulating materials can be charged with static electricity.

- **Insulators** are materials that do not conduct electricity. Examples are plastic, rubber, glass, stone, wood and paper.
- **Conductors** are materials through which an electric current can flow easily. Examples are metals and graphite (or pencil 'lead').

Pure water is an insulator. But water that has anything dissolved in it is quite a good conductor. That is why you can get an electric shock. Most of your insides are watery cells. If you touch a live source of mains electricity, you may be lucky. The current wants to flow through you into the earth. Fortunately, your skin is covered with a layer of dead cells that do not conduct. If your skin is dry, it will have high resistance. If you are wearing shoes with synthetic soles, these also have high resistance. However, if your hands are wet and you have bare feet, there could be an easy path for the current to flow into your body and through you into the ground. If the current flows through the muscles of your heart, it may stop beating, and you may die. That is why it is dangerous to use electrical appliances near water, for example in a bathroom.

Activity Measuring your own resistance

You will need
- an electrical multimeter

Method
You can measure resistance using a multimeter. Simply switch to the resistance setting and connect the item between the terminals. A tiny current flows – the voltage is too small to give you a shock.

1 Hold one terminal in each hand (Fig. 13.36). Note the reading.

Fig. 13.36 Measuring your body's resistance using a multimeter.

2 Dip your fingers in water and repeat. Note the new reading. Is it different from before?

3 Touch one terminal to each ear. Why is the reading very high?

Discuss

Why should you avoid using mains-powered appliances in the bathroom? What other precautions can be taken to avoid getting a shock in the bathroom?

What you should know

- The force of friction can give insulating materials a static electric charge when they are rubbed.
- There are two types of electric charge: positive and negative.
- Opposite charges attract; like charges repel.
- Insulators are materials through which electricity cannot flow.
- Conductors are materials through which electricity flows easily.
- Water is a fairly good conductor, and so is your body.

Questions

1 What force causes an insulating material to become charged when it is rubbed?

2 Copy the sentence below, choosing the correct word from each pair. (There are two correct versions. Can you find both?)

   A material that gains/loses electrons is given a positive/negative charge.

3 A student rubs three different plastic rods so that they become charged.
   - Rod A attracts rod B.
   - Rod B repels rod C.
   - Rod A has a negative charge.

   What types of charge do rods B and C have?

4 Research the work of Benjamin Franklin and his (dangerous!) experiment that proved the connection between thunderstorms and static electricity. How did it work? What causes thunder and lightning? Research the different types of lightning.

Electricity and magnetism

13.7 Magnets and electromagnets

▶ Objectives

After studying this topic you should be able to:
- describe the basic features of magnets
- say how magnets attract and repel each other
- describe the basic features of an electromagnet.

Fig. 13.37 This train at the Epcot Center, Walt Disney World, Florida is fitted with electromagnets and runs on a special track. The electromagnets hold the train just above the track, so there is no friction, and the train can reach very high speeds.

You have probably played with magnets. It is mysterious how they can attract and repel one another without touching. Magnets have many different uses (Fig. 13.37). They may simply keep the fridge door closed, or fix a notice to a board. They also play a vital role in important devices such as loudspeakers, motors and electrical generators.

The Chinese discovered how to use magnets as compasses over 2000 years ago. Christopher Columbus used a magnetic compass to direct him during his expeditions in the fifteenth century.

▶ Activity Facing north

You will need
- a bar magnet
- paper and thread
- a wooden clamp and stand

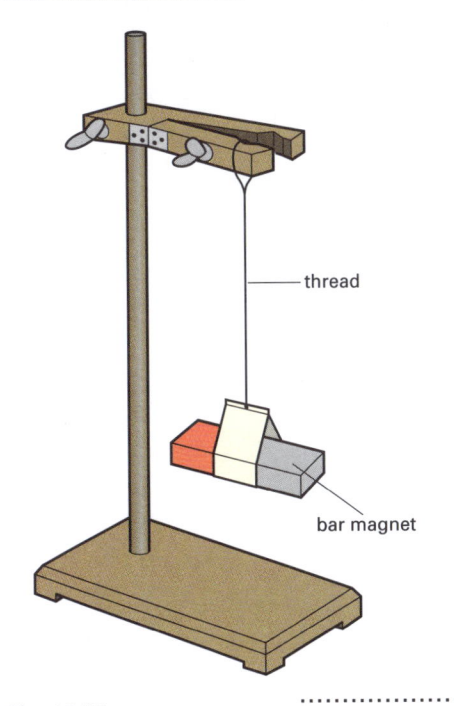

Method
1 Make a paper 'yoke' to go round the middle of the magnet.
2 Attach a thread to the yoke so that the magnet hangs freely from the clamp (Fig. 13.38).

Record
Notice the direction in which the magnet points. Push it gently round and let go. When it settles down, in which direction does it point? Compare the direction of your magnet with others in the class.

Discuss
1 Why should you not use a metal clamp and stand in this experiment?
2 You have made a simple magnetic compass that points north–south. What uses do compasses have?

Fig. 13.38

Magnetic materials

Permanent magnets (such as bar magnets and compass needles) are usually made from steel (an alloy made from iron). Once magnetized, steel keeps its magnetism for a long time. It will attract other pieces of iron and steel – these are magnetic materials. Only a few metals are magnetic – iron, nickel and cobalt. Others such as copper and aluminium are non-magnetic.

➔ Activity Testing materials

You will need
- two bar magnets
- a selection of materials (metals and non-metals)

Method
1 Test each of the materials in turn, and make two lists: 'magnetic' and 'non-magnetic' materials.
2 Hold a bar magnet in each hand with a gap between them, so that they attract each other. Ask a partner to place different materials in the gap, so that the material does not touch either magnet (Fig. 13.39). Does the force of attraction change?

Discuss
1 Which materials are magnetic?
2 Which materials will the magnetic force pass through?
3 What general rule can you make about materials and magnetism?

13.7 Electricity and magnetism

Fig. 13.39 Hold a piece of aluminium foil between two magnets. How does it affect the force of attraction? Try other materials.

Magnetic poles

Magnets are strongest near their ends. This is where the **poles** are situated. A bar magnet has two poles, north and south. We call them this because:

- a north pole is attracted towards the Earth's north pole – it is 'north-seeking';
- a south pole is attracted towards the Earth's south pole – it is 'south-seeking'.

The influence of a magnet spreads all round it. We say there is a **magnetic field** in the space around the magnet. You can use iron filings to show up the field. Figure 13.40 shows how we can draw lines of force to represent

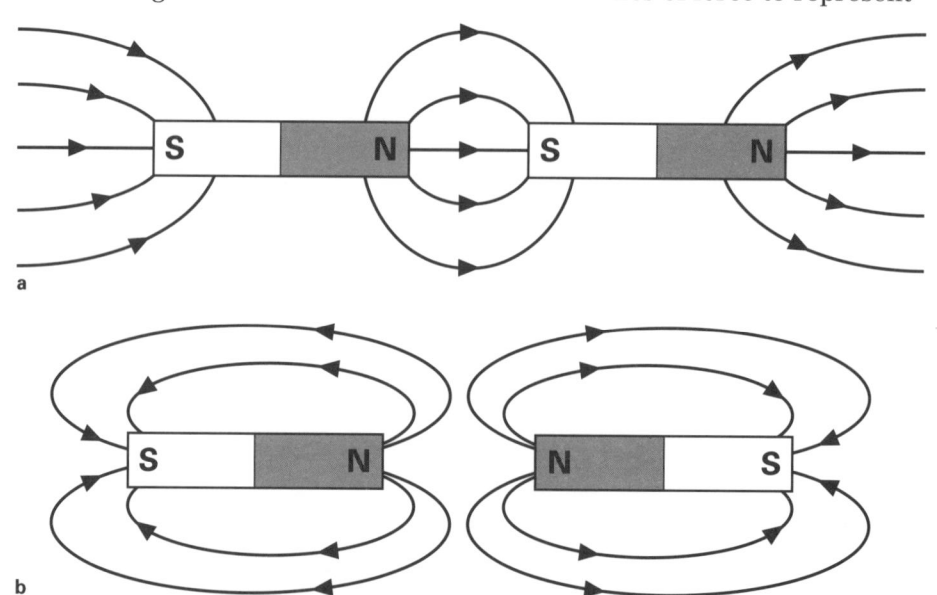

Fig. 13.40 Lines of force around magnets: (a) with opposite poles attracting; (b) with like poles repelling.

Magnets and electromagnets 13.7

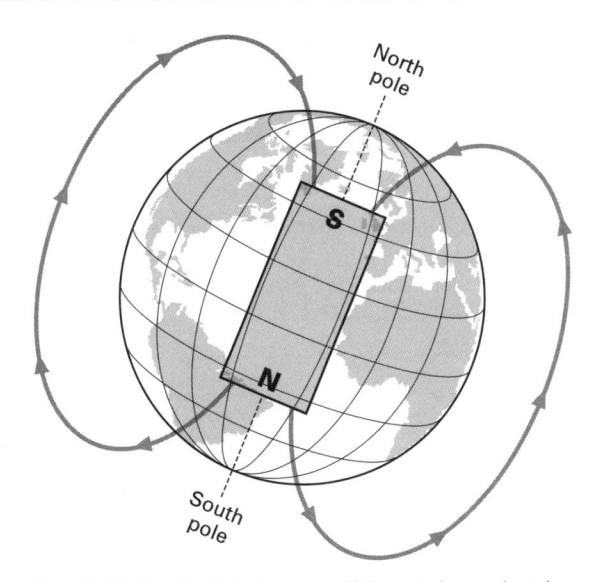

Fig. 13.41 The Earth behaves as if it contains a giant bar magnet with its south magnetic pole close to the Earth's geographic North pole.

the field. They come out of the north pole and disappear into the south pole. (Notice that the poles are slightly inside the magnet, not right on the ends.)

Two magnets will attract each other if the north pole of one is close to the south pole of the other. Otherwise, they will repel each other. Hence we can say:

- opposite poles attract;
- like poles repel.

This tells us something about the magnetic field of the Earth. The Earth behaves as if there is a giant bar magnet inside it (Fig. 13.41). A bar magnet turns so that its north-seeking pole points north. This means that there must be a south magnetic pole attracting it.

Did you know?

The Earth's magnetic poles are actually some distance from the true North and South Poles. At present the northern magnetic pole is about 1300 km from the actual North Pole, and the southern magnetic pole is about 2600 km from the actual South Pole. The magnetic poles move slowly over time, at about 10–15 km each year. They are even known to have swapped positions several times during the Earth's long history.

Activity Looking at magnetic fields

Eye protection must be worn

Danger!

Work carefully so that you do not spill any of the filings. Avoid getting filings on the magnets or on your hands.

You will need
- two bar magnets
- stiff paper
- iron filings in a shaker

Method
1. Place a sheet of paper over one of the magnets.
2. Sprinkle iron filings over the paper (Fig. 13.42). Tap the paper gently to allow the filings to line up.

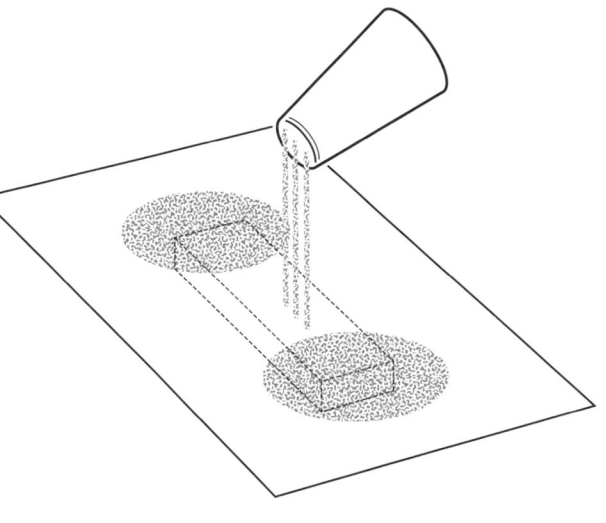

Fig. 13.42 Looking at the lines of magnetic force.

13.7 Electricity and magnetism

3 Sketch the pattern you see.

4 Carefully lift the paper and filings off the magnet. Tip the filings back into the shaker.

5 Repeat with two magnets under the paper. Try with the magnets attracting and then repelling. Sketch the filing patterns. Do they look similar to the diagrams of lines of force (shown in Figure 13.40)?

6 Cover good patterns with a damp paper towel and leave them for a few days until you have a permanent record in rust!

Electromagnets

When an electric current is passed through a coil of wire, it becomes magnetized – one end becomes a north pole, the other a south pole. This is called an **electromagnet**. There are three ways of increasing the strength of an electromagnet:

- use a bigger current;
- use more turns of wire;
- add a soft iron core inside the coil (Fig. 13.43).

One advantage of an electromagnet is that it can be switched on and off. Without an electric current flowing through it, it is no longer magnetized.

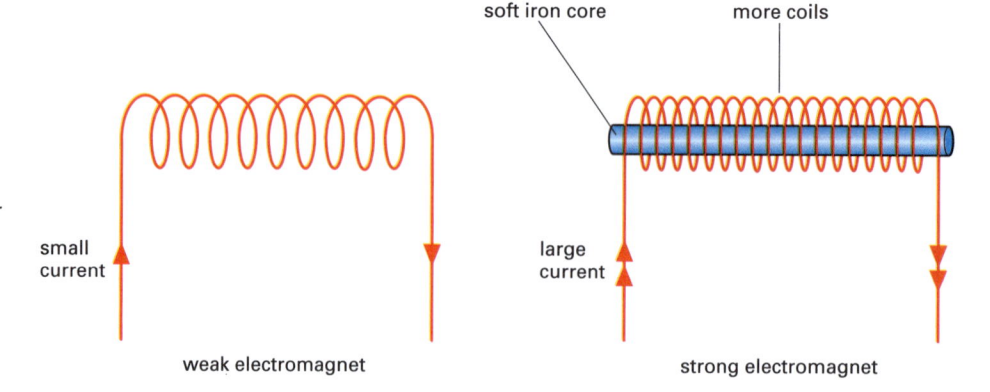

Fig. 13.43 You can make an electromagnet stronger by increasing the current, adding more coils of wire, and putting a soft iron core through the centre.

weak electromagnet — small current

strong electromagnet — large current, soft iron core, more coils

➔ Activity Testing an electromagnet

⚠ Danger!

Do not leave your electromagnet connected too long. The wire will become hot and the battery will run down quickly.

You will need
- flexible insulated wire
- a battery
- a variable resistor
- a thick iron nail
- pins or paperclips

Magnets and electromagnets 13.7

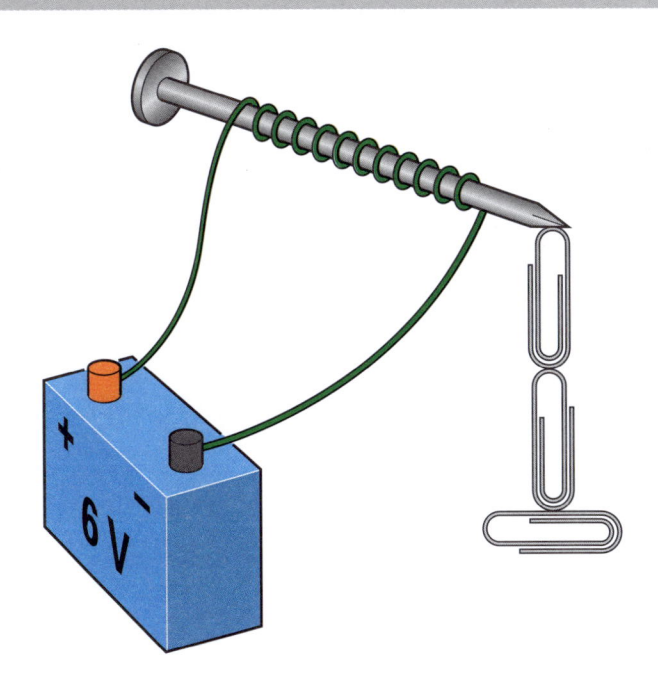

Method

1 Wind a coil of wire around the nail (Fig. 13.44).
2 Connect the bare ends of the wire to the battery.
3 Try using your electromagnet to pick up some pins or paperclips.

Discuss

1 You can test the strength of your electromagnet by hanging pins end-to-end from the iron core. How many will it support?
2 Include a variable resistor in the circuit. How can you adjust the strength of the electromagnet?

Fig. 13.44 A simple electromagnet picking up paperclips.

ⓘ What you should know

- Magnetic materials usually contain iron, nickel or cobalt.
- Magnets have a north pole and a south pole, close to either end, where the magnetic effect is strongest.
- Opposite poles attract; like poles repel.
- The magnetic field around a magnet can be represented by lines of force.
- Passing an electric current through a coil of wire produces an electromagnet. An iron core makes it stronger.

ⓠ Questions

1 If you think of the Earth as a giant bar magnet, where is its north pole and where is its south pole?

2 Copy the following sentences, choosing the correct word from each pair.
   a Aluminium/nickel is a magnetic metal.
   b The north/south pole of a compass always points to the Earth's magnetic south pole.
   c The lines of force/attraction appear to come from the fields/poles of a magnet.

3 Look around your kitchen. How many magnets can you find? (Don't forget that there are permanent magnets in many locks and catches; and that there are electromagnets in every electric motor.)

Electricity and magnetism

13.8 Uses of electromagnets

▶ Objectives

After studying this topic you should be able to:

- list some uses of electromagnets
- describe how electric doorbells and buzzers work.

We saw in Topic 13.7 that an electromagnet is basically a coil of wire that acts like a magnet when an electric current flows through the wire. Electromagnets can be made in various forms. Some have small coils, use small electric currents, and are weakly magnetic; others use many coils of wire and large currents to produce a powerful magnetic field that will lift heavy objects. Electromagnets are used in many different ways; some examples are:

- to lift iron and steel bars and sheets at steelworks;
- to lift scrap iron in scrapyards (Fig. 13.45);
- in relays (electromagnetically operated switches);
- to magnetize the tape during recording with a tape recorder.

Fig. 13.45 This scrapyard crane uses an electromagnet to lift large pieces of steel. Some can even lift whole cars!

Electric bell: An electric bell, for example a doorbell, includes an electromagnet. This is a clever design that vibrates back and forth automatically when someone closes the switch (Fig. 13.46). Here's how it works.

When someone presses on the bell push, the circuit is completed. Current flows from the battery round through the electromagnet coil and the springy strip, and back to the battery via the contact point X. The coil is now magnetized and attracts the springy strip. The hammer strikes the gong, and at the same time the circuit breaks at point X. The current stops, so the coil is no longer magnetized and the strip springs back to its original position. Now the circuit is complete again, and a current flows once more. The coil is magnetized and attracts the iron again, the hammer strikes the gong, and so on.

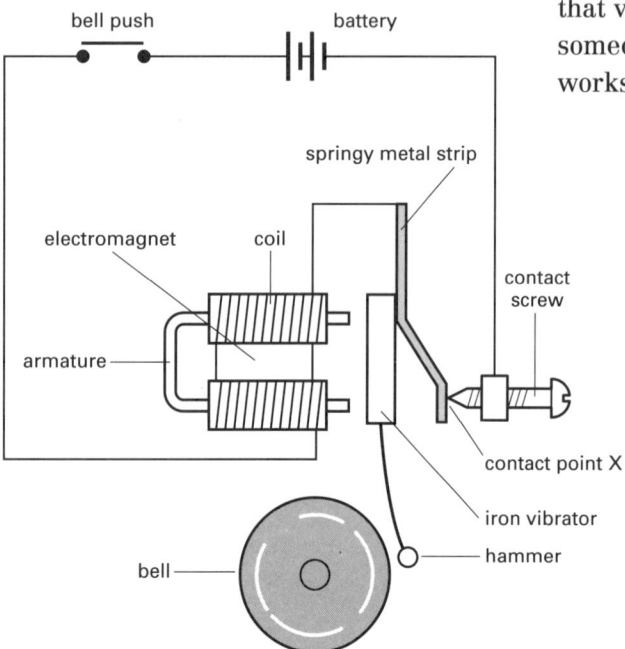

Fig. 13.46 The parts of an electric bell.

13.8 Uses of electromagnets

→ Activity Making a buzzer

You will need
- a flexible hacksaw blade
- an electromagnet (such as the one made in Topic 13.7)
- a low-voltage a.c. power supply
- clamps and stands

⚠ Danger!

Care needed when handling the blade!

Method
1. Set up the equipment as shown in Figure 13.47. The blade should just touch the point X.
2. When the circuit is connected up, the blade will be attracted to the electromagnet.

Discuss
Why does the blade buzz back and forth? (You may see sparks at point X. Why is this?)

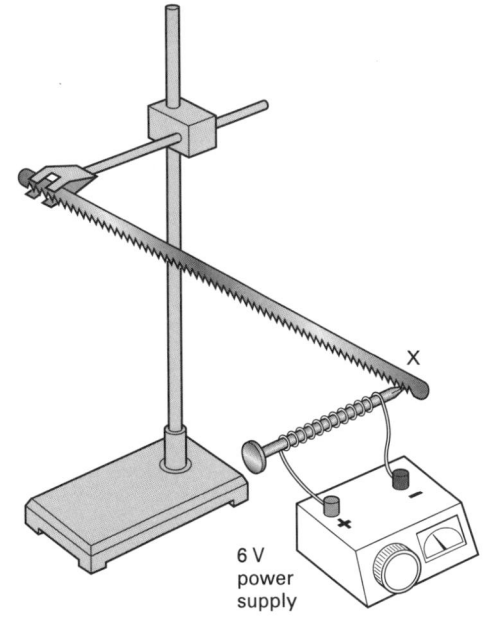

Fig. 13.47 Making a buzzer using a nail electromagnet and hacksaw blade.

◻ What you should know

- Electromagnets have many uses in devices such as electric bells and tape recorders.

@ Questions

1. State whether each of the following statements about electromagnets is true or false.
   a. They are always magnetized.
   b. Their power is increased by adding a lead core.
   c. They always have 100 coils of wire.
   d. They work better with an iron core.
   e. They are used in tape recorders.
   f. They always point north.

2. Suppose you are the operator of a crane fitted with a huge electromagnet, like the one shown in Figure 13.45. Decide which of the following materials you can pick up (you might need to experiment with a bar magnet first!):
   - an old washing machine
   - a leather armchair

13.8 Electricity and magnetism

- a fibreglass boat hull
- an old water tank
- some metal window frames
- rubber tyres
- a car wheel

3 How can electromagnets be used to separate soft-drink and food cans at a recycling centre?

4 Your electromagnet is not strong enough to pick up a load. How can you make it stronger? Think of more than one way.

5 No-one is quite sure why the Earth has a magnetic field. One theory is that electric currents flow around and inside its iron core – the Earth is a giant electromagnet! Research the latest theories on the Earth's magnetism. Why does the Earth's field change direction? Do other planets have magnetic fields?

Questions

Unit 9: Looking at non-living things

Multiple choice

1. Which of the following is NOT true about a gas:
   A it spreads out in all directions
   B it has a definite shape
   C it is a fluid
   D it can be squashed

2. Which is the correct sequence?
   A solid melts → liquid boils → gas
   B solid evaporates → liquid melts → gas
   C gas evaporates → liquid melts → solid
   D gas melts → liquid boils → solid

3. It is possible to grow a large crystal by:
   A dissolving a small crystal in water
   B suspending a small crystal in a saturated solution
   C suspending a small crystal in water
   D suspending a small crystal in a dilute solution

4. When a solid dissolves in a liquid, the liquid is called the:
   A solute
   B dissolver
   C solution
   D solvent

5. A compound:
   A is the smallest particle in an atom
   B has identical properties to its elements
   C is the smallest particle of an element
   D has different properties from its elements

6. Which method would you use to separate the blue and yellow components of a green dye?
   A chromatography
   B evaporation
   C filtration
   D fractional distillation

7. Acids and alkalis react to form:
   A metals   B oxides
   C bases   D salts

8. Which of the following is formed when a dilute acid reacts with a carbonate?
   A air   B carbon dioxide
   C carbon monoxide D hydrogen

Short answers

1. What are the three states of matter?

2. The melting points and boiling points of some compounds are given in the following table.

compound	melting point in °C	boiling point in °C
P	−182	−161
Q	−114	78
R	−78	−34
S	10	330
T	17	43
U	318	1390

   a Give the state (solid, liquid or gas) of each compound at 25°C.
   b Which of the liquids would freeze by placing it in the freezing chamber of a refrigerator?
   c Which substance(s) would be difficult to evaporate over a water bath?
   d Compare the arrangements of particles in P, S and U at 25°C.

3. What is a solvent? Give three examples.

4. The following table gives properties of some substances.

	state at room temperature	texture	colour
K	liquid	like water	colourless
L	liquid	oily	colourless
M	solid	crystalline	white
N	solid	waxy	white
O	solid	crystalline	pink

177

a Which of the substances would you expect to dissolve in water? Explain your answer.
b Which of the solids would you expect to melt most readily? Explain your answer.
c Which of the substances would you select for growing crystals?

Essays

1 Describe what happens when liquid water is (a) heated and (b) cooled. Use the correct words to describe the changes of state.
2 How are the bubbles put into a fizzy drink?
3 Iron filings do not combine with lead even when the lead is powdered and the mixture is strongly heated. How would you show that no compound is formed?
4 Write a letter to your pen pal describing to him/her how the juice from sugar cane is made into sugar.

Unit 10: Resources for life

Multiple choice

1 If water is added to soil, small bubbles of air rise to the surface of the water. What does this show?
   A soil reacts with water
   B soil is acidic
   C soil contains air
   D micro-organisms in the soil are drowning

2 Which of these statements is correct?
   A peat makes soil alkaline
   B lime makes soil acidic
   C coastal areas are high in salt content
   D humus destroys the soil crumb

3 Which of the following food chains is correct?
   A bird → cat → grass → worm
   B cat → bird → grass → worm
   C grass → worm → bird → cat
   D worm → bird → grass → cat

4 A food web is:
   A a collection of food chains in an ecosystem
   B a group of the largest animals in the environment
   C the producers that are found in a food chain
   D an interaction between the living and non-living parts of the environment

5 A food chain shows:
   A animals that live together
   B decomposition in an ecosystem
   C energy transfer between animals
   D energy loss amongst animals

Short answers

1 Which gases are present in air?
2 Which gas in air is needed for burning?
3 Draw a diagram to compare the sizes of sand, gravel and clay grains.
4 Soil takes thousands of years to be formed, yet soil can be lost in a few minutes. Name three ways in which soil is formed and three ways in which it can be lost.
5 Give the meanings of the following terms:
   a carnivore   b consumer
   c omnivore   d producer
6 What is the original source of all the energy on Earth?
7 Write down five food chains that may occur in your school garden.

Essays

1 Why is it important to use the correct type of fire extinguisher for different fires?
2 Draw and label a diagram of a soil profile.
3 Draw and label diagrams of:
   a the nitrogen cycle
   b the carbon cycle.

Unit 11: Systems in animals

Multiple choice

1 Athletes usually drink glucose drinks to:
   A advertise for companies
   B boost their energy levels
   C quench their thirst
   D strengthen their muscles

2 Sickle-cell anaemia is a:
   A blood disorder
   B digestive condition
   C nervous condition
   D skin disorder

3 Which condition is caused by the over production of abnormal white blood cells?
   A AIDS   B haemophilia
   C leukaemia   D sickle-cell anaemia

4 From which chamber of the heart is the blood pumped out to the body?
   A the right atrium   B the left atrium
   C the right ventricle D the left ventricle

Short answers

1 Describe the journey that the pulp of a mango would make along the digestive tract from the mouth to the small intestine.

2 Why is fluoride added to water and to toothpaste?

3 Why are high cholesterol levels in the blood considered to be dangerous?

4 Why does the human body need a transport system?

5 Name the vessels through which a molecule of oxygen would pass from where it is picked up in the right lung, to a cell in the big toe of the right foot.

6 The heart is a powerful pump in the body. What does this statement mean?

7 Why shouldn't you take drugs prescribed for another person?

Essays

1 Describe the 'multimix' principle. Name the food groups that make up the multimix and explain why it was designed.

2 Your dentist has discovered a cavity in your molar tooth which has penetrated to the pulp cavity. Draw a diagram to show the structure of a healthy tooth. Label the regions of the tooth through which the cavity has developed.

3 Describe that actions that occur in the chest as you breathe in and breathe out.

4 Explain what happens if someone's kidneys fail, and how they can be helped.

5 Your pen pal has told you that she or he wants to start smoking to look more grown up. Write a letter explaining why you think this is a bad idea.

Unit 12: Support and movement

Multiple choice

1 The term sessile means:
   A cannot swim   B can float
   C cannot walk   D fixed in a position

2 An animal without a backbone:
   A is an invertebrate   B is a vertebrate
   C has a spine   D has legs

3 When a muscle fibre contracts it:
   A gets longer
   B gets shorter
   C stays the same length
   D twists around

4 Which structure is responsible for the coordination of the body?
   A brain   B heart
   C kidney   D liver

5 The point where two bones meet is called a:
   A cartilage   B joint
   C ligament   D tendon

6 A support system which lies outside the body is known as the:
   A exoskeleton
   B endoskeleton
   C hydrostatic skeleton
   D protective skeleton

Short answers

1 Give three reasons why some animals move from place to place.

2 What are the four basic structures required to bring about movement?

3 Name three types of joints found in the body, and give an example of each type.

4 What is meant by the term 'oxygen debt'?

Essays

1 Describe how a bird's body is adapted (suitable) for flight.

2 How is movement brought about in man?

Unit 13: Electricity and magnetism

Multiple choice

1 The wires used to connect an appliance to its plug are colour coded. Which row of the table shows the correct colours?

	live	neutral	earth
A	red	green	black
B	brown	black	green and yellow
C	red	black	green and yellow
D	brown	blue	green and yellow

2 Which voltage might be used for the electricity supply in a house?
A 1.5 V
B 12 V
C 110 V
D 25 000 V

3 Ammeters and voltmeters must be connected correctly in circuits. Which row of the table shows how to do this correctly?

	ammeter	voltmeter
A	in parallel	in parallel
B	in parallel	in series
C	in series	in parallel
D	in series	in series

4 Which quantity is measured in kilowatt hours?
A electrical power
B electrical energy
C electrical resistance
D electrical voltage

5 The teacher blows up three balloons: red, green and blue. She rubs them with different materials to give them an electric charge: red, positive charge; blue and green: negative charge. The teacher then shows the class how the balloons attract and repel one another. Which row of the table shows correctly what they observe?

6 Which of the following is not magnetic?
A iron

	red + blue	red + green	blue + green
A	attract	attract	repel
B	attract	repel	repel
C	repel	repel	attract
D	repel	attract	repel

B copper
C cobalt
D nickel

7 An electric saw rated 2 kW was used for 6 hours. How much electrical energy was used?
A 2 kilowatt hours
B 3 kilowatt hours
C 6 kilowatt hours
D 12 kilowatt hours

Short answers

1 What is the difference between a cell and a battery?

2 What source of energy does a solar cell make use of?

3 A current of 5 A flows through a resistor R when a voltage of 10 V is connected across it. What is the resistance of R?

4 List four uses for variable resistors.

5 Three 10 Ω resistors are connected together in series. What is their combined resistance?

6 Three 10 Ω resistors are connected in parallel with a 6 V battery. What is the voltage across each resistor?

Questions

7 What can you say about the electric charge of an object which is described as neutral?

8 A bar magnet is hung from a thread. It turns round to point north–south. Explain why it does this.

9 A flashlight has a bulb, a switch and two cells.
  a Draw a circuit diagram to represent the flashlight.
  b Mark the positive and negative terminals of each cell.
  c Add arrows to show the direction in which the electric current flows.
  d Explain why no current flows when the switch is open.

10 Soraya's mother is worried that the landlord is charging too much for the electricity they use. Soraya noted down the reading on the electricity meter at the start of the month, and at the end.
  Meter reading at start of month = 23 045 Units
  Meter reading at end of month = 23 165 Units
  a How many Units of electricity were used in the month?
  b Each Unit of electricity costs 25 cents. The landlord charged Soraya's mother $50. Was this too much?

11 The circuit diagram shows two resistors, A and B, connected to a battery.

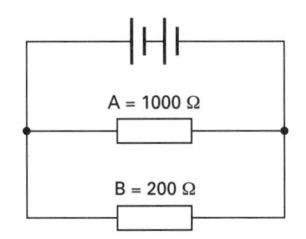

A = 1000 Ω
B = 200 Ω

  a Are the resistors connected in series or in parallel?
  b Is the current flowing through A greater than, less than or the same as the current through B? Explain your answer.
  c If resistor B was removed from the circuit, would the current flowing through A increase, decrease, or stay the same? Explain your answer.

12 A piece of plastic is rubbed with a cloth. It gains a negative electric charge.
  a What type of charge does the cloth now have?
  b What force causes the materials to become charged?
  c What particles have been transferred between the plastic and the cloth?
  d Which material has gained these particles?
  e Will the plastic and the cloth now attract or repel each other?

13 In an experiment, a 100 Ω resistor is connected up to a 10 V power supply.
  a What current flows through the resistor?
  b If the supply voltage is increased to 20 V, what current will flow?
  c What voltage is needed to make a current of 1 A flow through the resistor?

14 a Draw a diagram to show how you would make an electromagnet using a length of wire and a battery.
  b List the ways in which the electromagnet could be made stronger.
  c Give one advantage of an electromagnet over a permanent magnet.
  d List three uses of electromagnets.

Essays

1 Imagine that the electricity supply to your home was only available for one hour each day. For what purposes would you make use of the electricity during that time? What would you find it impossible to do without electricity?

2 George was examining a flashlight in the school laboratory. It would not light up. Wayne said that the batteries must be flat. Shirley thought that the bulb might have blown. Edgar suggested that the batteries might be the wrong way round. Their teacher suggested they should check these ideas, using equipment from the laboratory. What should they do to test each idea?

Science words

Here is a list of some important science words you have read in this book.

acid a substance of which a solution in water turns blue litmus paper red; it reacts with a base to give water and a salt
alimentary canal (gut) the tube that runs through the body from the mouth to the anus, in which digestion of food takes place; also known as the gut
alkali a substance of which a solution in water turns red litmus paper blue; a soluble base
alveoli (singular **alveolus**) tiny air sacs in the lungs, where gas exchange takes place
amino acids the units that proteins are made of
ammeter an instrument for measuring electric current
amp (ampere) the unit of electric current (symbol A)
amylase the enzyme in saliva that breaks down starch into maltose
analgesic a drug that prevents pain
antibiotic a drug that kills bacteria
antibody a special protein that attacks germs
aorta the largest artery through which oxygenated blood leaves the heart to go to the rest of the body
appendix a thin closed tube at the place where the small intestine meets the large intestine; causes appendicitis if it becomes inflamed or infected
artery blood vessel that carries blood from the heart to other body organs
arthropod an invertebrate with jointed legs (e.g. insect, spider, crab)
atom the smallest particle of an element
atrium one of the upper chambers of the heart

base a substance that reacts with an acid to give water and a salt
battery a number of electrical cells connected in series
bile a liquid produced by the liver that helps in the digestion of fats
blood vessel tube that carries blood around the body
bronchus one of two tubes into which the trachea divides

canine a sharp pointed tooth, used for tearing food
capillary the narrowest of blood vessels
carbohydrate energy-giving food such as starch and sugar
carnivore an animal that eats meat
cartilage a tough tissue that strengthens some parts of the body
cell (electrical) a device that produces electricity as a result of chemical reactions
chemical formula a set of symbols which gives the ratio of the numbers of atoms that combine to make a compound
chemotherapy use of drugs to treat cancer
chromatography a method of separating a mixture by letting it move across a medium such as paper; different parts of the mixture move at different speeds
circuit breaker a device that breaks an electrical circuit if too large a current flows
compound (chemical) a substance made up of different elements
conductor (electrical) a material that will allow an electric current to flow through it
coronary artery one of the blood vessels that supplies blood to the heart muscle
crown the top part of a tooth, visible above the gum
crude oil a mixture of different kinds of oil, found underground
crystal a solid in which the particles are arranged in a definite pattern (e.g. calcite, quartz, sodium chloride)

decomposer an organism that decomposes (breaks up) dead matter
deficiency disease a disease caused by lack of a particular nutrient in the diet
dehydration when the body does not have enough water or salts
denitrifying bacteria bacteria in the soil that break down nitrates to form nitrogen gas, which returns to the air
dentine the hard inner material of a tooth
desiccant a material that absorbs water easily; a drying agent
dialysis the process by which a machine cleans the blood of a person whose kidneys do not work properly
diaphragm the sheet of muscle that separates the chest cavity from the abdomen; it assists in breathing
diffusion 1. the movement of molecules from an area of high concentration to an area of low concentration
2. the scattering of light in different directions
distillation evaporating a liquid and then condensing the vapour to get the pure substance; a process of separating a solvent from a solution (e.g. water from a solution of sodium chloride in water)

egestion the passing out of undigested food as faeces from the body
electrolysis breaking down substances when molten or in solution, by passing an electric current through them
electromagnet a magnet created by passing an electric current through a coil of wire wound around an iron core
electron a tiny, negatively charged particle in an atom
element a substance that cannot be broken down into anything simpler

Science words

enamel tough, white material on the outside of a tooth

endoskeleton a skeleton that is inside an animal's body

enzyme substance that acts as a biological catalyst; it speeds up reactions in cells, but is not changed itself in the reactions

excretion the removal of waste products from the body

exoskeleton a skeleton that is on the outside of an animal's body

faeces solid waste that is left after the body has digested food and is passed out of the body unchanged

filtrate the liquid which comes through the filter paper in the process of filtration

filtration separating a solid from a liquid by passing the mixture through a filter

food calorimeter apparatus used to find the amount of energy in a sample of food

food chain the transfer of food energy from plants (called primary producers) through a series of living organisms

food web a network of interlinked food chains

fractional distillation separating a liquid mixture into fractions that boil at particular temperature ranges

fuse a wire made of a metal that melts at a fairly low temperature; it is included in an electrical circuit so that it melts and breaks the circuit when an excessively high current flows

gastric juice the digestive juice produced in the stomach

glycogen the form in which excess sugar (glucose) is stored in the body

haemoglobin the red pigment in red blood cells that transports oxygen

hallucination something that a person sees or hears or feels, but which is not really there

herbivore an animal that eats only plants

heterogeneous mixture a mixture in which you can see the separate parts quite easily (e.g. soil)

homogeneous mixture a mixture where the parts are so well mixed that it looks like a single substance (e.g. salt solution)

humus the organic matter in soil, formed from the decaying remains of plants and animals

incisor a chisel-shaped tooth at the front of the mouth, used for cutting food

insulator (electrical) a material that does not conduct electricity

intestinal juice the digestive juice produced in the intestine

invertebrate an animal without a backbone

kidney an excretory organ that gets rid of waste from the body and produces urine

kidney tubules tiny tubes inside the kidney where blood is cleaned of waste matter

kilojoule (symbol **kJ**) a unit of energy

kwashiorkor a deficiency disease caused by lack of protein

larynx the voice box; a chamber in the throat containing the vocal cords

legume one of a family of plants which includes peas and beans

ligament tough, elastic tissue that holds bones together at joints

litmus a substance used as an indicator; it turns red in acid and blue in alkali

lymph node a swelling in a lymph capillary that makes white cells for fighting diseases

lymphatic system a system of vessels that carry tissue fluid (lymph) around the body

lymphocyte a kind of white blood cell that produces antibodies to protect the body from germs

magnetic field the area in which the effect of magnetism can be detected

marasmus a disease caused by lack of food; starvation

milk teeth a human's first set of teeth

mixture several different substances mixed together, but which can be easily separated

molar a large grinding tooth, found at the back of the mouth

molecule two or more atoms joined together

mucus a slimy fluid that is produced by some cells in the body

nitrogen-fixing bacteria bacteria which live in the soil or on the roots of plants and can change the nitrogen of the air into nitrogen compounds of use to plants

obesity being overweight

oesophagus the tube between the mouth and the stomach; the gullet

ohm the unit of electrical resistance (symbol Ω)

Ohm's law the law which states that the current which flows through a resistor is proportional to the voltage across it

omnivore an animal that eats both plants and animals

permanent teeth a human's second (and last) set of teeth

phagocyte a type of white blood cell that attacks and eats germs

photosynthesis the process by which green plants make food and oxygen from carbon dioxide from the air, water, and light energy from the Sun

plaque a furry layer on teeth caused by bacteria feeding on bits of food

plasma the liquid part of blood

platelets particles found in the blood which help in the clotting of blood

pole a place where an effect is concentrated; a magnetic pole is the point where the magnetic force of a magnet seems to come from

power rating the amount of electrical energy consumed by an appliance

predator an animal that hunts other animals for food

premolar a large grinding tooth, found near the back of the mouth

prey an animal that is hunted by another animal

primary consumer an animal that eats food made by a producer

producer an organism such as a plant that makes food from non-living things in the environment

protein body-building food

Science words

pulmonary artery artery that carries deoxygenated blood from the heart to the lungs
pulmonary vein vein that carries oxygenated blood from the lungs to the heart
pulp cavity the area in the middle of a tooth that contains the nerves and blood vessels

radiotherapy use of radiation to treat cancer
reaction equation a shorthand way of writing what happens when substances react with each other
recycling using waste materials to make new things, thus saving material and energy
red blood cells cells in the blood that carry oxygen
residue anything left over, e.g. the material left on the filter paper when a liquid is filtered, or the solid left in the dish when a liquid is evaporated
resistance opposition to the flow of the electric current in a circuit (measured in ohms)
resistor a conductor that offers opposition to the flow of electric current
respiration the process by which cells produce energy by the oxidation of chemicals from food
resting heart rate the rate at which your heart beats when you are sitting quietly
rheostat a device for altering the resistance of a circuit; a variable resistor
roughage plant fibres in food that are not digested but which help food to move through the gut

saliva a digestive juice produced in the mouth by the salivary glands
salivary glands glands in the mouth that produce saliva
salt the product of neutralization of an acid by a base
saturated solution a solution which cannot dissolve any more solute at a particular temperature
secondary consumer an animal that eats primary consumers
sedative a drug that makes people feel calm
solute a substance that dissolves in a liquid to make a solution
solution a mixture of a solute and a solvent
solvent a substance, usually a liquid (although it could be a solid or a gas) that dissolves another substance
static electricity an electric charge that does not move
subsoil the layer of soil below the topsoil; it has less humus
suspension solid particles floating in a liquid

tendons the structures that connect muscles to bones
tertiary consumer an animal that eats a secondary consumer
tissue fluid the liquid between the cells in tissues
topsoil the dark, fertile top layer of soil, containing humus
trachea the windpipe; the main passage that takes air into the body; starts at the back of the throat
tranquillizer a drug that makes people feel calm
tumour a mass of abnormal tissue; cancer

ureter the tube from the kidney to the bladder
urethra the tube leading from the bladder to the outside of the body

vegan someone who does not eat any animal products, including milk and cheese
vegetarian someone who does not eat meat or fish
vein a vessel that carries blood towards the heart
vena cava (plural **venae cavae**) one of two very large veins through which all the blood flowing back from the body organs enters the heart
ventricle one of the lower chambers of the heart
vertebral column the backbone (spine)
vertebrate an animal that has a backbone
villi (singular **villus**) folds in the surface of the small intestine, where the products of digestion are absorbed into the bloodstream
vitamin a substance needed in the diet in small quantities
volt the unit of voltage (symbol V)
voltage the 'pressure' of electricity which causes an electric current to flow
voltmeter an instrument for measuring voltage

white blood cells cells in the blood that help to defend the body against germs
withdrawal symptoms the distressing symptoms experienced by someone who stops taking a drug they are dependent on

Index

acidity indicators 26, 27, 31
acids 26–27, 29, 31, 34, 182
    and carbonates 35–36, 37
    and metals 32–33
air
    composition of 38–39, 42–43
    pollution 61
    sacs (alveoli) 103, 105, 109, 182
alcohol 119–120, 122
alimentary canal 77–78, 81, 83, 182
alkalis (bases) 26–27, 28–29, 31, 37, 182
alveoli (air sacs) 103, 105, 109, 182
amino acids 64, 83, 182
ammeters 153, 154, 182
ammonia 41, 60–61
amps (amperes) 148, 153, 155, 182
amylase 78, 79, 182
anaemia 69, 99
analgesics (painkillers) 116, 182
antibiotics 115, 182
antibodies 93, 182
anus 82, 83
aorta 95, 182
appendix 82, 182
arteries 94–95, 97, 100, 101, 182
arthropods 137–138, 140, 182
atherosclerosis 99–100
atoms 16, 18, 19, 182
attraction 164–165, 167, 168, 171, 173

bacteria 43, 46, 49, 52, 61–62
bases (alkalis) 26–27, 28–29, 31, 37, 182
batteries 141–143, 146, 182
Benedict's test (for sugars) 66
bile 81, 182
biological control 55
birds 134–135, 140
biuret test 66
bladder 111–112
blood
    banks 95
    cells 92–94, 101
    circulation 95–96
    clotting 94
    disorders 98–99, 102
    groups 101
    transfusions 101
    vessels 94, 182
body temperature in humans 77
boiling points 6–7
bones 126, 130–131
breathing 103–109
    apparatus for diving 40
Brownian motion 1
burning, effects of 38–39

calories 70
canine teeth 86, 90, 182
capillaries 83, 94, 101, 110, 182
carbohydrates 53, 58, 63–64, 76, 83, 182
carbon cycle 58–60, 62

carbon dioxide 13–14, 16, 36–37, 38–41, 43
    in air 58–59
    in blood 105–106, 109
    and petrol (gasoline) 60
    produced by photosynthesis 53
carbonates 35
carnivores 54, 63, 86, 90, 182
cartilage 126, 131, 135, 182
catalase 78
cellulose 64
changing states of matter 5–8
chemical, formulas 18–19, 182
chlorides 30
chlorophyll 52–53
cholesterol 64, 99–100
chromatography 22–23, 25, 182
cilia 104, 121
circuit
    breakers 147, 182
    diagrams 151–152
circuits 161–162
circulation of the blood 95–96
clay 47–48, 51
coal 59
compost 46
compounds 16–18, 19, 182
concentration of solutions 15
condensation 8
constipation 83
consumers in food chains 53–54, 57
cooling substances 6, 7
coordination 128–129, 131, 133, 137
crude oil 24–25, 182
crystals 9–11, 182

decomposers 54, 57, 58, 61, 182
decomposition of compounds 18
deficiency diseases 68–70, 76, 182
dehydration 83, 119, 182
denitrifying bacteria 61, 62, 182
dentine 88, 90, 182
depressant drugs 115–116, 117
desiccants 41–42, 182
dialysis 114, 182
diaphragm 78, 103, 105, 182
diarrhoea 82–83
diet 63–64, 70, 76
diffusion 105, 182
digestion 77–78, 83, 105–106
dilution of solutions 15
dimmer switches 159–160
diseases of joints 131
disorders of the blood system 98–100, 102
dissolving materials 12–13, 14, 15
distillation 24, 25, 182
drugs 115–118, 120
    addiction to 116–118, 122
dry
    cells (batteries) 141–142, 146
    ice 41

earthworms 48–49, 138–139, 140
egestion 82, 182

electric
    bells 174–175
    currents 153–155, 157–158
electrical
    cells 141–143, 146, 182
    charges 164–165, 167
    circuits 151–153, 161–162
    conductors 164, 166, 167, 182
    energy 154–155
    resistance 157–158, 160, 166–167, 184
electricity 141–143
    mains 143–149
    paying for 144–146
    safe use of 147–149
    static 163–164, 166, 167, 184
    Units of (kilowatt hours – kWh) 145, 146
electromagnets 168, 172–173, 174–175, 182
electrons 153, 165, 182
elements 16, 18, 19, 182
enamel 88, 90, 182
endoskeletons 124, 131, 183
energy
    in different foods 71
    electrical 141–142, 154–155
    needs of the body 70–72, 76
enzymes 54, 64, 77–78, 81, 83, 183
eutrophication 61
evaporation 8, 21, 24
excretion 110–111, 114, 183
exoskeletons 124, 137, 140, 183

faeces 82, 83, 183
fats 53, 63, 64, 66, 76, 83
artificial fertilizers 61
filtration 20–21, 25, 183
fish 123–126, 140
fixation of nitrogen 60–61, 62
fizzy drinks 13–14, 15
fluoride 90
food 63, 74–75, 76, 83
    bolus 80
    calorimeter 70–71, 183
    chains 52–53, 55–56, 57, 183
    contaminants 74
    processing 74–75
    testing 66–68
    traditional Caribbean 75
    webs 52, 56, 57, 183
fossil fuels 59, 62
fractional distillation of crude oil 24, 183
freeze-drying 8
freezing points 6–7
fuses 147, 149, 183

gall bladder 78, 81
gases 2–4
gastric juices 80, 183
global warming 59
glucose 78, 83, 105, 109, 129
glycogen 64, 183
gullet (oesophagus) 78, 80, 103, 183

Index

haemoglobin 93, 105, 183
hallucinogenic drugs 115–116, 117
heart 94–97, 101–102
    attacks 100, 121
    rate 97, 184
heating substances 5–6
herbivores 54, 63, 86, 90, 183
heterogeneous mixtures 20, 25, 183
high blood pressure 99
HIV 92, 118
homogeneous mixtures 20, 25, 183
hormones 72
humus 44–45, 46, 50–51, 183
hydrogen 34, 143

incisor teeth 86, 88, 90, 183
indicators of acidity 26, 27, 31
injuries 130, 131
insulation materials 147, 149, 164, 166, 167, 183
iodine test for starch 66, 79–80
iron(II) sulphide 18

joints 126–128, 131

kidneys 111–114, 183
kilojoules (kJ) 70, 76, 183
kwashiorkor 65, 183

lactic acid 129
large intestine 78, 82, 83
larynx (voice box) 103, 183
legumes 60, 61, 183
leukaemia 99
ligaments 126, 183
lime (calcium hydroxide) 23, 51
    lime water (calcium hydroxide solution) 35–36
limestone (calcium carbonate) 50, 59
liquids 2–3, 5, 6–7
litmus 26–27, 183
liver 119–120
loam 47–48, 51
lungs 103, 109
    diseases of 108, 121–122
lymph nodes 101, 183
lymphatic system 81, 101, 102, 183
lymphocytes 93, 183

magnetic
    compasses 168–169
    fields 170–172, 173, 183
    materials 169, 173
    poles 170, 171, 183
magnets 168–170, 173
mains electricity 143–149
marasmus 73, 183
metal oxides 36
metals, and acids 32–33
mineral salts 68–69, 76
mixtures 16–17, 19, 20, 183
    separation of 20–25
molar teeth 86, 88, 90, 183
molasses 24, 25
molecules 18, 78, 105, 183
movement in animals 124, 126–128, 131, 133–134
mucus 104, 183
multimix principle (food guide) 75
muscles 126–127, 129

neutralization 28, 37
night blindness 69
nitrates 30, 43, 60–61
nitrogen 39, 41, 43, 58
    cycle 60–62
    fixation 60–61, 62, 183
noble (inert) gases 39, 43

obesity 73, 184
oesophagus (gullet) 78, 80, 103, 183
Ohm's law 158–159, 160, 183
ohms (symbol Ω) 157, 160, 183
oil refineries 24–25
oils in diet 64, 83
omnivores 54, 63, 86, 90, 183
organ transplants 94
oxygen 38–39, 40, 43, 95–96, 105, 109
    debt 129, 131
    and photosynthesis 53
    and respiration 53

pacemakers 98
parallel circuits 161–162
peat 50–51, 59
petrol (gasoline) and carbon dioxide 60
pH scale vi, 26–27, 31
phagocytes 93, 183
photosynthesis 40, 43, 52–53, 57, 58, 62, 183
pink mealy bugs 55
plaque 89, 183
plasma 94, 183
platelets 92, 94, 101, 183
pollution 61
power ratings of appliances 144, 183
predators 54, 55, 183
premolar teeth 86, 90, 183
producers in food chains 53–54, 57, 183
proteins 41, 43, 63, 64–65, 67, 76, 83, 111, 183
pulmonary arteries and veins 95, 97, 184

reaction equations 19, 184
reactivity 33
rectum 82
recycling 46, 55, 184
red blood cells 92–93, 101, 184
repulsion 164–165, 167, 168, 171, 173
residues 21, 184
resistors 157, 159, 160, 184
respiration 40, 43, 53, 57, 58, 62, 105, 109, 120, 184
rheostats (variable resistors) 159, 184
roughage 64, 76, 83, 184

safe use of electricity 147–149
salivary glands 78, 184
salt (sodium chloride) 9, 26, 69
salts 26, 29–31, 33–35, 37, 184 see also mineral salts
sandy soils 47–48, 51
saturation 10, 11, 12, 13, 184
separation
    of crude oil 24–25
    of mixtures 20–25

series circuits 161–162
skeletons 124–125, 130–131
skull 127
small intestine 78, 81–82
smoking 120–122
soil 44–49, 51
    acidity 29, 50
    animals in 48–49
    formation of 50–51
    pH values 29
    profile 44–45
    texture 47–48
solids 2–3
solutes 9, 11, 184
solutions 9–10, 11, 184
solvents 9, 14, 15, 184
starch 64, 66, 78
starvation 72–73, 76
states of matter 1, 5–8
static electricity 163–164, 166, 167, 184
stimulant drugs 115–116, 117
stomach 78, 80
sublimation 8
subsoil 45, 51, 184
sugar 66, 78
    sugar cane 23–24, 25
sulphates 30
sulphuric acid 34
Sun 52, 57
sweat 110
swimming creatures 135–136

teeth 85–87, 90, 184
    decay of 89–90
    structure of 87–89
three-pin plugs 147–149
tissue fluid 101, 184
topsoil 44–45, 51, 184
traditional Caribbean food 75
transformers 144, 146
transplants 114
tumours 121, 184

Units of electricity (kilowatt hours – kWh) 145, 146
universal indicator vi, 27
urea 110–111, 114
ureter 111–112, 184
urethra 111–112, 184
urine 111–113, 114

van de Graaff generator 166
varicose veins 99
vegans 70, 184
vegetarians 70, 184
veins 94, 95, 97, 99, 101, 184
vena cava 95, 184
villi 81, 83, 184
vitamins 53, 63, 68–69, 70, 76, 89, 184
voice box (larynx) 103, 184
voltage 155–156, 184
voltmeters 154, 184

water 37, 53, 68, 76, 109
    vapour 42–43, 106
white blood cells 92–94, 101, 184
windpipe (trachea) 103, 184
withdrawal symptoms 116, 118, 119, 122, 184